D1423074

# THE PRIVATE ROD

VICTORIAN LITERATURE AND CULTURE SERIES

Karen Chase, Jerome J. McGann, *and* Herbert Tucker, *Editors*

# THE PRIVATE ROD

*Marital Violence,*
*Sensation, and the Law*
*in Victorian Britain*

Marlene Tromp

UNIVERSITY PRESS OF VIRGINIA
*Charlottesville and London*

The University Press of Virginia
© 2000 by the Rector and Visitors of the University of Virginia
All rights reserved
Printed in the United States of America

*First published 2000*

∞ The paper used in this publication meets the minimum requirements of the
American National Standard for Information Sciences—Permanence of Paper
for Printed Library Materials, ANSI Z39.48-1984.

Library of Congress Cataloging-in-Publication Data
Tromp, Marlene, 1966–
   The private rod : marital violence, sensation, and the law in Victorian
Britain / Marlene Tromp.
      p.   cm. — (Victorian literature and culture series)
   Includes bibliographical references and index.
   ISBN 0-8139-1949-5 (cloth : alk. paper)
   1. English fiction—19th century—History and criticism.   2. Marriage
in literature.   3. Family violence—Law and legislation—Great Britain.
4. Domestic fiction, English—History and criticism.   5. Law and
literature—History—19th century.   6. Family violence in literature.
7. Sensationalism in literature.   I. Title.   II. Series.

PR878.M36 T76   2000
823'.809355—dc21                                                      00-026131

*For those who are working to end violence against women*

*The rod of iron with which he rules her never appears in company—it is a private rod, and is always kept upstairs.*

Wilkie Collins, *The Woman in White*

# Contents

# Acknowledgments

As with any feminist project, a host of people were involved in making this book possible, from the women with whom I worked at the SAFE domestic violence and sexual assault shelter to the readers, colleagues, and supporters who encouraged my work. I am deeply grateful to Elizabeth Langland, who reminded me that an academic could choose to write and think about those things for which she cared most deeply, who offered untiring and supportive feedback throughout the project, and who provided a professional role model that I could admire. She, Daniel Cottom, Flash Silvermoon, Stephanie Becker, Lesley Gamble, Amy Murphy, Susan Hearn, and Stephanie Smith helped bring the earliest drafts of this project to paper, and many at the University of Wyoming, including Eva Brumberger, Beth Kolko, Susan Aronstein, Janet Constantinides, Bob Torry, and Caroline McCracken-Flesher, helped me see it through. I am grateful to the Women's Studies Programs and scholars at the University of Florida, the University of Wyoming, and Denison University who nurtured my intellectual growth and provided a supportive community. The joy of collaborative work and conversation, especially with Pamela Gilbert (both in and outside of academe) and Aeron Haynie, and the discovery of like minds and mentors such as Gail Turley Houston, whose warmth, grace, and intellectual insight challenged and encouraged me, have helped me see the best in the academy and remain committed to my work here. The beloved and beautiful people who provided me with friendship, delight, and sometimes even late-night conversations about *Daniel Deronda*—Teresa Pern Reed (most steadfast and wonderful), Samantha Goldstein, Sandy Runzo, Sylvia Brown, Tamra Horton, Toni King, Lakesia Johnson, Linda Saum, Mary Lutz, Lanette Dennis, and the whole Emmaus community—gave me the sunshine Ohio sometimes lacked. My dear family, Eileen and Hans Tromp, Mary Tromp Gardner, and all of the Eisenhauers, provided me the emotional, spiritual, and sometimes physical space in which to write. The English department I now call home, the students, the community of scholars, support staff, administration, and friends I have at Denison made finishing this project a delight and provided the means that made it possible. Finally, and with heartfelt sincerity, thank you God, Dave, Mugg, and Sheb, for making music and giving of your love so generously.

A portion of chapter 3 appeared in different form as "Mary Elizabeth Braddon's Sensational (En)gendering of Domestic Law" in *Beyond Sensation: Mary Elizabeth Braddon in Context,* edited by Marlene Tromp, Pamela Gilbert, and Aeron Haynie. It is reprinted by permission of the State University of New York Press. © 2000 by the State University of New York. All rights reserved.

A portion of chapter 5 appeared in different form as "Gwendolen's Madness" in *Victorian Literature and Culture* (September 2000). It is reprinted by permission of Cambridge University Press. © 2000 by Cambridge University Press. All rights reserved.

# Introduction: Sensation, Violence, and Privacy

*He, he, he! To lose a wife is to get a fortune.*
(sings) *Who'd be plagued with a wife*
    *That could set himself free*
    *With a rope or a knife,*
    *Or a good stick, like me?*

—*Punch and Judy,* 1827

## Textual Play, Textual Pleasure, and the Application of the Rod

*There are no longer any innocent words. The objective effect of unveiling destroys the apparent unity of ordinary language.*

—Pierre Bourdieu, *Language and Symbolic Power*

THERE ARE NO INNOCENT WORDS. Despite the childlike qualities of the song from *Punch and Judy*, the popular puppet show offers us a means of opening a discussion on Victorian texts to explore the investments of texts and words, social codes and law, and it also provides insight into violence, the domestic space, and economic relations in that realm. Punch sings the song after murdering his baby and "belabour[ing] [Judy] till she is quite dead. He [then] 'tosses the body down with the end of his stick' and laughs" (Leach 11). The violence of this drama begs analysis when contrasted to representations of the Victorians as genteel, stoic, and proprietous, particularly in what has been considered the morally stringent middle classes.

Though primarily working-class entertainment performed to street audiences early in the nineteenth century, Punch and Judy made appearances in middle-class drawing rooms and in children's literature by mid-century. The increasingly pervasive drama produced much disruption and often drew disapproval as well. In 1863, *Chambers* magazine remarked that it was "'a pity [Punch and Judy] should be known' at all, and argued that 'the "sensation dramas" now demanded by the theatregoers are to better plays what Punch is to Fantoccini'"[1] (qtd. in Leach, 95). The puppet show, whose ubiquity suggests how complexly embedded it was in the culture's understanding of itself and in the creation of a middle-class ideology, was also linked to the "sensational novels" that predominated at mid-century.[2] The alignment of Punch and Judy with sensation and the contention regarding its performance in the home point to some of the central questions I take up in this argument. How did the Victorians define the propriety of a text—which kinds of words and narratives did they perceive as "innocent"? How did identifying a text as "sensational" marginalize and manage its content, precluding it from "serious" consideration?[3] How did they imagine and legislate gendered violence and violence between "man and wife"? How were text, class ideology, and, often more subtly, the fervor for imperial growth entangled in their answers to these questions? Finally, how have we, as modern critics, imitated the ideological entanglements of our predecessors in the texts we have chosen to study,[4] and in what ways has this tendency reproduced the invisibility of some cultural, intellectual, and fictional patterns?[5]

The responses I examine in Victorian fiction, nonfiction, and law suggest that there was a complex range of unspoken assumptions regarding these issues, and furthermore, that these assumptions often came into conflict, producing disruptive cultural tension. Such tension, however, does not demonstrate that these texts were generated outside of "middle class control," as Winifred Hughes argues in her excellent study of sensation fiction (42). Rather, I will argue that the phenomenon of sensation was fundamentally produced by middle-class reading practices (in spite of the increasing literacy in the working classes), middle-class writing, and middle-class anxieties. They participated in the production of a new middle-class consciousness—in spite of the fact that these novels "attack[ed] the most cherished middle-class values" (Hughes 42). I am interested in what we can learn not only about generic conventions and their implications, but about violence in even middle-class marriage from a wide variety of texts, including those that may seem, like Punch and Judy, to be pure of ideological investment or less pressing subjects of scholarly inquiry because of their distance from intellectual and philosophical pursuits. In "The Spectre of Ideology," Slavoj Žižek notes that "the very gesture of stepping out of ideology pulls us back into it" (10),[6] the move in which I see seemingly nonideological texts such as sensation complexly implicated as one of the "fictions" that expose and denaturalize ideology (7). I am also compelled by the question of why violent dramas, such as the Punch plays and the sensation novels that followed, made an appearance in the homes of the middle class, a place where such narrative representation had heretofore been unseen. To that end, this study positions sensational fiction in its market and against high-culture realist fiction and the law to trace the path of these developments.

The sensation novel, a genre characterized by its scandalous narratives and emotionally and socially provocative dialogue and plots, had its heyday in the 1860s and early 1870s, in the midst of growing concern about codes of behavior in marriage.[7] Essentially excluded from the canon of the late twentieth century, sensation novels and their impact on and in Victorian culture have only recently come under serious consideration in Victorian studies.[8] Often couched in the popular frames of bigamy, marital abandonment, and "cruel" relationships,[9] and resulting narratively in threats and women's responsive violence—up to and including murder—sensation explicitly addressed themes that often were eschewed in what was considered moral, didactic, high literature. I examine this generic classification by rethinking the dichotomies that place sensation outside of and opposed to realist fiction and truth and proposing a closer relationship between the genres, exploring the ways in which sensation both derived from and revised realist fiction, a revision that long outlasted sensation's seemingly temporary sway over the public. I have chosen to do this using the central metaphor of marital violence,[10] considered in itself a sensational topic that multiplies the tensions I explore.

To examine the evolution of both literary and legal negotiations of marital violence, I begin with a novel that precedes the critical articulation of sensation as a genre, and with a novelist who was widely considered a forefather of sensation: *Oliver Twist* by Charles Dickens. I then turn to two popular sensation novelists, Wilkie Collins and Mary Elizabeth

Braddon, who for many define the genre. Next, I move through the disappearance and social critique of the genre to Margaret Oliphant, a novelist who was considered to have written realist portraits of life, occasionally infused with sensation. Finally, I examine the impact of sensation on the discourse of realist fiction through a novelist who frequently has been cited as the model of Victorian realist fiction, George Eliot.[11]

Studying the novels chronologically provides a historical frame for examining the shifting legal discourse, mapping it against the changes in sensation, and speculating on a conversation between sensation and the law. In addition, it allows us to examine progressively the ironic ways that early narratives claiming to represent truth relied heavily on socially constructed assumptions about race, class, and gender to describe marital violence in the domestic space. It also allows us to study the means by which sensation, as a genre and a methodology, reproduced but also disruptively resisted those stereotypical assertions later in the century, offering a very different image of violence in the home than that contained in official reports or drawing-room conversations. The generic shifts that loosely defined a mode of fiction we know as sensation participated in a reframing of the Victorian vision of marital violence, and sensation's break with realism, "at the height of the trend toward realism" (Hughes 47), provided the Victorians—and provides us—with a new means of reading realist fiction and of understanding and responding to violence materially and discursively.

I demonstrate the re-visioning that sensation offers and the impact that it has on high culture by moving between realist and sensation fiction and between fiction and the law. The distance between fictional narrative, an active dismantling and reassembling of social discourse to produce an engaging and entertaining textual experience—what Derrida calls "playing the law," a process of emerging from the sanction of, revising, and resisting, and thus making the law (*Acts of Literature* 216)—and legal text itself, a sober and earnest inquiry into the social and political context, may seem immense. In fact, narrative may seem to differ as dramatically from law as sensation does from realism, yet the law is no less marked by an exploration evocative of textual play than the most spectacular fictions.

I cross this diverse body of texts to isolate discursive patterns that reveal a significant engagement between them all. In this engagement lie responses to the questions I posed at the opening of this introduction.

Breaking down faith in the presumed innocence of some words and fictions allows us to break down the boundaries between various forms of representation and to find in them tensions that serve as a rich ground for study. Rather than perceiving sensation or the friction it generated as a solution to violence in the home, I regard it as the marker of a liminal moment, the pivot on which a cultural shift occurred, generating a kind of chaos in understanding and necessitating new dialogues about violence and married life. Indeed, in A. James Hammerton's study of marital violence in the period, he finds (though he does not comment on) women speaking of reading as a means of responding to violence in their homes, pointing to the role of fiction in at least some women's reconsideration of the legal and social terms of these issues. By the end of the century, the (always tenuous) legal and social fiction of a stable and natural social authority was undone by new readings of the relationship between domesticity and violence, a disruption revealed in part through sensation.

### Disrupted Frameworks: Theorizing Sensation

*[L]iterature seem[s] . . . to be the institution which allows one to say everything [tout dire], in every way. . . . To say everything is no doubt to gather, by translating, all figures into one another, . . . but to say everything is also to break out of prohibitions. To affranchise oneself—in every field where law can lay down the law. The law of literature tends, in principle, to defy or lift the law. . . . It is an institution which tends to overflow the institution.*

—Jacques Derrida, *Acts of Literature*

Many scholars have pursued interests in marital violence exclusively through the study of legal documents, historical events, and nonfiction debates. Important works by Maeve Doggett, Mary Lyndon Shanley, and A. James Hammerton have advanced our understanding of the issue with this kind of research. Literature, however, equally a product of (and productive of) its historical moment, provides us with another means of insight into the construction of the terms through which we can chart cultural shifts.[12] Michel Foucault has argued that all discourses are constructed by the interplay of "a series of discontinuous segments whose tactical function is neither uniform or stable" but that, in their poly-valence, are the very stuff that produce, as well as undermine, social notions (such as marital violence) (*History of Sexuality* 100). As Doggett notes, marital violence began to develop its modern configuration during the Victorian period, an age that has been the launching site of much of Foucault's work. In *Discipline and Punish,* Foucault explored the move from corporeal violence to juridical control through self-monitoring, and in *The History of Sexuality* he inquired into the myth of Victorian sexual prudery, two accounts that crisscross the landscape of marital violence I lay out here. In the interstices of those cross-hatchings, I find the terrain for my own study, and in positioning my study there, I must account for both the theoretical framework I take up and the texts I choose to examine.

### Disruption of the Theoretical: Writing Social Change

In Foucault's methodologies, I find two gaps I must bridge in order to frame my argument. First, his accounts of the Victorian period fail to consider the way in which corporeal violence, though unacceptable in the public space, may still have been a part of the privatized, domestic space.[13] Further, his discussion of sexuality and power, which speaks to the "deployment of sexuality [through which] each individual has to pass in order to have access to his own intelligibility," does not address the role of gendered violence in the formation of subjectivity. I read these problems as the first gap, a product of Foucault's failure to consider gender, along with the many other social and political structures he investigates, as one of the primary avenues of power exchange and management. As Lois McNay notes in *Foucault and Feminism,* "despite Foucault's theoretical assertion that power is a diffuse, heterogeneous and productive phenomenon, his historical analyses tend to depict power as a centralized, monolithic force with an inexorable and repressive grip on its subjects. This . . . arises, in part, from the fact that Foucault's examination of power is one-sided; power relations are only examined from the perspective of how they are installed in institutions and they are not considered from the point of view of those subject to power" (38), a concern that points to the question of gender, among others. Certainly, for Foucault, anyone subject to power deploys it as well, but McNay vexes the simplification of the material impact of power's circulation. Thus, the inclusion of questions regarding gendered power and the position of those who were literally subject to—but not necessarily defined as "subject" by—the law enriches Foucault's methodologies as a means of exploring the period, rather than dismantling them. This strategy is particularly important for an analysis that focuses on violence between men and women, "man and wife." Like many before me, then, I have employed the insights of feminist critics to illuminate the space that Foucault's theories had previously left obscure, a reconsideration of his work that accords with his own notions of discursive interchange.[14]

Second, Foucault's work focuses on the totalizing effect of discourses and thus produces, as Elaine Hadley notes, "a rather static archeological model to account for change, movement and resistance in its historical record of 'power'" (10). I respond to this second gap by reconsidering Foucault's subject matter and by offering a further revision of his methodological approach. As both D. A. Miller and William A. Cohen note, Foucault circumvents the literary in his studies, a site at which a more frankly playful engagement with pressing, but not less significant, cultural concerns may have been enacted.[15] Exploring this territory lends us the opportunity to map more fully the social understanding of these issues. Moreover, since I am concerned explicitly with disruption—the moments in which generic, legal, and social discourses were particularly and visibly unstable—as a means of more fully understanding the process of social change, my work has been influenced by the insights of Jacques Derrida. Derrida's theories provide me with the means to theorize this instability and the role of disruption and excess, which are perhaps the most distinctive elements of sensation fiction. Deconstruction scrutinizes the collapse and transgression of boundaries, asking about the place of these functions in the discursive processes. Derrida's work gives me the means to discuss the way that sensation as a discourse emerged out of the tensions in the law, then participated in the reinvention of the law.

To establish the modified theoretical grounds from which I propose to make claims about sensation fiction, I must return not only to the question of textuality, but to my assertions about the impact of sensationalism on realist fiction, the law, and cultural understanding of marital violence to establish a connection between text and material conditions. In "Revolution in Poetic Language," Julia Kristeva argues that "textual experience reaches the very foundation of the social—that which is exploited by sociality but which elaborates and can go beyond it, either destroying it or transforming it" (*Kristeva Reader* 117). Derrida concurs, remarking that literature "is an institution which consists in transgressing and transforming, thus in producing its constitutional law; or to put it better, in producing discursive forms, 'works' and 'events' in which the very possibility of a fundamental constitution is at least 'fictionally' contested, threatened, deconstructed, presented in its very precariousness" (*Acts of Literature* 72).

I was concerned with the ways in which literature might (dis)engage constructions of gender that left fictional women, in the depictions of violence we have traditionally read from the period, at the mercy of their partners and violence itself nearly invisible in dangerous domestic situations. Though I cannot examine the material conditions of women in violent relationships themselves for a host of reasons, not the least of which is Elaine Scarry's questions about the reproductivity of pain or the distance that lies between this text and its subjects, I can speak to the discourses that shape and were shaped by those material effects. Canonical fictional accounts may have led us to believe that the women of the nineteenth century saw no alternative to violence in their homes.[16] I maintain that sensation fiction provided early portraits of resistance to (as well as capitulation to) violence, and that sensational narratives, profoundly popular in a culture often believed to have been silent on these issues, participated in a transformation of the terms of the legal debates and ultimately disrupted the Victorian vision of violence. Indeed, significant changes in the status of women and of marital violence did occur during the period in both the fictional representations (culminating in the New Woman novel of the 1890s) and in nonfictional discussions (especially evidenced by Frances Power Cobbe's "Wife Torture in England," as well as through landmark legal changes regarding divorce, child custody, and married women's property, and agitation for social changes such as women's suffrage.

Derrida argues that the terms upon which we build cultural coherence are often structured around perceived limits and histories that collapse upon investigation. This insight offers shape to this kind of study; it figures the space in which to ask about resistance and transformation. Furthermore, this type of argument provides the theoretical framework for the feminist project at the heart of this text. It allows us to imagine ways in which we might continue to deconstruct the law and, through a range of cultural responses, the patterns of violence in the home that have remained in many ways unchanged to this day. Derrida argues that there is

> *distinction between the law, that is the history of right, of legal systems, and justice. . . . [T]here is a history of legal systems, of rights, of laws, of positive laws, and this history is a history of the transformation of laws. You can replace one law by another one. There are constitutions and institutions. This is a history, and a history, as such, can be deconstructed. Each time you replace one legal system by another one, one law by another one, or you improve the law, that is a kind of deconstruction, a critique and a deconstruction. So, the law can be deconstructed and has to be deconstructed. That is the condition of historicity, revolution, morals, ethics, and progress. But justice is not the law. Justice is what gives us the impulse, the drive, or the movement to improve the law, that is to deconstruct the law. That is why I said that the condition of possibility of deconstruction is a call for justice. (Caputo,* Deconstruction in a Nutshell *16)*

In their search for justice, the Victorians revised their law and rewrote their fiction to imagine new means of speaking to the presence of violence in the domestic space.

### Disruption of (the) Material

At the level of the material, both in terms of the texts that I examine and the circumstances in which they were generated and read, I turn to the question of what the Victorians conceived of as possible. Many critics have argued that the principle of realism reigned in Victorian fiction, and, indeed, realism has been implicitly regarded by modern critics as the central source of materials for significant intellectual inquiry. My study asks not only about these texts, but about those that fell "beyond the pale" and seemingly outside the structure of social, economic, and political power relations. Anthony Trollope, an important Victorian novelist of the "prosaic reality . . . [of] everyday life," positioned novels, novelists, and readers in two camps, the sensational and anti-sensational: "The novelists who are considered to be anti-sensational are generally called realistic" (qtd. in Hughes, 39). Trollope both polarizes these modes and defines sensation as a form one must oppose, calling realism "anti-sensational," not "non-sensation." Richard Altick has recognized the work of both of these forces in concert, studying both novelistic efforts to produce the most "real" novel in pursuit of critical acclaim and the work of a sensational media as a counterpart in this process to create the "real." [17] Realism often was the ground on which Dickens, Trollope, and Eliot were praised and sensation fiction writers condemned. The complexly entangled notions of gender, class, and imperialism, particularly as they were conceived of as realistic or sensational, inflected the shifting discourses governing marriage, the domestic space, and notions of violence and erected the seemingly firm boundaries between the realist and sensational.

Despite the dearth of literary criticism concerning marital violence,[18] I found voluminous material about all of the unseemly, improprietous issues of this study—marriage, violence, and resistance—in the sensation novels of the 1860s and early 1870s. Contrary to its reputation as literary triviality, sensation was significant in many ways. Its tone and subject matter, the very things for which critics censured it,[19] opened a wide range of possibilities concerning what might be represented. Because the same social limitations, by virtue of their definition, did not apply to sensation fiction—it was expected to be sensational—and because it was regulated by different standards of propriety for its publication and sale,[20] it became the site of a discourse that offered an alternative way of perceiving gendered relationships and the violence that might lay at their core.

At several levels, sensation—regardless of the author's intentions for the narratives or the reading audience's perceptions—served as a voice for these concerns. Judith Walkowitz, in her study of the "dreadful delights" in Victorian England, suggests that W. T. Stead's "Maiden Tribute," a "sensational" newspaper account of the forced prostitution of young girls, "provided a language of emotion in stark contrast to the disembodied voice of reason and science that presumably set the tone" for discussions of sexual danger (*City of Dreadful Delight* 144). Sensation in any media, however, provided far more than an emotional experience; it seemed to touch the very core of reason. In fact, according to Thomas

Boyle, popular newspapers carried stories that were as graphically explicit in their depiction of sexuality and violence as sensation novels, often even more so. He further explains that "news and novels were regularly associated" (129); the truth of the news (and novels) and the sensation of the news (and novels) blurred so effectively that critiques of both were fraught with ambivalence and contradiction (60). Altick concurs, arguing that "[f]iction . . . however sensationalized, could be regarded as a faithful transcript of contemporary life: there were the newspapers to prove it. They added verisimilitude to extravagance, and thus made the extravagant credible" (*Victorian Studies in Scarlet* 79). Altick further notes the anxieties of critics who faced the crumbling boundaries sensation drew into focus. He indicates that Henry James's 1865 review of sensation, in which James suggested that Wilkie Collins "introduced into fiction those most mysterious of mysteries, the mysteries which are at our own doors," was met with cultural disquiet:

> *James's jaunty tone was at odds with the deeper concerns expressed, or implicit, in what his English contemporaries wrote on the same subject. It was no light matter to see fell purposes and deeds attributed to the social class that by the mid-Victorian era had become the prime wielder of political, social, and economic power and the center of attention in imaginative literature, above all fiction: the self-consciously and proudly moral middle class. Its primary interest in literary matters was to read about itself, to find its comfortable world mirrored in fiction. To the distress of most arbiters of taste and morality in such matters . . . sensation novelists turned the reverential ideal of home and family inside out, purporting to discover lurking behind the innocent facade of decorous life a prodigious quantity of illicit behavior. (152–53)*

It is this tension, the ambivalence in the presentation and understanding of the truth, particularly as it regards the domestic space, that I examine in sensation. This framework urges a destabilization of generic boundaries as well, moving away from the renaturalization of the boundaries between sensation fiction and realist fiction.[21] It also points to a disruption of content that urged critics to label certain texts sensational, a label that has stuck to many novels for almost a century and half.[22] Their categorization, the critical move that located them outside the center, calls into question a center that naturalizes and does not fully see itself. In part because of this ambiguity, and perhaps as a byproduct of the resistance on the part of critics (Victorian and otherwise) to expose the "unseemly" social matter I have chosen to discuss, many of the patterns I trace here are suggestive rather than explicit correspondences, exploring what Athena Vrettos calls "semiotic drift."[23] By crossing this range of texts and identifying their repetitions and successive transformations, I hope to render the logic of my argument realistic and reasonable. I wish to establish the ways in which sensation's re-presentation of the discourse of marital violence might have offered not only women, but the men who wrote the legislation that has often been perceived as providing a frame for their lives, a means of addressing sexual violence, of imagining what might be real.

## The Publication of the Private: Rewriting the Law

*Paradoxically, at the very moment when the transformation of marriage from an economic institution to a private relationship was being consolidated, its privacy was compromised by intrusive scrutiny and surveillance. This was facilitated by the contemporaneous spread of literacy, newspapers and reading habits that encouraged a shared newspaper culture among the middle class.*

—A. James Hammerton, *Cruelty and Companionship*

*What then, if by perpetual provocation, [the wife] should awaken the tempest of his wrath! We will not contemplate that thought.*

—Sarah Stickney Ellis, *Wives of England*

Ultimately, I believe, the reconception of sexual violence occurs through the repositioning of terms, their movement from a place of occlusion (not absence) to illumination, the publication of the private. Issues that were closely guarded as subjects of individual, domestic privacy[24] were exposed for mass public consumption,[25] inverting explicit standards of propriety.[26] In his study of wife abuse, A. James Hammerton indicates that "respectability worked as a deterrent to exposure" (50). Understanding marital violence and making it utterable are two features of the texts I study here that respond to the anxiety of exposure and silence. They defy

Sarah Stickney Ellis's injunction "not [to] contemplate," not to speak of, a husband's wrath, even if he be what she describes as a man in the "unreasonable class." As Anthea Trodd points out, much mid-century fiction "lifted the roof" off the secrets of the middle class, a move that was produced by and produced anxiety. Ann Cvetkovich argues in *Mixed Feelings* that the ideological management of sensation functioned more effectively to suppress contention, to soothe; she points out that "within middle-class American culture in particular, a discourse about affect serves to contain resistance, especially from women. Rather than leading to social change, the expression of feeling can become an end in itself or an individualist solution to systematic problems" (1). Cvetkovich discusses the ways in which the sensation novel (a part of the apparatus that culturally produces and manages affect as a construct) became a site for the naturalized association between women's bodies, sensation, and the construction of gender, ultimately reinforcing the domestic ideal. We must bear in mind this analysis of sensation, examining the ways in which it feeds into Victorian constructions of womanhood, privatization, and disempowerment.[27] I do not focus on sensation and its production of affect being potentially liberating (in the text itself or in the reader through the novel's expression of anger or frustration, as Showalter describes[28] and Cvetkovich critiques).

I shift the terms of these questions, focusing on the possibility that sensation might expose the contradictions in the mainstream social and legal conceptions of marital violence. I suggest that sensation might embody a kind of extasis, a ventriloquism that both distorts the mainstream discourse and speaks through it, for it, and about it, producing a seemingly counter but functionally medial discourse to high-culture fiction and realism. Sensation locates the ways in which realist discourse fails to establish, in Garrett Stewart's words, "the social subject it purports to inscribe or address" (*Dear Reader* 168), offering a disruptive, postmodern reading of the decentered subject, a subject who may not be the white middle-class Englishman and instead be his bruised and battered wife. It is in this trajectory that I find an equally present and productively subversive expression of the relationships between women and violence, women and sensation, and sensation and realism that dismantles the very constructions it seems to uphold, offering new methods of perceiving gender and gendered relations.

Ultimately, developing an understanding of the impact of sensation in all of its contradictory functions is a necessary hermeneutic device through which to read the tensions in realist fiction such as Eliot's.[29] In *The Realistic Imagination,* George Levine argues that Victorian realist authors were self-conscious about the conventions of realism, and that over the course of the century they inverted the terms of realism to recreate the genre. Experiments, Levine notes, "are not aberrations from some realistic norm, but intrinsic to its nature. Resisting forms, it explores reality to find them; denying excess, it deserts the commonplace self-consciously asserted as its subject. Positing the reality of an external world, it self-consciously examines its own fictionality. . . . The realistic novel persistently drives itself to question . . . the nature of . . . itself" (21). I argue that sensation was "intrinsic to [the] nature" of realism, created by the drive toward realism (this may suggest why sensation was condemned by critics but not eliminated by boycott or deflated by lack of sales), and participated in the transformation that took place across the century, supplying the medium through which the tensions about what defined the real became figured.[30]

Comparing the shape of sensation to the shifts in legal discourse and the realist fiction that succeeded it provides evidence of its impact on and engagement with social issues—not simply in terms of the legal/social management of the themes represented, but in the exposure of this management and the development of an alternative representation for these terms. We can read sensation as more than the simplification of cultural constructs in which transgressive heroines are punished or mysteries are solved to "rationalize intense affect and make it safe" (Cvetkovich, *Mixed Feelings* 7). Indeed, Cvetkovich notes that sensation novels sometimes contain "subversive elements" and that it is impossible to separate "the mechanisms of subversion and recuperation or [designate] a particular literary text [as] intrinsically liberatory or reactionary" (*Mixed Feelings* 55). Her work carefully critiques the recuperative elements of sensation, yet as she indicates, there is value in examining the other possibilities a text provides. Her study has made us sensitive to the repressive elements in sensation; mine attempts to discern the ways in which the progressive rewriting of this genre offered up a critique of contemporary constructions of gender and marital violence. Sensation's mysteries and transgressions provide a powerful engagement with the discourse of violence, "overflowing the institution" itself, as Derrida suggests: not simply sub-merged or conventional, but public, transgressive, and fruitful for analysis and discussion.

### Textual Play and the Rod

To uncover what I propose is an embedded and sometimes contradictory discourse of marital violence, as well as the generic changes attendant upon this discourse, I focus on the text of several novels in detail, using close readings to point to the competing threads embodied in each piece. This allows me to make theoretical, historical, and literary claims about the complexities of the systems of internal symbolic logic, exposing that aspect of sensation fiction that has often been obscured in studies of the genre. Rather than pointing primarily to the gross elements of plot struc-ture and a few selected passages in the text, I want to venture into the intricacies of narrative evolution and language. The theoretical position I have taken, a position that speaks to the subtle complexities of novelistic narrative, demands this kind of attention to textual minutiae—what I would argue points to the theoretical tensions in the text. In 1857, Henry James opined that "registering the anarchist underworld, a world defined through its own obscurity . . . through its articulation in a novel, would [cause it to] lose its essence." "Vagueness," James suggested, might be read as "authenticity" (Maynard 188, 189). Such a notion of realism has domi-nated the texts we have chosen to study—particularly in the terms under which sensation fiction has been dismissed as less dense and intellectually rich than, for example, George Eliot's prose—and the methods we have employed as literary critics. I prefer to see the vagueness, the underworld of the text, as ripe for interrogation, for it is precisely in the generation of these global notions of vagueness that we might lose the tensions James hoped to evoke. Baudrillard's notion that the real cannot be figured into representation belies our attempts to uncover the reality of Victorian life in the narrow world of realist fiction; I would extend that claim further to suggest that it also disturbs gestures toward analysis that all function in the same fashion. By resisting the reduction of what James called the "loose baggy monster" of the Victorian novel to a summary argument, I hope to resist traditionally dismissive readings of sensation fiction and to uncover trends that have been overlooked before. Though I do not argue that these texts or methods (not new, but resurrected with the revisions this theoretical framework can provide) leave us any closer to an unassailable reality than those offered by other analyses, they offer another reading, in both kind and content, that might enrich those performed before by other scholars.

In part 1, "Fictional Records," I lay the groundwork for this argument and look at *Oliver Twist,* a narrative of violence between partners produced prior to sensation fiction. The infamous scene of Nancy's graphic, bloody murder by her common-law husband, Bill Sikes, presages the advent of a sensational reimagining of violence in the domestic space. Although *Oliver Twist* hearkens back to the eighteenth-century tales of family violence in *The Newgate Calendar,* a popular series of true-crime narratives, Dickens revises many of their narrative techniques in his sympathetic portrayal of Nancy's life and death, in spite of her identity as a prostitute. Consistent with an evangelical fervor for moral rescue, this move may seem an uncomplicated amelioration of the violated woman's dilemma, but this narrative of salvation is deeply implicated in other ideological currents, specifically those undergirding a burgeoning industrial capitalism. Ultimately, Nancy's redemption depends not upon her ethics or a code external to her that overlays the tale, but upon her monetary worth to her social "betters." She and others are favored only as they participate in the generation of a proprietous middle-class identity, achieved through financial stabilization and metaphoric disembodiment, both subtly underwritten by the circulation of text—wills, letters, narratives—much like the one Dickens himself created in this novel. However, moments in Dickens's narrative gesture toward more dramatic shifts in the depiction of marital violence. The Artful Dodger's linguistically unorthodox response to the legal system provides an unconventional yet comprehensible use of language that makes possible a less dangerous, but still sharply caustic, critique of the law. This move hints at the rhetorical structure of the genre labeled as sensation fiction.

In part 2 I turn to what I call "Sensational Revision," beginning with Wilkie Collins's *The Woman in White,* one of the novels to which the term "sensation" was first applied. In this narrative we see, perhaps for the first time in the nineteenth century, a character of genteel birth display bruises on her arms and neck left by an aristocratic husband's attempts to extort capital from her. A virtuous middle-class man usurps the position of her violent patrician husband and restores order to the domestic space. This novel follows on the heels of the Divorce Act of 1857, legislation that was designed, in part, to prevent "unworthy" husbands from violently "sweeping away" the earnings of their working-class wives. Though the act characterized violence in the home as a working-class phenomenon, Collins's novel moves violence out of the working class of Dickens's fiction and Parliament's laws.

I see in these narratives two important phenomena. First, the implicit critique of the legislation and the embodiment of upper-class women embedded in the narratives earn them the appellation "sensation," an attempt to delegitimize that fails, however, to silence. Collins's extraordinarily popular novel still left its revisions reverberating against the reigning fiction of violence in the home. I also read the novel against the grain of its own overt narrative, uncovering vexed visions of class and propriety that remark the villain as nonaristocratic, remarginalizing the violence and, as in the case of *Oliver Twist,* enlisting the violence in service of sanctifying middle-class identity.

In the third chapter, I discuss Mary Elizabeth Braddon's *Aurora Floyd*—a novel that helped earn Braddon the title "Queen of the Circulating Libraries"—and examine the ways it evokes the language of the Contagious Diseases Acts. These acts, designed to check the spread of venereal disease in her majesty's navy, marked the prostitute as the central threat, indeed the very source of the danger. Yet the law permitted what amounted to repeated assaults on suspected prostitutes, and many feminist protesters suggested that the women were in danger, rather than the men. Significantly, demonstrations against the law were launched only after the acts had been effortlessly passed and were repeatedly extended. I argue that these dilatory critiques were made possible by the imperfect mimesis of *Aurora Floyd,* which, though strikingly similar to the language of the acts, disrupts the discourse of the acts in ways that invert its claims. Though a "horsey woman" (a description powerfully associated in the period with prostitutes) who seems to be responsible for the death of her husband, Aurora finally is positioned as a victim. The defamed heroine's innocence calls into question the construct of the dangerous woman as the vessel to contain danger in the home and, in the unexpected transposition of victim and victimizer, models the rhetoric that made possible the repeal of the Contagious Diseases Acts.

In the final section of the book, "Realism Reconsidered," I address Margaret Oliphant, a writer who explicitly critiqued sensation, yet was thought to have exploited sensation techniques herself. Here, I open the exploration of sensation's impact on realist novels and techniques. In *Salem Chapel,* Rachel Hilyard shoots her estranged, abusive husband in the head at point-blank range to "end his horrid career." This explosion of physical boundaries, along with other transgressions in the novel, shatters the middle-class vision of domestic peace and propriety embodied in the parallel plot line's decorous leading family, the Vincents. Most critics have bifurcated the tale of Rachel's abusive husband and the spiritual struggles of the Dissenting minister Arthur Vincent, calling the former a sensation story that interferes with the latter, a realist narrative worthy of consideration. I read this interference differently than other critics have, however, examining the way it provides a figurative static in the transmission of the real. I interrogate the relationship between the two through generic boundaries slippages, the blurring of sensation and realism. I argue that Oliphant's use of language, madness, and the woman's body offers us the means to see both realism and the undefiled middle class contaminated by sensation. The disruption of these seemingly inviolable constructs provides evidence of boundary betrayals that resist critics' attempts to maintain the safe dualities established in earlier fictional modes.

Finally, I take up George Eliot, one of the most important realist novelists of the nineteenth century. I argue that in *Daniel Deronda* Eliot offers one of the most powerful illustrations of sensation's impact on realism by demonstrating, through her heroine Gwendolen's relationship to her cruel husband, that violence is a real possibility in the ranks of the elite and that the real itself must be read and understood through the sensational. Faced with the paradoxical impossibility of violence in a polite world where such violence was thought not to exist, Gwendolen must renegotiate her understanding of social reality to justify her fear of her husband. Thus, she abandons realism, escaping into sensationalized, performative madness, a gesture that expresses the tensions between decorous social convention and her material experience. I interrogate the discourse of reason, which produces the notions of realism in the novel, eschewing the strategy of many critics to declaim the novel's sensational moments and locate the tensions of Gwendolen and Henleigh's marriage in Gwendolen's failures. This argument not only points up Eliot's exposure of violence in genteel marriages, but Gwendolen's "yeasty mingling of dimly understood facts with vague but deep impressions, and with images half real, half fantastic" (402) furnishes us with the key to decode this revised discourse of realism/sensation.[31]

# I

## FICTIONAL RECORDS

# I

···⟨∞⟩···

## A "Pound" of Flesh: Morality and the Economy of Sexual Violence in *Oliver Twist*

*I hope to do great things with Nancy.*

—Charles Dickens, letter to E. M. Forster

### Truth, Tears, and Death: Dickens's Disembodied Angels

FOR THE VICTORIANS, the flesh of a woman had a value, a clearly economic value. A woman's body was the ground upon which complicated financial settlements were arranged prior to and after matrimony, and her reproductive capacity provided her husband with heirs—issues that have been the focus of much significant scholarship. Here, I am interested in exploring both the ways a poor woman was marked by the middle and upper classes as a means of determining the value of her body when her husband saw fit to damage or destroy it, and the ways that a middle-class woman's body served as a counterpoint to the working woman's physicality, providing instead a means of social embodiment that denied the physical body and therefore made it seem impervious to violence. This sleight of hand was accomplished through text—in both its consumption and production. In the working class, however, the thoroughly corporeal woman who labored, produced, and reproduced (without the benefit of a discreet confinement) bore also the textual materialization of physical danger in both a social and legal sense. Though violence certainly did occur in the middle and upper classes, I speak here to the effacement of violence in those classes and its containment in the body of the working-class woman, a move that helped shaped legal changes in years to come.

There was a significant social similarity between the working-class woman and other women in that, like her more prosperous sisters, the working-class woman's flesh had a price, and not only for the sake of the income she provided for her family. The appraisal of a Victorian working woman's worth when she was threatened by violence in her home was dependent on her materiality—specifically, upon the ways she might materially benefit her "betters." Early in the century, rituals such as charivari and rough music (or "riding the stang," the phrase used in northern England) had been used by rural working-class communities to punish excessive marital violence. A man might be publicly humiliated with verbal taunts ("Shame! shame! Who beats his wife?") and a serenade of raucous music played on homely instruments such as frying pans and tea kettles for physically abusing his wife beyond the community's sense of reason (Chambers 510).[1] A punishment also used for other excesses ("henpecking" wives or shrews or cuckoldry), it deteriorated with the growth of judicial and legal involvement in small communities and the growing power of text (and its middle- and upper-class producers) to define the boundaries of social violations. Thus, when a working woman was beaten, her economic value was often spoken to by those with the social authority to define such transgressions, and, significantly, these transgressions were often articulated in spiritual terms, rather than in crude pecuniary language that might confute the naturalized separate-spheres ideology that purported to place women beyond the scope of economic questions. A poor woman's value—and thus the role of civic and social law in demonstrating compassion for, protecting, or disciplining her endangered body—was determined by her economic worth in a variety of contexts, depended upon her virtuous service to a developing industrial capitalist culture, and was screened by the discourse of salvation. Early representations of middle- and upper-class women marked them as innately spiritual, disembodied creatures—angels who required no protection from the kinds of abuses believed to be common in the working class; their spiritualized bodies could not be harmed by physical acts.

Charles Dickens's *Oliver Twist* dramatizes such a pattern and illuminates the complex means by which the culture may have begun to construct its understanding of violence in the home and between domestic partners. Critics have long been aware of the way in which privileged women were disembodied, textually domesticated and framed by the fiction they consumed and through which they wrote themselves.[2] My argument interrogates the role this phenomenon played in the legal and social conception of marital violence and the way that *Oliver Twist* serves as a landmark of these attitudes and in the evolution of sensation, depicting a transition between early nineteenth-century narrative efforts to negotiate the questions surrounding violence in marriage and the sensation fiction that later in the century so powerfully reembodied these women and spoke to violence so distinctively. By positioning *Oliver Twist* between the poles of an earlier tradition and the genre that followed, I hope to render the dramatic legal and social transitions made visible by the rise of sensation more clear and to demonstrate Dickens's role as an important generic and thematic bridge to the sensation fiction and cultural attitudes evident later in the century.

### Morality and God's Truth

In his preface to the third edition of *Oliver Twist,* Dickens repeatedly identifies the novel as a realistic depiction of criminal life in England, defending with special vigor the prostitute Nancy, her housebreaking lover Bill Sikes, and their disturbing and violent relationship. Nancy, according to Dickens's reading of the critics, exhibits an "unnatural" devotion to a wicked man (36). He elucidates his position by explaining that the representation of "stern truth . . . was a part of the purpose of this book" (35) and describes the narrative as "truth" or "true" five times in the last few paragraphs of the preface. At one point, with regard to Nancy, he underscores his attention to "truth" by capitalizing each letter of the word. These assertions form Dickens's response to objections about the novel's morality. He argues that his emphasis on the "established truth" gives him the authority to provide "a lesson of the purest good," to "serve . . . a moral" (33). He goes so far as to lend a biblical quality to the narrative by referring to it as "emphatically God's truth" (37).

In this emphasis on morality, Dickens was generating a new moral code, one over which there was enough tension to arouse resistance and to require such effusive assertions, and one that impinges on the questions I wish to address here. There are several threads embedded in these assertions. First, Dickens's attention to God and morality in his depiction of characters suggests that the ethics of domestic life and a proper understanding of criminality[3] are bound together. Further, these remarks suggest that this triad of terms (morality, the domestic, and criminality) may be successfully mapped out in a particular form of textual representation, as they are here, novelistically. Second, the preface specifically points up the veracity of Nancy and Bill's characterization, lending a centrality to Bill's repeated assaults and to Nancy's brutal murder. The fundamental quality of this violent relationship to Dickens's preface and to the action of the narrative explains its significance to my discussion about violence in domiciliary relationships. Dickens's depiction of Bill and Nancy provides evidence of a transition taking place in the literature, one that reveals a quickening of the patterns fully born into the sensation fiction I will discuss in chapters 2 and 3 and that demonstrates a textual transformation from a narrative that preceded this novel, *The Newgate Calendar; or, Malefactor's Bloody Register.*[4] Finally, I am interested in the thematic role of Dickens's emphasis on morality plays in regard to both this textuality and the framing of intimate relationships, particularly as it serves to screen particular economic transactions and violence in the narrative.

### Angels Blind with Weeping

To a large extent, *Oliver Twist* concerns salvation, a notion that had powerful implications in the primarily Christian world of Dickens's early Victorian readership and that bears significantly on the interrelationship between morality and violence in the novel. The salvation of Oliver, Rose, and, finally, Nancy figures centrally in the narrative. Exploring the elements in their distinct forms of salvation reveals a great deal about the underlying codes. Oliver seems to be saved from a variety of dangers: the criminal element that wants to use and destroy him, the cruel Poor Laws, and his wicked half-brother Monks, who attempts to deny him his fortune by seeking to foster his degeneracy under the tutelage of the fence, Fagin. Rose Maylie also appears to be saved repeatedly. She is rescued from poverty and from the home of the poor cottagers, who had taken the nameless girl in but had run out of compassion after learning of her sister Agnes's illegitimate child (Oliver) and being persuaded that Rose would also behave badly. Rose's beloved, Harry Maylie, seems to rescue her by giving her a new name, unsoiled by her sister's illicit behavior.

Both Rose and Oliver escape these injurious material circumstances by virtue of their virtue—an attribute made apparent in their angelic gentleness and beauty, not in their physical resistance to temptation or the bodily hardships they endure. Indeed, their salvation comes in spite of remarkable odds because they are already saved, a move that binds safety to morality and angelic disembodiment (and lodges violence in the body of the working class). A benevolent force protects Oliver from surrendering to the dangers of Mrs. Mann's baby farm, the workhouse, Mr. Bumble's cruelty, and apprenticeships to the chimney sweep and the undertaker before he ends up in the hands of Fagin. Even after Oliver has been absorbed into the criminal world and Fagin's young thieves take the naive boy on his first pickpocketing expedition, he still appears angelic. Their victim, Mr. Brownlow, refuses to believe that Oliver is guilty of any wrongdoing because the child's face and expression are so innocent. Upon first seeing Oliver, Brownlow remarks, "'*Can* he be innocent? He looked like—By the by,' . . . [He] halt[ed] very abruptly and staring up into the sky [exclaimed,] 'Bless my soul!'" Brownlow recalls friends who had been "taken up from earth only to be set up as a light, to shed a soft and gentle glow upon the path to Heaven" (119). The references here to God, Heaven, and seraphic guides evoke not only Oliver's lost parents, but the angels to which Oliver is so often compared. Although the construct became insistently gendered later in the century, women had no corner on the angel market in 1843 when Sarah Stickney Ellis explained that truly good men possessed the "nature and capacity of angels" (58). This angelic purity protects Oliver from the criminals, whose efforts to corrupt him through mistreatment, bribery, and fear repeatedly fail.

Neither is Rose's salvation a surprise. Significantly, we are told that "if ever angels be for God's good purposes enthroned in mortal forms, they may be, without impiety, supposed to abide in such as hers" (264). As Nina Auerbach has argued in *Woman and the Demon,* the fluidity of notions like the domestic angel made their containment in firm categories ultimately unsuccessful. Still, they have great symbolic power in the novel, and Rose's angelic identity evokes the crystallized images that would later appear in Coventry Patmore's renowned "Angel in the House" and John Ruskin's *Sesame and Lilies.* The narrator of Patmore's "Love at Large" describes the presence of a woman as a panacea: "How sad soever I was before / Then is my sadness banish'd far" (10–11). Rose's appearance lends the same remarkable effect; her "sweet female voice . . . quell[s]" disquietude and commotion. The domestic angel makes the home a haven; she has the heavenly power to bring light in darkness, tranquility in chaos, and joy in sorrow. Rose's intelligence "seemed scarcely . . . of the world; and yet the changing expression of sweetness and good humour, the thousand lights that played about the face, and left no shadow there; above all, the smile, the cheerful, happy smile, were made for Home, and fireside peace and happiness" (264). Despite her misfortunes, Rose's wisdom comes not from the hard realities or experiences of her past, but rather is other-worldly, appropriate to her angelic demeanor. In her presence, "Home" becomes a sanctified place, the word capitalized to reveal its sacred quality. In Rose, the recipe for a peaceful domestic space, we find a defiance of the very possibility of violence. Rose's virtues are rare enough to in-spire Harry Maylie, who describes her as his "peace and happiness" and "a creature as fair and innocent of guile as one of God's own angels" (314), to give up a career in Parliament for love of her.

In spite of the novel's gestures toward the possibility of their corrup-tion or a fall through death, these characters remain miraculously un-scathed. When Oliver ends up in the hands of the Maylies after the thieves attempt a robbery and leave him behind with a gunshot wound, Dr. Losberne, a family friend, insists that Oliver's angelic aura may be misleading. "Vice . . . takes up her abode in many temples; and who can say that a fair outside shall not enshrine her" (268). When Rose falls ill, the doctor, Mrs. Maylie, and Harry all indicate that "it is not always the youngest and best who are spared" death (295). Yet the narrative militates against these claims; Oliver is as blameless as he looks, and Rose is spared. Always pure, and thus always safe, they are protected from bodily harm by their identity.

Rose and Oliver make no moral transition in the narrative, despite the fact that their lives are significantly transformed. Rather, they make a fully naturalized economic transition that is linked to a host of other vir-tues, such as gentility, purity, solvency, and security, characteristics iden-tified with the middle class. Oliver regains his fortune and Rose becomes respectably self-supporting in her marriage to Harry, no longer depen-dent on the grudging charity of others. The criminals, however, are the only ones who candidly acknowledge the profit margin of such angelic qualities. Toby Crackit, a housebreaker, remarks of Oliver's face, "His

mug is a fortun' to him" (209), for he could easily pick "old ladies' pock-
ets in chapels" without arousing suspicion. Fagin, the criminal gang's
leader, complains that the "looks" of most criminal youth "convict 'em
when they get into trouble, and I lose 'em all. With this boy, properly
managed, my dears, I could do what I couldn't do with twenty of them"
(192). Oliver, as Dickens argues in his preface, is the very "principle
of Good" (33). His angelic demeanor, his goodness, underscores his
economic value; he is a golden child, worth a fortune to whomever pos-
sesses him.

The link of economics to this purity indicates that both separate-
spheres ideology and gender constructs were vexed and deeply intertwined with those aspects of culture that were to provide their antithesis,
such as the marketplace, a phenomenon Lenore Davidoff and Catherine
Hall have described in *Family Fortunes*. Still, the construct of the angel
and its corollaries had powerful material effects. In the next section, I
examine some of the ways that these terms play out, using their articulation to read, as David Paroisien has described it in regard to *Oliver Twist*,
"the external signs of the new urban culture . . . whose impact . . . rendered unreliable previous assumptions" (14). As I read the novel, the attempt to consolidate these shifting terms is further an attempt to position
middle-class identity, and to do so safely against the possibility of violence
and horror. Decoding the intricacy of these connections requires close
attention to the internal landmarks of morality in the narrative.

Rose and Oliver's incessant weeping is one feature that signals this
construct. In the magistrate Fang's courtroom, during Oliver's arraign-
ment, the narrator remarks that the legal system made "angels blind with
weeping" (123). The angels in this narrative are conspicuous, and weep
they do. Oliver sheds tears at almost every point in the narrative's turn.
The story opens in anticipation of his first cries and closes with the tearful
baptism of his newly declared relationship with Rose. Oliver cries when
he leaves the cruel Mrs. Mann's baby farm, when he is placed in workhouse solitary, when he is fed, when he is hungry, when he is presented
to the workhouse board and to his friends, when he is ill, and when he is
well. Though he has good reason to be unhappy, the frequent textual
enactment of his tears lends emphasis to this particular representation of
his grief. The device becomes increasingly significant when we pair it
with the fact that the other character who frequently dissolves into tears

is Oliver's young and gentle aunt, Rose Maylie. Rose weeps at the sight of Oliver, at the plans to save Oliver from the police, when she becomes ill, when the man she loves is sad, and when he is happy.

Weeping becomes a kind of symbolic baptismal purification that points up the good and, in its absence, the evil. Bill, the housebreaker and murderer, never cries despite his increasingly horrible prospects. We learn to trust Nancy, despite the fact that she is partly responsible for returning Oliver to Fagin, because she weeps over the boy's situation. She is, in fact, the only criminal who ever weeps for any reason. When Nancy first debates whether or not to go to Rose, she "burst[s] into tears" (355), an indication that we may read her anew. Her tearful breakdown in Rose's presence teaches us to value her and is an indicator to Rose and Mr. Brownlow that her disclosures can be trusted. Mrs. Maylie, Giles, and Harry also weep briefly in the novel (though they don't achieve the persistent downpours of the angels). We are told, for example, that we may regard Giles as an "honest fellow; [he] had not been feigning emotion, [which] was abundantly demonstrated by [his] very red eyes" (302). These characters' momentary spells are marked as genuine and thus as gestures that demonstrate their goodness. When Rose and Oliver learn of their relationship to one another, the narrator says: "Let the tears which fell, and the broken words which were exchanged in the long close embrace between the orphans, be sacred" (463). Genuine tears are, like those who drop them, sacred.

According to Fred Kaplan in *Sacred Tears,* this form of Victorian sentimentality grew out of eighteenth-century moral philosophy and was contrasted not to reason, as late nineteenth-century and twentieth-century constructs would have it, but to immorality and untruth (17). Kaplan indicates that this philosophical idealism was a means of resisting the Hobbesian notion of innate moral decrepitude, which formed the basis of philosophical realism. Kaplan's antipode to sacred tears is philosophical realism, a contrast that does not eliminate the possibility that they would have been compatible with the literary realism of the age— a genre in which Dickens was anxious to position himself and that is disrupted not in Rose's tears, but in the violence against Nancy, a new tension Dickens's novel introduces. In fact, the gesture toward an ideal truth, as Dickens so clearly lays out in his introduction, links the weeping not only with fact but with moral authority, signaling the narrative effort to reconsider contemporary understanding of these issues. Like the melo-drama's terms of good and evil that Elaine Hadley describes as a "form of strategic dissent" (112), the unstable dichotomies of good and evil in *Oliver Twist* offer a means of reforming the domestic middle-class space and the roles within that space, including a textualization that defies vio-lence in the middle class.

### Alligator Tears

Simulated tears, then, provide a counterpoint to the angels and indicate the distance of the actors from the virtue they attempt to affect. We see this particularly in the characters of Mrs. Sowerberry and Mrs. Bumble, who use their tears to manipulate their husbands. In both cases, their artificial weeping is aligned with episodes of violence in the home. In our introduction to the Sowerberrys, Mrs. Sowerberry deploys "a very com-mon and much-approved matrimonial course of treatment . . . [which] reduce[s] Mr. Sowerberry to begging, as a special favour, to be allowed to say what Mrs. Sowerberry [is] most curious to hear." She calls him a "brute," though she is the one who "threatened violent consequences" and "frightened Mr. Sowerberry very much" (78). Her performance of victimization and the pretense of his violence frames their marriage. Her alligator tears violate the ethics established in the novel and not only dem-onstrate immorality, but render visible the "cause" of violence. When Mr. Sowerberry learns that Oliver has fought with Noah Claypole, the cruel charity boy, Mrs. Sowerberry demands Oliver's punishment, pun-ishment Mr. Sowerberry seems reluctant to give. Mrs. Sowerberry thus bursts into "a flood of tears," a flood that "left Mr. Sowerberry no alter-native. If he had hesitated for one instant to punish Oliver most severely, it must be quite clear to every experienced reader that he would have been, according to all precedents in disputes of matrimony established, a brute, an unnatural husband, an insulting creature, a base imitation of man. . . . The flood of tears left him, however, no resource; so he at once gave [Oliver] a drubbing which satisfied even Mrs. Sowerberry herself" (94–95). Though Mrs. Sowerberry seems the violent one—she threatens her husband, beats Oliver, and demands that Mr. Sowerberry do the same—he is the character who bears the title of brute. Violence and im-propriety such as this arises from marriage; Mrs. Sowerberry calls upon the "precedents of matrimony" with her false tears to generate violence. Her shamming indicates her failing, a failing that precipitates a "drubbing" of Oliver.

We see a similar situation with Mr. Bumble and his new wife, the former Mrs. Corney. Though Mr. Bumble insists that it is "the prerogative of a man to command," Mrs. Bumble clearly has the upper hand. When she fails to achieve her end, she "drop[s] into a chair, and with a loud scream that Mr. Bumble was a hard-hearted brute, [falls] into a paroxysm of tears." These performed tears again warn of looming violence. Moments later, Mrs. Bumble, having "great experience in matrimonial tactics," "clasp[ed] [Mr. Bumble] tightly round the throat with one hand, [and] inflicted a shower of blows . . . upon [his head] with the other. This done, she created a little variety by scratching his face, and tearing his hair. . . . [Finally,] she pushed him over a chair . . . and defied him to talk about his prerogative again, if he dared." Rich with the military discourse of tactics and battles, Mrs. Bumble's prose and behavior leave her "in full possession of the field" (324–26). Her assault, preceded by the dramatized weeping, suggests what might have happened to the fearful Mr. Sowerberry had he not responded to his wife's tears.

The counterfeit weeping of these two women reveals two things: an abandonment of propriety so severe that it turns gender roles on their heads, and an embodiment of violence that seems explicitly linked to their fraudulent tears. Their false weeping distances them from the disembodied domestic ideal that Rose represents and marks them as failed women. We may read their lack of purity, their failings, as the triggers for the violence that follows. A woman's moral failings, therefore, cause violence in the home. The comedy immanent in these two scenes derives from the inversion of gender roles and suggests that we should read them less as an aspersion on marriage in general than on a particular kind of marriage with a particular kind of wife. Unlike Rose Maylie, whose marriage late in the novel offers a model of pure delight, these women are an inversion of her identity in more ways than one, for their relationships are marked by a profound physicality not evident in Rose, a physicality that seems possible only in the lower-middle and working class.

In Nancy's murder, brutality and domesticity are again linked to the weeping woman. Although as the narrative progresses Nancy begins to shed genuine tears that indicate a growing goodness inside her, we are reminded, with profound violence, that this moral metamorphosis does not alter the characteristic that Nancy has in common with other poor women. Her flaw is the capacity for physical damage that Rose transcends in her angelic demeanor, an attribute linked particularly to her class. Nancy has a body, a body upon which this violence can be enacted and have particular results—in her case and that of many others, death. This aspect of Nancy's identity, made apparent by her relationship to Rose, emphasizes the role of socioeconomic class in the production of wealth and the enactment of violence.

### Material Remains: Death, Finance, and the Body

*Oliver Twist* is a narrative as much fascinated with death as with weeping, not only in the form of Nancy's sensational murder, Bill's dramatic hanging, or Fagin's anticipation of his execution, but as a powerful metaphoric code for embodiment or the lack of it. In the opening moments of the narrative, Oliver barely escapes death—and this isn't the only time his life seems to be at risk. In his poverty and during the course of his criminal life, and even at the Brownlows' and the Maylies', the character and the narrator refer several times to the likelihood of the boy's death. His father dies before, and his mother just after, his birth. He more than once thinks of himself as "more dead than alive" and remarks, "I feel as if I should die!" even on happy occasions, such as his rediscovery of Brownlow. Other characters associate him with death as well. When Monks sees Oliver in Chertsey, he exclaims, "Death! . . . [H]e'd start up from a marble coffin, to come in my way!" (297). Oliver threatens death, yet seems to be impervious to the death all around him. What makes it possible for this frail child to survive these hardships?

True to the pattern, the other character who miraculously avoids death is Rose. She too is an orphan whose parents expire early in her childhood. She also is sickly and frail. She falls seriously ill, and all around her believe her death is imminent. Despite the diagnosis that she lies on "grave's verge" and the conviction that "it would be little short of a miracle, if she recovered" (298), she lives on.

Indeed, Rose is a miracle. Like Oliver, she is "[c]ast in so slight and exquisite a mould; so mild and gentle; so pure and beautiful; that earth seemed not her element, nor its rough creatures her fit companions"

(264). God himself authorizes Rose's continued sojourn in this physical world. During her illness, the narrative denies us any details of her ailment, nor do we see her in her sickbed. She is simply removed from our view. When the Maylies' servants shoot Oliver during a robbery, we never see his lacerated flesh or gore, a form of representation Nancy's murder scene clearly indicates was possible to narrate. Though a host of children at Mrs. Mann's fall graphically ill and die at her hands, Oliver survives. When Oliver, Noah, Charlotte, and Mrs. Sowerberry engage in battle, Noah's black eye and "dreadful wounds" (91) figure prominently in the description of the scene, but despite the excessive punishment inflicted upon Oliver—scratching, punching, kicking, caning, and finally, a drubbing by Mr. Sowerberry—the marks one would expect to see on his body are never delineated.

Rose and Oliver are impervious to violence and death because they are angels in the most elemental way—their immateriality. Helena Michie argues in *The Flesh Made Word* that the angel in the house bears a "bodiless body" of representations "that haunt Victorian representation of women" (90). Sally Mitchell indicates in *The Fallen Angel* that "the spiritual was a woman's provenance and the material was man's" (xii), suggesting that materiality itself belonged to the workplace and that middle-class women lacked this embodiment. I agree that these frameworks are indeed laid out in the novel, but argue that such dichotomies collapse when examined under the lens of economics and are used to mask the engagement of the domestic sphere in the attainment of not just money, but of middle-class identity and respectability, with the violent use of working-class women to achieve that goal. Though Sarah Stickney Ellis "strongly advocated maintaining a strict separation of the domestic and social spheres, arguing that women develop their moral superiority only by their exclusion from the marketplace" (qtd. in Gallagher, *Industrial Reformation* 119), women in the novel still end up maneuvering in the economic and being fixed in the material. Susan Walsh has described how women (particularly climacteric women) figured centrally in the Victorian economy as silent partners to financial development, and here we see both Nancy and Rose bound up in negotiations over the wealth of those for whom they care. Nancy and Rose shepherd great wealth to Oliver's guardians, and Rose's financial considerations become pivotal in her marriage to Harry. The difference between these two women would seem to be their bodies or lack of them. Rose manages funds without recourse to a body, but Nancy becomes so material by the novel's end that considering her salvation seems almost oxymoronic. Though this notion of the bodiless angel evolved over ensuing decades, becoming increasingly domesticated and material (marked by the impressions of sensationalism and its radical embodiment of the heroine into vexed creatures both ephemeral and eternal), Dickens's early angels seem to melt under the touch.[5] Michie notes the complexities for women in both living in and absenting their bodies, "suggest[ing] that the distance between the heroine's body and the words used to describe it are not simply *différance,* but an intervening between a subject and its representation" (84). Michie notes how some women appear to recede into language, such as *Middlemarch*'s Dorothea Brooke; they are then positioned as "presence and absence" (87). In their present absence, they cannot be harmed, but can serve as the locus for material gain and symbolic articulation of the middle-class space.

In contrast, the narrative provides characters who seem to be little more than bodies. When Nancy, for example, attempts to keep an appointment with Brownlow and Rose to give them information, Bill physically restrains her, and her body becomes an impediment to her will. Bill, "pinioning her hands dragged her, struggling and wrestling . . . and held her down by force . . . [until] wearied and exhausted, [she] ceased to contest the point any farther" (400). In addition, when Bill murders Nancy, not only is her body his focal point, but it is a narrative obsession. We are offered gruesome details of the crime, and for Bill, nothing besides Nancy's body seems to exist. He attempts to cover the body with a rug, then, in fear of what it might do when out of his sight, as if it were animated by its materiality rather than a soul, he hastily removes the rug. "And there was the body—mere flesh and blood, no more—but such flesh, and so much blood!" (423). He is so attentive to the corpse that he "never once [turns] his back upon [it]" (424). Nancy's profession, a trade in the body, and her death scene ground us completely in the material, highlighting precisely the kind of details that we are denied in Oliver's beating and Rose's illness.[6] In fact, Bill doesn't even refer to Nancy by name by the end of the novel. He simply calls her "the body" (447).

Nancy's physicality is also emphasized by the sustained comparison between her and Bill's dog, Bull's-eye. This parallel points up Nancy's animalistic qualities—qualities that often were associated with working-class women[7]—despite her ultimate goodness. Bill addresses Nancy "with a growl like that he was accustomed to use when addressing his dog" (166). Dutifully, when the dog is told to "mind [Oliver]! Mind him!" (158), he obeys with an alacrity that pleases his master, as does Nancy. Reflective of the inner battle that "turns [Nancy] against [her]self, and all of [the criminals]" (240) and later leads to her death, she fights with Bill to protect Oliver from the dog. She cries, "Keep back the dog; he'll tear the boy to pieces" (164). Bull's-eye, like the target after which he is named, takes Bill's hits just as Nancy does. Echoing the scene in which Nancy defends Oliver and Bill wrangles with her until she faints, Bill "drop[s] on his knees [and] beg[ins] to assail the animal most furiously" when the dog dares to resist admonition and beating (153). This fight, like the one between Bill and Nancy, is interrupted by Fagin, and Bill demands, "What the devil do you come in between me and my dog for?," troping the more common phrasing, "me and my wife." Indeed, Bill misses important signals between Fagin and Barney while dealing with the injuries inflicted on him by the dog, as his focus on Nancy's betrayal will lead him to miss Fagin's manipulative gestures. Bull's-eye, "well used" to kicking and commands, "coil[s] himself up in a corner very quietly without uttering a sound" when Bill orders him to enter (136), just as Nancy does after she shows Oliver her bruises then sits quietly by the fire without stirring (201). At one point, Bill chastises Bull's-eye for seeming to be "ashamed of [its] master" (136). Nancy's shame, the characteristic that leads her to speak to Rose Maylie, is perhaps the prime mover in the chain of events that lead to Bill's final assault on Nancy.

Only Bull's-eye witnesses Nancy's murder, and with its feet saturated with her blood it inadvertently gives away Bill's location (440), just as Nancy had. Ultimately the dog pays for its loyalty to Bill by having its skull crushed, just as Nancy had. When Bill is hung on the roof of the crib from which he's trying to escape, the dog lets up a "dismal howl, and collecting himself for a spring, jumped for the dead man's shoulders. . . . [H]e fell into the ditch . . . striking his head against a stone [and] dash[ing] out his brains" (453). Indeed, as Fagin notes, Bill "treat[s] [Nancy] like a dog" (401).

If death makes "all men equal," as the narrator remarks (259), then it is especially significant that Oliver and Rose consistently escape death and a character such as Nancy is positioned inside it for a good portion of the novel. It reveals an inequality that plays out clearly along socio-economic lines. Screened by the morality that is immanent in Rose and Oliver and by text in various forms—yet inescapably articulated in narrative tensions—finances and economic serviceability play vital roles in the negotiation of violence. Again, by overlaying the economic questions with morality, the narrative authoritatively names the rules for propriety. This suggests that such rules were a point of contest in the culture, notions up for grabs, positioned for revision. Indeed, text—such as this narrative, public speech, naming, and, through these, wealth—is the very thing that resolves characters such as Rose and Oliver into being, making them apparent in spite of their immateriality. Significantly, it is also what dematerializes, ends the life of, the working-class and criminal characters in the story. Text makes violence seem possible and present only in the working class.

### The Economy of Resolving Bodies and Embodied Words

The physicality of working-class figures plays out in several ways in *Oliver Twist,* through the body, through the violence enacted on it, and, as we will see below, through textuality and speech. Most poignantly, Nancy's murder makes grotesquely apparent her physicality. (Many critics believe that Dickens's dramatization of Nancy's murder, in which he performed the parts of both Bill and his victim, had the same function because it both filled Dickens's coffers and hastened his death.) By countering this famous scene with the narratives of the body that precede it, I hope to demonstrate its significance as a phase in the evolution of the terms of violence and the role of economics in its articulation.

#### The Calendar

Beginning in 1719, the authors of *The Newgate Calendar*—prison chaplains who wished to earn a profit while maintaining their anonymity for the sake of their ecclesiastical posts—culled tales from the session papers of trials and the Ordinaries of Newgate, records made by prison chaplains. *The Calendar* was reprinted, and new cases were entered, up to the year 1841. These documents, compiled in *The Complete Newgate Calendar,* contain surprisingly graphic depictions of violence in the home, with details of severed limbs, grotesque murder strategies, and women burned alive, both at the stake for a spouse's murder and at the hands of a husband. These stories provide a formula for domestic propriety and for the behavior of "man and wife," one that was mirrored in the fictional narratives produced at roughly the same time.[8] The typical formula of the Newgate tales is the authoritative narrator(s) who adjudicates on the ethics of the criminals and victims and justifies the punishment of crimes; the insistence on the text's truth; the graphic, almost gothic, details; and the focus on the immorality of the perpetrators and often the victims. Most often, beaten or murdered working-class women were depicted as savages along with their husbands, a pattern repeated in the Divorce Act that was passed a few years after the cessation of *The Calendar*'s publication.[9] In one case reported in *The Complete Newgate Calendar,* Henry Griffin, a brutal journeyman blacksmith, sliced his wife's windpipe with a razor. The text does not only impugn Mr. Griffin in the case; Mrs. Griffin, we are told, was a woman of "vicious habits, such as infidelity, drunkenness, etc." (65). Indeed, her behavior was deemed so offensive that Mr. Griffin was obliged only to pay a small fine, although he openly admitted to the murder.[10]

*Oliver Twist* reconfigures this model by exalting the woman-victim and marking her as a candidate for salvation, rather than describing her as flawed. This difference illuminates one means by which nineteenth-century paradigms of family violence and middle-class identity were shaped and highlights what I believe to be a foundational thread in the construction of the complex web of social notions surrounding the means of determining the ethical social response to family violence and the proprietous middle-class home. It reveals a shift in the identity of the working woman from a removed "Other" to a far more familiar, and essential, economic conduit for the middle and upper classes, while maintaining her as a repository for violence.

### The Calendar's Nichol Brown

The relationship between Nichol Brown and his wife is in many ways analogous to the relationship between Nancy and Bill. The Browns were a cohabiting working-class couple, and Mrs. Brown's violent murder was not precipitated by a charge of sexual infidelity. In the person of Nichol Brown, we are granted a detailed account of a man who was an "atrocious monster," very like the vicious hooligan Bill Sikes. Brown ate flesh cut from the leg of a recently executed convict still hanging from the gibbet and burnt his wife to death in the fireplace when he came home drunk to find her intoxicated as well. The scene I quote here is strikingly similar to that of Nancy's murder; however, there is a significant difference.

> *After having been drinking at an alehouse in Cannongate, [Nichol Brown] went home about eleven at night, in a high degree of intoxication. His wife was also much in liquor; but, though equally criminal himself, he was so exasperated against her, that he struck her so violently that she fell from her chair. The noise of the fall alarmed the neighbours; but, as frequent quarrels had happened between them, no immediate notice was taken of the affair.*
>
> *In about fifteen minutes the wife was heard to cry out "Murder! help! fire! the rogue is murdering me! help, for Christ's sake!" The neighbours, now apprehending real danger, knocked at the door; but, no person being in the house but Brown and his wife, no admission was granted; and the woman was heard to groan most shockingly.*
>
> *A person, looking through the key-hole, saw Brown holding his wife to the fire; on which he was called on to open the door, but refused to do so. The candle being extinguished, and the woman still continuing in her cries, the door was at length forced open; and, when the neighbours went in, they beheld her a most shocking spectacle, lying half-naked before the fire, and her flesh in part broiled. In the interim Brown had got into bed, pretended to be asleep, and, when spoken to, appeared ignorant of the transaction. (240)*

In spite of his conviction for the murder, Brown showed no remorse, and reports from his prison stay described him as so hardened a man that he was capable of making an "ancient minister" weep. After his execution, the community expressed its outrage and horror by repeatedly stealing and finally destroying Brown's corpse. (The fact that the assaults were enacted on his corpse, not his living person, again suggests that for the working class, identity is lodged primarily in the body.) Clearly, the authors of *The Calendar* disapproved of Brown, and they represented an entire community sharing in their disapproval; in fact, they remarked, "It is impossible to express sufficient horror at the crime of which this man was guilty . . . it is therefore the less necessary to make any remarks on his case, as no one can be tempted to think of committing a similar crime till he is totally divested of all the feelings of humanity. From a fate so wretched as this may the God of infinite mercy deliver us!"

Despite the criticism of Nichol Brown, however, no great sympathy is expressed for his deceased wife. She is a "shocking spectacle," a visual horror, who isn't in "real danger" when she is habitually beaten by her husband. They both are, according to the narrative, "equally criminal" preceding the murder. Both Brown and his wife are depicted as social and moral failures who dismissed their obligations to the community and became "obnoxious to their acquaintance[s]" long before the murder. The narrators never call upon their readers to pity Mrs. Brown's horrible fate, as they do many "innocent" figures in the series of tales, nor do they depict her favorably. Instead, they offer a lengthy commentary on the Browns' marriage—in spite of the editors' insistence that it is "unnecessary." This indicates the drive to articulate and reinforce what is described as a natural code of morality regarding not just inanimate property and goods, as in *The Calendar*'s cases of burglary and destruction of property, but marriage and violence.

These naturalized codes lay heavy emphasis on several issues: first, the couple's moral and social misdeeds, she as a drunk who failed to please her husband, and he as a cannibalistic, heartless monster; second, their mutual failure as human beings and the poor habits inculcated by their class that seemed to make their violence possible. Furthermore, the authors repeatedly insist upon the accuracy of the account (a move Dickens reclaims in his novel), suggesting an almost sacred quality for the sentiments expressed. Indeed, the fact that these tales emerged from the Ordinaries reinforces their "spiritual," "naturalized" truth. Finally, the graphic and carefully detailed violence of this narrative serves to further emphasize the depravity of those involved. We might, for example, find Nichol Brown's attempt to abdicate responsibility for the crime by slipping into bed and claiming that he was asleep during the assault on his shrieking wife—in spite of the witnesses—farcical, if it weren't for the grotesque, excessively detailed violence, including the description of

Mrs. Brown's bubbling flesh that precedes his denial. *The Calendar's* discursive method, referencing the natural ethical guidelines derived from the "truth" inherent in the text, as well as the journalistic detail, reinforces the often unspoken, but persistently present, moral codes, the authority to speak to them, and, through these, the construction of the working-class woman and man as inherently flawed and violent.

In the late 1830s, after more than a century of consistent reprintings and enlargements, the republication of *The Newgate Calendar* abruptly stopped and the Newgate novels, a genre that imitated *The Calendar,* "attracted a new kind of attention, genuinely hostile" (Hollingsworth 15). I argue that many early nineteenth-century novels take up the social project of these criminal narratives, deploying many of the same strategies, deferring—with one prominent modification—to the patterns established in *The Newgate Calendar* that had pleased the public and generated tremendous profits for its authors. Beth Kalikoff points to the distinct motives and manners of middle-class fictional narratives and those written in street literature style, but it is the role *The Calendar* played in its heyday and the similarities between *The Calendar* and later fiction that urge me to point to this contrast. Dickens argued that (like *The Calendar*) he had resisted the idealization of his working-class characters' behavior and depicted them in all their horror so he could most effectively provide a moral. His preface and the body of the novel *Oliver Twist* emphasize all those characteristics I noted in *The Newgate Calendar*—the appeal to the truth, the self-evident morality, the detailed horror of the crime. Yet, significantly, in *Oliver Twist,* the abused woman is a sympathetic figure, unlike the ill-fated Mrs. Brown.

This shift in terms reveals an unspoken shift in ideology—one that significantly alters the role of the other elements in the text and appears at a crucial moment in British industrial, economic, and social history: a revised notion of the working woman's economic and moral relationship to the middle and upper classes. In *Oliver Twist,* the depiction of true-to-life violence functions, as it had in *The Calendar,* to naturalize the depiction of some working-class people as ghastly perpetrators of vicious crimes and to mark them as the fit and only victims of such crime—but in this case, only the male villain is at fault. Bill's victim is only his. Nancy is not victimized by her culture or the economic system; her grinding poverty and apparent lack of opportunities are transcended in the moment Rose makes an offer of moral deliverance. Divorced from her social context, but still thoroughly corporeal and fallen, Nancy is depicted charitably, her moral choices identified as the source of the salvation she is promised.

The compassion we feel for Nancy deflects our attention from the economic relations between the working-class woman and her "betters" in the novel and turns it to the benign didactic and moral nature of the narrative in which the "true" villain is punished. Thus, the brutal murder of Nancy by Bill Sikes focuses on the kind of graphic events we saw in the Brown case. The narrative tells us how Sikes struck Nancy down with a gun butt, then a heavy club, while she begged for the salvation of them both and insisted on her loyalty to him; how he beat her again and again while she prayed, moaned, and raised her hands to heaven; how her hair, which clung to the club with which he battered her, blazed in the fire and floated up the chimney when he tried to destroy evidence of the crime. Though depicted as a graphic, physical horror, like Mrs. Brown's death scene, Nancy's murder is staged centrally as a scene of moral horror, in which we are reminded over and over that Nancy has at last been saved by the angelic heroine Rose Maylie. Nancy cries out, just before her death,

> "[L]et us both leave this dreadful place, and far apart lead better lives, and forget how we have lived, except in prayers, never to see each other more. It is never too late to repent. They told me so—I feel it now." . . . [H]e beat [his gun butt] twice with all the force he could summon upon the upturned face that almost touched his own. She staggered and fell: nearly blinded with the blood that rained down from a deep gash in her forehead; but raising herself, with difficulty on her knees, drew from her bosom a white handkerchief—Rose Maylie's own—and holding it up, in her folded hands, as high towards Heaven as her feeble strength would allow, breathed one prayer for mercy to her Maker. (422–23)

This story is unlike those in *The Calendar*; despite the horror of Mrs. Brown's death, we are not called upon to pity her, to pray for her salvation, as we are in Nancy's case. Nancy's narrative operates to evince great sympathy for a fallen woman, a woman marked as innately unworthy of the gentrified Rose Maylie's attention. Nancy's grievous difficulty in obtaining an audience with Rose seems to point to the gulf we must cross in feeling, with Rose, a desire to pull Nancy from the clutches of Bill and her miserable life.

In his essay on *The Old Curiosity Shop* and Marx's account of capital, Matthew Rowlinson considers the sublime form of capital and the ways it remarks questions of materiality and the site of exchange. Most relevant here is the way in which his argument about excess materiality in a system of exchange disrupts that system. I shift focus here to the most undeveloped portion of Rowlinson's argument, gender, to suggest that in *Oliver Twist* we might read Nancy's excessive materiality and her role in a series of economic exchanges as evidence of another form of the manifest historically situated tensions Rowlinson sees in *The Old Curiosity Shop*. In *Oliver Twist*, Nancy secures the economic exchange, serving as the material conduit, the body that bears the violence of the transaction. Yet, her death disrupts the easy comfort of the fiduciary processes, creating an anxiety the narrative cloaks in the rhetoric of morality. Thus, we pity Nancy, but she successfully provides and provides for, as the novel would seem to suggest, those who are most worthy. In fact, the host of arguments that position Dickens as increasingly critical of the poor and criminal, after describing his early attitudes as generous and liberal, fail to take into account the way that figures such as Nancy operate beneath the rhetoric of sympathy, serving the middle classes at the cost of their lives. As Philip Collins has argued in *Dickens and Crime,* Dickens's notions about crime are often far more complex than his critics are willing to admit. In this discussion, I hope to enrich our understanding of Dickens's complexity and vex those notions of a simple transition from liberality to conservatism along the lines of gender and through a kind of crime to which we have rarely attended in critical study: economic and marital violence.

### Savings Accounts

Despite the emphasis on Nancy's salvation in Rose's interactions with her, Nancy does not come to the attention of the kindly gentlewoman as a hardened prostitute in need of moral salve. Nor is she the subject of the narrator's sympathy because Bill beats her. Our first encounter with Nancy does nothing to separate her from the character with whom she is introduced, Bet, another prostitute and criminal. Indeed, Dickens's novels are as filled with anonymous women who fall under the hands of brutal men as are the pages of *The Newgate Calendar.* Nancy's relationship to her benefactress differs from the rest of the criminal element in a significant way—she serves as a valuable avenue to Oliver's fortune, providing all the vital clues about his whereabouts, identity, and history. Even the language in which she communicates her information to Rose emphasizes the role that economics plays in this scenario: "[Monks] said that he had got the young devil's money safely now . . . after making a good profit besides" (363). Nancy becomes the means of transferring the wealth and property that were formerly held by the "villains and thieves" in her criminal working-class circle into the hands of Oliver and his benefactors, Mr. Brownlow and Rose Maylie. In fact, although Monks believes that Rose and Mr. Brownlow might give "many thousand and hundreds of thousands of pounds" to get the information Nancy provides, they are required to give nothing, and are instead richly rewarded for their connection with Nancy.

Reading this scene in the framework I have provided here allows very different aspects of the women's conversation to emerge for analysis. Rose promises Nancy salvation, diverting the focus from financial questions: "'[Y]our evident contrition, and sense of shame; all lead me to believe that you might yet be reclaimed. Oh!' said the earnest girl, folding her hands as tears coursed down her face . . . 'let me save you yet'" (364). Rose's tears overlay the scene with morality and salvation. Yet, in spite of Rose's insistence that she must protect Nancy and cannot let her return to her criminal life knowing the danger Nancy will face, she does, just as Nancy predicts. Rose inquires, "Of what use, then, is the communication you have made?," a remark that resists the suggestion that Nancy's salvation is what is at stake (365). Finally, Rose solicits Nancy's services again, despite her awareness of the danger Nancy faces. When Rose openly discloses her encounter with Nancy to Mr. Brownlow, Mrs. Maylie, Dr. Losberne, and Mr. Grimwig (breaking the solemn promise she has made to speak to only one other person and calling into question Rose's absolute fidelity), the only object of the group is "the discovery of Oliver's parentage, and regaining for him the inheritance of which, if this story be true, he has been fraudulently deprived" (373). Mr. Brownlow has long ago discovered Oliver's parentage, which lays increased emphasis on the inheritance as the primary gain in this situation. Indeed, Brownlow will not bring down the criminals based on Nancy's information, despite the fact that this might provide them with the proofs of Oliver's parentage currently in Fagin's possession. Brownlow's reason for avoiding this course? That it would be "in direct opposition to our own interest— or at least to Oliver's which is the same thing" (374). In addition to the fact that Brownlow's remarks reveal the party's concerns as somehow primary, the term "interest" carries monetary connotations into his motives. Indeed, the term evokes the increasingly complex system of savings and credit in industrial capitalism, a system that Patrick Brantlinger argues was foundational in constructing national identity, and that I would argue was just as vital in securing individual identity—particularly as a metaphor for respectability and probity in the middle class that defied the representation of middle-class violence. By securing information on the inheritance, they reap a remarkable profit—three thousand pounds, half of the money still in Monks's possession (475).

Once Nancy has provided the necessary information in her last interview with Rose and Brownlow—a confirmation of Brownlow's beliefs about Oliver's identity and the location at which they might apprehend Monks—Brownlow immediately attempts to terminate their contact, indicating that Nancy has wasted the "priceless treasures" the Creator bestowed upon her (414). The link of treasures to Nancy's fall, rather than the wealth she transfers, again masks finances with morality. Though Brownlow offers Nancy asylum, a necessity for the myth of salvation proffered here, he confidently assures Rose that Nancy could not be persuaded to accept the offer—a remark that is stunningly premature and dismissive, especially in such dire circumstances. Contrary to Brownlow's claim, Nancy does experience a struggle. Without a mention of any apprehension by Nancy, Brownlow urges, "We compromise her safety, perhaps, by staying here. We may have detained her longer than she expected already" (415), clearly a dismissal of the young woman. Through Nancy, we have the most ironic disavowal of economic gain. She begs that Brownlow and Rose understand she has "not done this for money." Indeed, she gains none. She refuses the small purse Rose offers and merely takes the handkerchief that will be so prominent in her death scene.

Nancy's possession of the purse would be as criminal as Fagin's secret stash or Bill's payments from Fagin. It would ethically soil her to possess money. She is not the proper receptacle for cash, but for the embodiment of a fallen and battered womanhood. She must bear the violence on her body, not the trappings of wealth. However, the thousands of pounds that Monks predicted Brownlow would give are transmitted to Brownlow instead, free of taint, without impunity, because they serve to shore up an identity that never was working class, Oliver's.[11]

The upper classes invest briefly in Nancy, but their investment is not a financial one. It is marked instead as moral. Their return, however, is profoundly economically rewarding. Nancy's value and the loss expressed at her brutal death do not depend on the soul that might have been saved. None of her comrades is offered the same chance at redemption, although they, like Oliver and Nancy, experience the same victimization at the hands of the older criminals because of their poverty and isolation. None of them has had protectors, as Oliver has, and even when Nancy identifies her relationship with other criminals and her concern for their well-being as the sole reason for her unwillingness to begin a virtuous life, salvation is never offered to them. Nancy is the only cooperative economic tool for her "betters," and therefore she is the only criminal offered moral deliverance. This particular working-class woman is valuable not because of the difficulties she faces in life, not because of her "heart of gold," but because of the gold she transmits. Once Nancy's economic usefulness ends, so does her life.

The transformation of the true crime narrative of family violence, from the early *Newgate Calendar* to the novels of Dickens, occurred alongside the rumbling progress of the industrial revolution, the rise to economic power of the middle class, and the dramatic increase in the numbers of the destitute in the economic centers of Britain. In this environment of economic instability, the emphasis on strict morality and the sympathy evinced for the fallen woman, particularly in cases of interfamilial violence as it is articulated in this narrative, may be revealed as suspect. By reading *Oliver Twist* against the grain and in the context of historical precedents, this pattern suggests that the nineteenth-century Evangelical project participated in a complex range of social issues, often veiling the economic structures that underlay the shifting Victorian scene.

*Embodying Text and Speech*

The shift from *The Newgate Calendar* as a voice of moral authority in relation to domesticity, violence, and the law to narratives such as *Oliver Twist* reveals the transition to a Victorian industrial capitalistic consciousness, fostered by the burgeoning middle classes, a move Davidoff and Hall link with a growing emphasis on morality, as opposed to particular religions, in the 1830s and 1840s (184). In this novel, these patterns are mapped out through textuality and speech, both significant in regard to understanding the relationship of fiction and the law to social codes because of what they generate: the fiction and law that laid out the gendered and class relations that made Nancy's murder (and those of people like her) possible, as well as a middle-class identity that denied such a possibility. A significant corollary to the issue of textual production is the question of self-production. If the "respectables" were marked by their distance from the body of the "roughs" and were performing a material disembodiment that obscured violence, then we must consider how their identity was generated. If not in the flesh, from what ground was the identity of non-working-class figures shaped? The most genteel form of embodiment was through self-narration, "getting the body into writing," as Peter Brooks describes it (1). Brooks indicates that identity depends upon marking the body with signifiers: "Signing or marking the body signifies its passage into writing, its becoming a literary body, and generally also a narrative body, in that the inscription of the sign depends on and produces a story. The signing of the body is an allegory of the body become a subject for literary narrative—a body entered into writing" (3). I would use the broader term "text" to suggest that although often written, as in legal documents (which provided a link to respectability and the shifting legal codes), this embodiment was also accomplished through storytelling (which might be verbal or textual, which Dickens both represents in and performs through his novels) and through verbalization (which in the novels is, again, always textual). Significantly, the working and criminal classes must avoid all public engagement in these activities—they cannot tell their stories publicly or represent themselves in legal text; indeed, this is a kind of death for them as it is for Nancy. Contrarily, this is precisely what Oliver must do to gain his fortune, and as the novel suggests, it is what all genteel men and women will do to improve their economic status, safe in the knowledge that the text screens any violence.

## Buy the Book: The Social Circulation of Text

Books engage the reader in several ways. I focus here on two: the introduction of the buyer into the economic cycle as he or she purchases and consumes the text, and, as Dickens noted in the preface to *Oliver Twist* and as several contemporary critics have recognized, the provision of a moral, a book's signification of cultural codes in the narrative, even when that is not its intent.[12] The latter theme returns to the importance of text in relation to social codes, such as those surrounding marital violence. I propose that textuality functions in *Oliver Twist* to position the consumer economically and morally and to obscure both the body and violence. The signified slips under the signifier in the way that Jacques Lacan describes in his essay "The Agency of the Letter in the Unconscious," kept in motion by the endless displacements and substitutions on the signifying chain (*Ecrits* 164). Because a halt in this process exposes the emptiness of the signifier, its inability to maintain the illusion of disembodiment on which propriety depends, the process must be kept in motion.[13] As Garrett Stewart notes, the fictional narrative "decenter[s] the social subject it purports to inscribe" (*Dear Reader* 168), thus the process continues, constant circulation holding the material in abeyance, reasserting the social construction on which it insists. Elizabeth Langland and Lenore Davidoff both note that signifiers were also kept in circulation to identify the genuine insider, one who could parley in the latest codes. These codes were also identifying in that the subject's identity must be constructed in these shifting terms—a tenuous process that must be vigilantly maintained.

I have suggested that the privileged in *Oliver Twist* are disembodied and that it is only in the working class that the novel depicts physical materiality. This disembodiment becomes visible in the narrative's relation to textuality, which further illuminates the active obfuscation of violence. Athena Vrettos, speaking to the role of illness in Victorian culture, argues that Alice James's diaries reveal a desire "symbolically to reconstruct her body in a more durable form. . . . [T]he body is not so much represented in as replaced by a narrative act" (*Somatic Fictions* 49); she describes this as a Victorian impulse to "transform bodies into narratives" (182). Though textuality serves as a no more lasting or secure embodiment than a social construction that places a woman well within her physical frame, it indeed marks her as less vulnerable to acts of physical violence.

We first see evidence of the relationship between body and text in Oliver's studies, which make apparent a mind/body dualism, suggesting that a gulf lies between. Though the categories of mind and body in Victorian England were not thoroughly stable, as Vrettos's work indicates, they had not yet been baffled by the development of the neurological or psychological sciences. This division makes possible a reading-induced half-sleep that "holds [Oliver's] body prisoner . . . and enable[s] [his mind] to ramble at its pleasure." In this alienation of mind and body, words predominate, forcing the imagination to accommodate itself until it is "a matter of impossibility to separate the two" (309).

This understanding makes a new reality for Oliver, a new way of thinking that assists him in erasing the life of criminality (as he erases Fagin and Monks, who mysteriously disappear without a trace when they arrive at the study window) and allows his physical body to mark his distance from the working-class child that he seemed to be earlier in the narrative. Here, Oliver takes up the life of the mind, not the life of the body, a sign of his new class. Indeed, the engagement with text is suggestive of Louis Althusser's interpellation of the subject: the hailing of the other that positions us as ideological beings.[14] This is not simply a passive process in which a reader is marked by the text, but rather an engagement with the text, the reader's textual production in response and the circulation of these texts, here described as "the life of the mind," because a life in textuality is the life of the privileged. This life requires that its focus be the immateriality of the mind translated into the materiality of text, rather than body. Stewart describes Erich Schön's claim, in *Loss of Sensuality,* that silent reading forces the reader to "giv[e] up [the] physiological register . . . [and] facilitates instead . . . a turn toward what [Schön] calls 'a controlled traffic in the specific reality of a literarily mediated world.'"[15] This shift then facilitates, according to both Schön and Stewart, the creation of the "new bourgeois citizenry" (Stewart, *Dear Reader* 77, 78). The site of social embodiment, then, lies in the material object in this scene: the book and its circulation.

From the moment that Oliver first sees Mr. Brownlow, the gentleman is associated with books. Brownlow, described as a "very respect-
able-looking personage," achieves respectability through his bottle-green
coat, his smart bamboo cane, and the fact that he stands at a bookstall,
"reading away . . . turning over the leaf when he [gets] to the bottom of
page, beginning at the top line of the next one, and going regularly on,
with the greatest interest and eagerness" (114). This book, carried from
the bookstall to Brownlow's and back again, emblematizes Brownlow's
honor and reveals Oliver's honesty to us. Oliver's first interview with
Mr. Brownlow, after he recovers from his illness, takes place in Brownlow's study, a room "quite full of books." Oliver wonders at "such a great
number of books as seemed to be written to make the world wiser.
Which is still a marvel to more experienced people than Oliver Twist,
every day of their lives" (144). These texts and their circulation among
those of a certain class make the world wiser, just as this novel might.
Brownlow offers the books as bait to Oliver, in a way that clearly indicates
an expectation of particular social codes, those Brownlow, and presumably his books, holds to be moral. "You shall read them, if you behave
well," he suggests (145).

When Oliver begins to settle into his new life with the Maylies,
books, reading, and writing are offered again to the boy. "Every morning
he went to a white-headed old gentleman, who lived near the little
church: who taught him to read better, and to write. . . . Then, he would
walk with Mrs. Maylie and Rose, and hear them talk of books; or perhaps
sit in some shady place, and listen whilst the young lady read. . . . Then,
he had his own lesson for the next day to prepare; and at this, he would
work hard" (291). This work does not simply promote Oliver's health.
More important, it allows him to engage with gentlemen and with Rose
and to secure his position in their social world in preparation for the
wealth he will receive. He can, in this way, become like Mr. Brownlow
and Harry Maylie, gentlemen who not only read books, but produce
proper text as well, text that can be shared and can stand in to demonstrate the identity of a gentleman.

Oliver is given his first chance to employ his new skills when Harry
returns to London after Rose's illness. Harry inquires of the boy, "You
can write well now? . . . I wish you to write to me—say once every
fortnight . . . you can fill up a sheet" (320). This activity not only estab-

lishes Oliver in Harry's good graces, but in the class to which he belongs. The transmission of the letter represents Oliver's proper fit in the signifying chain of his world. Dick, Oliver's former companion at Mrs. Mann's baby farm, makes a similar request of Bumble—to write for him because he lacks this genteel skill: "I should like . . . if somebody that can write, would put a few words down for me on a piece of paper . . . to leave my dear love to poor Oliver Twist" (172). The child's inability to write not only prevents him from communicating with one who would have the power to save him, but grounds him firmly in the working-class identity that forces him out of circulation himself. Bumble notes in this request for speech the danger of Dick's "demogaliz[ation]" by Oliver. This bumbled word seems to suggest that Dick has been corrupted, perhaps by his desire to reach beyond his position, and Bumble reveals this in a significant way. "They're all in one story," he exclaims (173). At this point in the narrative, the only thing separating Oliver from Dick is his material situation, and the evocative reference to the story that Dick cannot tell—and Oliver (and Dickens) can—suggests that the narrative and economic transition are linked. Writing and textuality, then, work to establish identity and generate money, complex processes that figure the site of gendered violence. Michael Ginsburg reads *Oliver Twist* as a "rhetorical marketplace," though he argues that this is evident only in sites of non-naturalized (and thus rhetorical) speech (230). I suggest that the novel points to economics everywhere, using text to screen this exchange, to stand in the place of money, as it does for the body. This becomes most apparent in the omission of text. No one speaks of Oliver's natural father's money, for example, only his will and its absence. Therefore, I will turn to the examination of text's failed circulation and the way it speaks to the questions of economics and textuality.

Those middle-class figures who fail to circulate text assault the social system and often literally disrupt the flow of money. For example, Mr. Fleming, Agnes and Rose's father, died "without a letter, book, or scrap of paper" (462). His omission left Rose nameless, penniless, and at the mercy of the bitter Mrs. Leeford's schemes. Similarly, Oliver's father, Mr. Leeford, failed to transmit the vital will that would have saved Oliver from early hardship and would have properly introduced him into the upper class shortly after his birth. This failure to dematerialize them in the text is the act that brings these characters the closest to experiencing violence. When Brownlow first narrates the senior Leeford's tale, he emphasizes the absence of this exchange: "leaving no will—*no will*—so that the whole property fell" to the wicked Monks and his mother (437). Leeford also failed to transmit a letter to Brownlow that would have further explained his situation with the fallen Agnes, his newborn child, and his wishes for his money. Similarly, the blank in which Leeford should have provided a surname on the ring he presented to Agnes represents another social and moral failing. This information would have identified and enfranchised Oliver at birth. Though Leeford had produced these texts, his failure to introduce them into the textual economy led to hardship for his youngest son. We know Mrs. Leeford's villainy, the only thing she "transmitted" to Monks (459), in part because she burns Leeford's will and secrets the letter, disrupting the transmission of documents and money. Monks safeguards her secrets, and it is only when he is forced to betray the contents of the papers and Fagin is required to give them up— when the text is recirculated—that Oliver and Rose are restored to their rightful places.

Significantly, Monks and Fagin produce the substance of these texts when they are at their most vulnerable: Monks, when he has lost half his father's fortune to Oliver, and Fagin, the night before his execution. Both of them die after these revelations. Indeed, all of the criminals evince a dislike not just for legal text, but for text in general. This distaste becomes apparent when Oliver is first recaptured by the gang. The boy has been sent on an errand carrying Brownlow's books. Brownlow and his friend Grimwig intend for this task, the transmission of text, to demonstrate the child's legitimacy or illegitimacy, his worthiness of their favor. When Nancy and Brownlow return Oliver to Fagin's gang, Fagin and Bill argue over who will take the cash Oliver carries and who will take the books; clearly, neither of them wants the handsome volumes. Fagin remarks that the money is "[m]ine, Bill, mine. You shall have the books." Bill threatens, when this offer is made, to "take the boy back again." Charley, one of the young thieves, mocks Oliver with his distance from the books now that he's back in the criminals' hands: " 'They're very pretty. . . . [B]eautiful writing, isn't it, Oliver?' At the sight of the dismayed look with which Oliver regarded his tormentors, Master Bates, who was blessed with a lively sense of the ludicrous, fell into another ecstasy." The link between text and economics is laid bare in the criminal class; when it is finally settled that Fagin will be the new owner of the books, Bill remarks, "You may keep the books, if you're fond of reading. If you a'n't, sell 'em" (163–64). To be textually embodied in the working class—on a police record, through the Ordinaries of Newgate—was to be lost, to endanger the body in its signifying displacement, to risk physical violence. The construction of identity in the working and middle classes had become increasingly divergent in recent decades, as Davidoff and Hall note in *Family Fortunes*. Though Oliver begs them to return the books, even if it binds him for life to Fagin's gang, the criminals recognize that Oliver's failure to participate in the circulation of the books will make him seem wicked to his new friends.

Significantly, the only book with which Fagin supplies Oliver is almost certainly *The Newgate Calendar:* "It was a history of the lives and trials of great criminals. . . . Here, [Oliver] read of dreadful crimes that made the blood run cold; of secret murders that had been committed by the lonely wayside; of bodies hidden from the eye of man in deep pits and wells: which would not keep them down, deep as they were, but had yielded them up at last, after many years, and so maddened the murderers with the sight, that in their horror, they had confessed their guilt, and yelled for the gibbet to end their agony" (196). Oliver's reaction to this text distinguishes it from the proper narratives "written to make the world wiser." For Oliver, the text evolves from a book to bodies themselves, obliterating the words and becoming criminality, carnality. The text was "so real and vivid, that the sallow pages seemed to turn red with gore; and the words upon them, to be sounded in his ears, as if they were whispered, in hollow murmurs, by the spirits of the dead" (196–97). The criminals failing to participate in the benefits of the new economic system remain trapped in a time past, in the pages of an outdated book whose pages they have "soiled and thumbed" (196), marking the text with their corrupted bodies. Oliver seeks instead a new and revised guide to living. It's not simply that *The Calendar* offers rules for misbehavior or working-class behavior and Oliver needs to do the reverse. Its entire epistemology is outdated. This way of perceiving the world is for naught, and Oliver must learn the new system. The criminals are damned by their failure to engage in another way of life; they don't, like the culture at large, participate in Victorian progress.

The "right" texts embrace change and evolve with the times, as *Oliver Twist* does, announcing their distance from physicality and violence. However, most of these texts remain outside the discourse and the economic grasp of those without means. Circulating texts, such as those transmitted through Mudie's Circulating Library, gained their socioeconomic mark in part by the price tag a subscription carried. In Trollope's *He Knew He Was Right,* Miss Stanbury, a painfully proprietous woman, refuses to have a subscription to anything too inexpensive in her home, deploring the disrespectability implied in their affordability. The only criminal in *Oliver Twist* who attempts to move beyond poverty-ridden textuality and into respectability is Nancy, when she tries to read a novel. Her attempt marks the way in which this activity seems bound to fail for the criminal element, for, as Nancy says to Brownlow and Rose, "I'll swear I saw 'coffin' written in every page of the book in large black letters" (409). For her, textual engagement represents a kind of death instead of the new life it presents Oliver. Indeed, all forms of text that produce the middle class may endanger those outside of that world.

### Public Speaking

For Fagin's gang, "peaching," or becoming an informer, serves as another form of representation, places them in circulation, and represents an unwelcome means of disclosure and potential death. The new discourse, being developed and resolved in the space of the bourgeoisie, endangers the poor and dispossessed for precisely the reason that it secures the position of the others. For figures such as Oliver and Rose text provides the kind of material textual body that allows them to efface their physical bodies and enter into the polite society of the middle and upper classes. Yet this disembodiment threatens to destroy the one thing with which the working class is associated and for which its members are valued— the physical: their labor and, as in Nancy's case, their bodies as the venues for economic exchange. Thus, the effacement of physicality that bourgeois speech implies means an effacement of life for working-class figures. Circulating his narrative among the Maylies, Brownlow, and their friends saves Oliver, remakes him in that small study filled with books that presumably provide other narratives of a similar sort.

Telling a story in the criminal world, on the other hand, means certain death. When Oliver, the Dodger, and Charley first spy Mr. Brownlow, the pickpockets silence Oliver, and the gang's first worry when Oliver disappears is that he will talk out of turn. Bill takes Oliver on the housebreaking excursion, and tells him, "[I]f you speak a word when you're out o' doors with me . . . that loading [from this gun] will be in your head without notice." Nancy translates Bill's intentions for Oliver by framing them in terms of the activity in which he was engaged at Mr. Brownlow's only days before. "[Bill] will prevent [your] ever telling tales afterwards, by shooting [you] through the head" (200). The house-breaker and his partner, Toby Crackit, constantly call upon Oliver to be silent.

In addition to the pragmatics of crime, there is a social value to public speech, one that does not accrue to the criminals and is, indeed, inverted in their case. When Nancy first becomes attached to Oliver, creating concern in the gang, neither Bill nor Fagin suggests that she might threaten to leave, rob them, or return Oliver. Rather, Bill reassures Fagin by saying, "[Nancy] ain't one to blab" (191). Indeed, public silence is precisely what's valued. Fagin explains to Oliver that other boys who "evinc[ed] a desire to communicate with the police, had unfortunately come to be hanged at the Old Bailey one morning" (177), linking speech and death in their circle. Bill performs a "dumb show," "tying an imaginary knot under his left ear, and jerking his head over on the right shoulder" (137), mutely indicating that death arises from speech, the same kind of social speech with which Fagin threatens Oliver. However, as Fagin admits, he cannot hurt Oliver because he "[is] not like other boys in the same circumstances" (244). Far more threatening is the possibility that Oliver will speak of them: "He has not peached so far. . . . If he means to blab us among his new friends, we may stop his windpipe yet" (142).

Significantly, though the men anticipate violence from those in the middle and upper classes, Nancy must fear the men in her own world. Here, we see how the question of text directly implicates gendered violence as an exclusively working-class phenomenon. Nancy begs Oliver for his silence when she hands him over to Bill, indicating directly the ways in which speech draws up and damages the body in the world in which they are operating: "Hush! Every word from you is a blow for me" (199). When Nancy attempts to leave to meet with Rose and Brownlow, to "peach," Bill threatens to sic his dog, Bull's-eye, on her and remarks, "[I]f I hear you for a half a minute longer, the dog shall have such a grip on your throat as'll tear some of that screaming voice out" (399). As we see in the novel's close, Nancy's words are such a threat that when she speaks, she must be murdered. Repeatedly in the narrative, "one word" is enough to end another's life (177, 240, 298).[16]

Nancy's increasingly public story precipitates her untimely death at the hands of her partner. When she prepares to go speak to Brownlow and Rose, Bill observes, "You look like a corpse come to life again" (357), foreshadowing the death that will result from her speech. After discovering Nancy's "indiscretion," Fagin asks Bill what he would do if anyone in the gang were to peach. Bill exclaims that he would "grind his skull under the iron heel of [his] boot into as many grains as there are hairs upon his head" (419). He proves his prediction about the fate of the informer when he crushes Nancy's skull. His first action, however, is to "[place] his hand heavily upon her mouth" (422), blocking her speech with physical force. She responds by tying up the language in paradoxical knots, indicating that she won't voice anything, despite the fact that she must speak to him in some fashion to protest her innocence and beg for her life: "I won't scream or cry—not once—hear me" (422). Already lost from speaking out, Nancy becomes trapped in a linguistic double bind: the speech that ends her life cannot protect her as well. For her, and others, words equal death, and she has just the body on which the repercussions of these deadly indicators can be deployed. As we see most graphically in Nancy's case, the middle and upper classes remain free from the taint of violence, while the violence that crosses all boundaries of class and gender is concentrated into the horrific domestic conflict between Bill and Nancy.

Though the novel offers no thoroughgoing rise from the lower ranks (Oliver's success is implied in his wealthy gentleman father), it does depict a descent. Monks originated in the upper class, but his choice to circulate in the criminal world makes speech the same threat to him as it is to the other lower-class characters. We see his working-class embodiment when Nancy informs on Monks, and she describes him with exclusively bodily indicators. She remarks on his height, weight, and coloring, but perhaps more significantly, speaks of his physical deterioration and corruption, indicating that "although he can't be more than six or eight and twenty, [he looks] withered and haggard. His lips are often discoloured and disfigured with the marks of teeth; for he has desperate fits, and sometimes even bites his hands and covers them with wounds" (413).

Brownlow responds by identifying another physical flaw, the "broad red mark, like a burn or a scald" on his throat. This materiality indicates Monks's move away from his origins, a move I would link to the story Monks wishes to keep silent, his disruption of the textual circulation of his father's documents. Once he has disposed of the signification that would efface his body and secure his genteel identity, his body becomes his central figuring metaphor.

Monks, then, like the criminals, can be destroyed by the speech of others, and indeed, he remarks that he has been brought down by "babbling drabs," thwarted in his attempts to crush Oliver's ascendance to the same class (459). Unsurprisingly, he resists this speech himself, a move that can only hasten the destruction of his plans. When Brownlow attempts to force him to speak, he struggles, "mutter[ing] some unintelligible words," and begs "with a faltering tongue" for some other penalty (434). As Brownlow publicly shares the narrative of Monks's and Leeford's lives, we are offered other indices of Monk's body: he bites his lips and shifts in his chair restlessly, complaining that Brownlow's "tale is of the longest" (436). Brownlow demands that Monks relate his narrative, and Monks points to a set of papers, indicating "you have the story there." Brownlow replies, "'I must have it here, too' . . . looking round upon the listeners" (457). Monks must make public his history in order to complete Oliver's. Although he has penned the text that will disown him and make him materially the poverty-stricken drudge he appears to have become, he must also put this text into social circulation to achieve the effect Brownlow desires. His speech, however, will have a different effect on him than Oliver's does. Oliver's establishes the boy as a noble figure; Monks has already slid beyond the reach of gentrifying language. The story he tells indicates how deeply entrenched he has become in the criminal class. Monks can only narrate his destruction of the legal documents that his father had produced to reform the mistakes he had made. When the narrative turns to the contents of the will itself, rather than its destruction, Monks becomes silent and Brownlow speaks. Monks speaks only of destruction and death, Agnes's and his mother's. His confession simultaneously unmakes Monks as a member of the elite and remakes Oliver in his former place. As the narrator suggests, Monks has "utter[ed] curses upon himself" (459), as his speech must inevitably be—it exposes him to

Fagin, reveals him to Nancy, and renders visible his attempts to slip beyond the reaches of text.

### Body Language

"Cant," the criminal discourse, functions as more than a code among thieves or a marker of class; it is a signifier of morality and material identity. Ginsburg notes that "Oliver's [cant-free] speech becomes 'pure' speech and has to be understood as a metaphor for the pure soul" (221). Contrarily, cant signifies the impure, the debased, the physical; it is the thieves' body language. The danger in deploying such speech is in positioning its speakers as a commodity for the use of the upper classes to be physically consumed, as Nancy is. The speech of the criminals is not text that substitutes for the corporeal and materializes them into the bourgeois, but rather it marks them as the social body. We see the manifestations of this attention to the body most visibly in Bill's material maledictions. His oaths include "Burn my body!" (166, 187, 210, 356), "Cut my limbs off one by one!," and "Wolves tear your cursed throats!" (254). He frequently interacts with other people by speaking about their bodies, with remarks such as "Bring in your body" (187). After the murder, Bill refers to Nancy's body as a thing (399) and asks, "Is—it—the body—is it buried?" (447). Ironically, the narrative sets up Bill as Nancy's victim (he is haunted by her eyes, her ghost, and, significantly, the information she has put into circulation), just as she is his, through the chain of events precipitated by her storytelling. In their deaths, the violence in the narrative seems to be safely contained in the acts of the one reflected back to the other.

This framework would seem to suggest that the threat of domestic violence is not a social problem caused by the devaluing of women, and within this frame, violence does not seem possible in the genteel classes. In the signifying economy of *Oliver Twist,* it is contained in Bill and Nancy, and once they die, their violence dies with them. This form of speech generates a system of individual guilt, making it possible to cleanse the narrative of all taints through the destruction of Fagin, Bill, and even Nancy. The focus on individual subjectivity and speech relieves us of the responsibility of attending to the system that underpins poverty, crime, and violence—specifically because these formations render the service of generating middle-class subjectivity. The return of Oliver's fortune (not Nancy's salvation) depends upon eliminating these dangerous embodied speakers and replacing the white-waistcoated gentleman on the workhouse board with a good board member, not eliminating the board. Once the Bumbles are out of workhouse management and in the workhouse, we can have a happy ending.

Significantly, the narrator resists the body language that the criminals speak, language that identifies the self as embodied in the physical rather than the textual. The maintenance of spiritual authority over the text requires avoidance or denunciation of this rhetoric. Sometimes the narrator simply calls remarks of this tenor "terrific imprecations" (212) or indicates that a character "gave utterance to about a couple of score of curses and threats, the rapid production of which reflected great credit on the fertility of his invention" (166). Despite the fact that we have been informed in the preface that the novel is strictly truthful, the narrative censors Bill's language. At one point, the narrator simply remarks that Bill spoke "in [the] cant terms, with which his whole conversation was plentifully besprinkled, but which would be quite unintelligible if they were recorded here" (137).

Dickens remarks in his preface that not a "word is exaggerated or over-wrought" (35), that he has given a truthful representation of the working class, yet he often expels their voices from the narrative because "speech [should not] offend the ear" (33). He attempts to "banish from the lips of the lowest character [he] introduced, any expression that could by possibility offend" (36). The thieves' cant, for which we are provided a glossary, testifies to the distance between proper speech and the discourse of criminals, which the reader should not understand without assistance. Oliver's difficulty in comprehending their speech reveals not only his own innocence, but the corruption of their language. Angus Wilson remarks in the introduction to the novel that in successive editions of the novel, there was "an increasing softening of the mild oaths" (21). Wilson suggests that Dickens was simply capitulating to public pressure for bowdlerization. I would argue, however, that as Dickens increasingly moved to secure his legitimacy, to take up a more lofty class position, he was forced, like his narrator, to expurgate the "incomprehensible" speech that marks the working classes or be forced to identify himself with them. In order to retain his social authority, Dickens must claim a social position, as his hero does, through the propriety of his speech. In *Dear Reader,* Stewart argues that just as the reader was conscripted in the act of reading, the writer was conscripted in his efforts to generate his social identity. Like those characters who must constantly keep text in circulation, so must Dickens—not just to fill his coffers with the funds that moved him away from the specter of the blacking warehouse and into his Gad's Hill mansion, but to reiterate himself as a figure who belongs there. "Dickens was yearning to acquire the legal and cultural status of a middle-class professional" (Hadley 118). Since the profits of *The Pickwick Papers* and *Nicholas Nickleby* had gone largely to the publishers and not Dickens, their production (and the production of the novels that follow) indicates they were written more than simply to increase Dickens's bank accounts. As Brantlinger has eloquently argued, the realist novel "is a perfect simulacrum of a social order based on nothing more substantial than public credit and 'speculative commerce'" (*Fictions of State* 168), an activity that is bound to reveal the emptiness of the signifier below. Brantlinger sees this empty space as the signifier (not the signified) of debt and credit; we may also read this as a form of empty social signification in terms of social class. Though we can only gesture largely at the unstable boundaries that defined respectability and economic success (did Mary Elizabeth Braddon, for example, attain these prestigious laurels?), there certainly was a volume of literature defining and positioning the ranks of the middle classes. These texts in themselves were a part of an effort to establish the author (upon whose authority we may define our own position), as well as a social space.

Dickens rose socioeconomically on the back of Nancy's murder, just as Oliver did. Dickens succeeded, as his letter to E. M. Forster suggested, in "[doing] great things with Nancy." Both externally, for Dickens, and internally, for Oliver, the role of working-class women in establishing their identities and bearing the burden of violence—serving as the pound of flesh with which they purchase their status—is veiled in the narrative. The once seemingly working-class male can ascend to his position as long as the violence of that ascent is obscured by the women and confined to the domestic scene. Indeed, the danger is marked as the author's. The necessity for an author to "bring upon the scene the very scum and refuse of the land"—as Dickens claims Fielding, Defoe, Goldsmith, Smollett, Richardson, and Mackenzie did—was a dangerous proposition for a man attempting to establish himself in the world, to move out of the corporeal materiality of the past and into the new industrial capitalistic materiality. In his study of Victorian repression, John Kucich argues that "Dickens needed to deny that his protagonists' use of repression intersected the mechanism of Victorian social power, even as he dramatized the in-evitability . . . of this interaction," a move Kucich links to Dickens's own desires for "social authority" (253). I concur with this evaluation, seeing the engagement with textuality and morality as a screen for economic and social functions. For an author, however, this move was fraught with obvious economic connections that were only tenuously veiled, sometimes unsuccessfully so. Trollope's popularity declined, for example, when his *Autobiography,* in which he elaborated on his economic motives, was published. The veils various discourses might throw over these eco-nomic questions were vital to the maintenance of respectability, and the ways in which those veils were manipulated (had Dickens politely man-aged the thieves' speech he presented?) were equally pressing. Tellingly, Brownlow's suggestion that Oliver become an author elicits an absolute refusal.

> *"How should you like to grow up a clever man, and write books, eh?"*
> *"I think I would rather read them, sir," replied Oliver.*
> *"What! wouldn't you like to be a book-writer?" said the old gentleman.*
> *Oliver considered a little while; and at last said, he should think it would be a much better thing to be a bookseller; upon which the old gentleman laughed heartily and declared he had said a very good thing. (145)*

Brownlow's response does not imply that authors are ignorant, failed, or weak; in fact, he indicates that one must be clever. Rather, the profession may complicate the articulation of a social position—for Oliver, it has been vexed enough already. When one engages in risky speech, that of the poverty stricken and low, one risks his or her position. Being a seller of books would require none of this threat, while still allowing one to engage in the circulation of the text and the economic cycle. The book-seller who saves Oliver from three months' hard labor publicly relates the tale of the boy's innocence in Mr. Fang's courtroom. The narrator calls him the "worthy book stall keeper" (123) who hasn't the class position to have freedom (he must find somebody to mind the shop before he can come to Oliver's rescue), but at least has respectability. Embodying this speech, then, is a risk for Dickens and his text because, in the narrative, he embodies himself. The fact that *Oliver Twist* was the first published work to which Dickens attached his name rather than a pseudonym (Ackroyd 275) indicates his desire to render himself legible as a professional, decorous, middle-class figure.[17]

### Arresting Legal Discourse

Perhaps surprisingly, as Oliver and Brownlow's run-in with Mr. Fang indicates, the law was not necessarily an ally in the bourgeoisie's early attempts to make themselves through speech. In later chapters, I discuss the way in which fiction and the law tangled in the articulation of marital violence. Here, I examine the way that figures such as Fang, Blathers, and Duff may even thwart the process of self-making, of generating middle-class authority and identity and erasing the middle-class woman's body. They serve an equivocal role in the narrative, which indicates the need for their reform. Mr. Brownlow, "the older gentleman, [speaks] like a gentleman" (120) in Fang's courtroom, but Fang pretends not to recognize this discourse. Instead, he insults Brownlow with the question, "What's this fellow charged with?," leaving Brownlow in a "perfect frenzy of rage and defiance" (124). Such mockery registers the reach and scope of the law, as well as the threat it may pose not only to Oliver but to Brownlow. Nor is this the only moment in which the respectables are at odds with the law. When Dr. Losberne tends to Oliver after his inauspicious arrival at the Maylies', he chooses to suppress Oliver's true story and misinform the police—this is not the community in which Oliver's narrative should be aired. From the moment they are introduced, the Bow Street officers mark themselves as debased by speaking in a corrupted discourse, like the criminals. Their cant includes phrases such as "This warn't a put-up thing" (277), which baffles Dr. Losberne and the Maylies. Entering Oliver's story into circulation with those who are clearly outside of this self-generating middle-class discursive cycle might corrupt his narrative, mark it with the elements of the others' distance from gentility. Oliver's tale is, thus, recited only to the Maylies, Dr. Losberne, and Brownlow.

Critics have argued about the role that Blathers and Duff play in the narrative, particularly with regard to their conversation about Conkey Chickweed, a "story better than a novel book." As with other working-class characters, the circulation of Conkey's story causes him to lose everything. Further, although the officers claim to have solved the crime of Conkey Chickweed, their solution is dubious, the detectives disagree with one another about the perpetrator (one arguing that his comrade arrested the proper villain, Conkey Chickweed himself, and the other twice suggesting that the family pet was the culprit), and they fail to solve the robbery at the Maylies'. They are depicted as incapable and buffoonish. Blathers clumsily "forc[es] the head of his stick in his mouth, with some embarrassment" (274) when they first arrive at the Maylies'—behavior that is certainly no formula for patriarchal and phallic authority. Their presence even disrupts the good-hearted efforts of Giles and Brittles, who involve themselves "in such a wonderful maze of fresh contradictions and impossibilities, as tended to throw no particular light on anything, but the fact of [their] own strong mystification" (282). These tensions, rather than helping to produce self-generating speech, might baffle Oliver in the same way. Therefore, Dr. Losberne insists that they conceal the truth: "the object is a good one, and that must be our excuse" (277). The object? As we have heard from Mr. Brownlow before, the object is to make Oliver's status as a young gentleman possible, even if that requires deception or violence.

Later, when Losberne wishes to involve Blathers and Duff again, his suggestions are marked as impractical "hot-brained" schemes that Brownlow claims would be a "very Quixotic act" (374). Not only are the representatives of the law at fault here, but the law itself. The law is, as Mr. Bumble infamously suggests, "a ass" for being out of touch with the rapidly changing social codes (461). The novel critiques the Poor Laws, as well as their administrators. Mrs. Mann is a cruel overseer who starves and beats children. Mr. Bumble is a cowardly and vicious man who cares only about his own interests. Dickens savagely attacks the absurd perception of the workhouse as "a regular place of public entertainment for the poorer classes . . . where all was play and no work" and where the inmates are allotted the ridiculously spare portions of "three meals of thin gruel a day, with an onion twice a week, and half a roll on Sundays" (55). When people succumbed to death on this diet, the narrator reports, "the board were in ecstasies" (55). As James Kincaid and Brian Rosenberg have argued, Dickens's complexity, and I would suggest, narrative complexity in general, belies an absolute and securely bounded series of codes.

The roles of text, law, and violence here are complexly inflected. Dickens's best intentions may not have freed working-class women from violence, but his efforts drew them into the textual conversation, a conversation developed and more radically refined in the sensation fiction of ensuing decades. In the clever Artful Dodger, we see evidence of the emergent tensions taken up by sensation. The Dodger, who experiences a "social death" at the hands of the law in the form of transportation (395), confounds all of these codes of speech, identity, and law by offering a linguistically scrambled speech that still conveys meaning. He speaks of the "deformation of his character" and his unwillingness to "abase himself by descending to hold" a conversation with an accuser (395). He asks of the jailer, "Did you redress yourself to me, young man?" (396). Though his threats to "make a parliamentary business of it" when the authorities prepare to commit him are clearly futile, his remark that the courts "ain't no shop of justice" rings throughout the novel. Indeed, the entire courtroom erupts in laughter—a disruptive, jarring laughter that exposes the absurdity of the legal claims for absolute authority and truth, and also that of the speech codes the narrative lays out. In this dangerous scrambled speech (the Dodger could have brought down even heavier penalties on himself, in spite of the laughter his speech produces), we begin to see how the novel can contribute to and act in the way that the Dodger's example suggests. The novel can participate in a conversation by calling into question the law as a part of a larger problem. However, as Brownlow and Losberne's reluctance to speak directly to the law indicates, language must be carefully managed, must walk the line of self-authoring and social authority cautiously. The Dodger's distorted yet meaningful speech provides a rare sample of the public speech that doesn't put a criminal to death. In later chapters, I will argue that sensation fiction capitalizes on these literary efforts and brings them to fruition within the body of the text to generate the kind of legal and social friction that the Dodger's brief speech makes here.[18] Thus I close this discussion of *Oliver Twist* where I opened it—with the preface—to point to the ways in which the revision of the law, the subject of much of the book, is to occur: "in the dress of this (in novels) much exalted race" (35), Dickens argues, the "stern truth" can be delivered and can be a "service to society" (34) as a whole.

This bold claim, that the novel can revise the culture, is one that I want to make as well, though not so simply as it seems to be offered in these few words. I would argue that this early pre-sensational account pointed to tensions in the law, and that sensational fiction that followed participated in the kind of revision that the Dodger represents—and in much the same way, by moving outside of normative codes, avoiding cant, but inventing a new language to rethink textual self-creation. The Dodger's speech demonstrates the role of text in challenging the discourse of social custom. What remains, the fact that the law does not protect figures such as Nancy, will be addressed in the following decades. The social and civic law has marked gaps, and sensational fictional accounts will contribute to the revision of the law and the culture's attitudes about it.

In the 1830s, working-class women were marked so as to make possible and visible violence against them, which, though it naturalized the abuse of working-class women, also had the important effect of drawing new attention to women such as Nancy. The corollary disembodiment of genteel women obscured violence against them and, in the case of *Oliver Twist,* made marriages in the non-working classes virtually invisible, as Kenneth Frederick has noted. Brownlow's engagement is terminated before its legal consummation, Mrs. Maylie's predates the narrative's action, and Rose and Harry's appears late in the narrative. There are several movements in the novel that call the nuclear family and the social constructs that mimic it into question; however, it just as powerfully asserts the ideologies upon which they are based in the tropes of salvation and the dissipation of bodies. The move to disembody privileged women also makes visible the role of economics in the abuse of women, as we see in Nancy's murder. Though this structure helped generate a new sensibility toward violence, it problematically naturalized the abuse against working-class women, making them likelier victims and denying them, because of this violence's inevitability, legal and social protection. It also made abuse in the upper and middle classes oxymoronic by evacuating the body that might have been violated.

SENSATIONAL REVISION

2

# II

## Brutality and Propriety:
## Wilkie Collins's *The Woman in White*
## and the Divorce Act of 1857

*There are novels now in circulation which will cer-*
*tainly puzzle the future student of the Victorian era.*
—"The
Sensation
Novel"

### The Sensation Novel and Wilkie Collins

FROM THE TIME OF THEIR IDENTIFICATION AS A GENRE, sensation
novels produced an alternative narrative framework in their language,
their plots, and their engagement with the sociopolitical discourse of Victorian Britain. The context in which they were published and received
became a part of their larger narrative structure, situating them ideologi-
cally, and situating our understanding of them now.[1] Sensation novels
were distinguished by contemporary critics from novels that maintained
a fidelity to nature or used artistic exaggeration; they identified them
instead as texts in which "nature [was] entirely disregarded" (review of
*The Woman in White, Sixpenny Magazine* 366). They were called "mysterious and unnatural" (review, *Spectator* 1428) and said to "sacrifice everything to the intensity of excitement" (review, *Critic* 233). Jonathan Loesberg argues that the genre was "created by reviewers" rather than created
by the texts, and was for these critics a product of intense debate (115).
Much of this debate regarding *The Woman in White* (1860) centered on
whether Wilkie Collins exhibited the foibles of the sensation novel or
had, as some critics claimed, adhered to "stern reality" (Henry James,
qtd. in Page, 122). Even Margaret Oliphant, who condemned sensation
novels for their "violent and illegitimate means," regarded the plot and

characters of *The Woman in White* as "natural and possible" ("Sensation Novels" 566)

This favorable interpretation was buttressed by the novel's teleological narrative that seemed to provide a neat closure with the woman's rescue and a final resolution through marriage and childbirth—a manufactured conventionality that appeared to contain any themes discordant with the current social harmonies. However, there were themes that ruptured the frame of the novel and remained exposed on the surface. Jenny Bourne Taylor explains this phenomenon of capitulation/resistance in Collins in relation to nineteenth-century psychology: Collins's notions of "consciousness and cognition can most radically question social perceptions and identities. . . . [I]n Collins's novels the struggle for control of the narrative itself—the struggle over who narrates, who appropriates and represents others' testimony and evidence as history which the story reconstructs as truth—is often bound up with both the undermining and the affirmation of a gendered, middle-class subjectivity" (*Secret Theatre* 26). Winifred Hughes, in her important study on Wilkie Collins, also finds this dual operation in his work, pointing out that the narrative is often disrupted by the host of narrators and minor accomplices (140). These critics have identified precisely the aspect that makes Collins an important study, but I find in these tensions a movement far less privatized than that suggested in the life of the mind or the secret machinations with minor accomplices. I locate in *The Woman in White* an exposure, a very public reconsideration of external, material tensions that ripple the surface of the novel. The apparent wedding of these various tensions in one tale, what we might now call a postmodern marriage, is described by Roland Barthes in *S/Z* through the concept of narrative codes: "Alongside each utterance, one might say that off-stage voices can be heard: they are the codes: in their interweaving, these voices (whose origin is 'lost' in the vast perspective of the *already-written*) de-originate the utterance: the convergence of the voices (of the codes) becomes *writing,* a stereographic space where [they] . . . intersect" (21). The hermeneutic code that drives toward the revelation and disclosure of mysteries and the resolution of complication is countered by a Bahktinian multivocity, recomplicating the terms that seem to have been successfully mediated. Thus, although the novel relies on moral platitude, exploiting class and flawed womanhood as veils for the enactment of violence, it still troubles representation of violence at these sites, launching an alternative discourse.

These multiple frictions—over the possibility of realism in a text that defined sensation and the regulation and unruliness manifest in the narrative—bring to the surface tensions over the critical relationship between sensation and what was understood as reality. The blurring of these terms threatened to undercut the authority of one of the most accepted of cultural realities, the law. Like the work of Dickens that preceded it, Collins's novel, by producing questions of legality, was bound to be disruptive. Yet the novels that fell into the sensational class did something to earn that name. They generated a more aggressive inquiry, and in the case of sensation, I would add to Barthes's formula the notion that this collapse into critical and narrative confusion and the creation of a new genre are perhaps inevitable in the always contentious production of social change. Indeed, this was a time of change. Caroline Norton's impassioned letters on infant custody, women's property rights (crusades shared by many feminists), and divorce had shaken the nation. Feminist committees had been formed to petition Parliament on these matters, and an early, deeply vexed Divorce Act had been passed. Thus, sensation novels tapped into ideological anxieties and contradictions, exposing and often exploding what seemed to be the real limits of discursive possibility. Deriving authorization for transgression from their classification in the literary taxonomy, and read by critics as increasingly transgressive (evidenced by the identification of the genre and the growing anxiety expressed in commentaries by critics such as Henry Longeville Mansel and W. Fraser Rae), these novels betrayed literary, as well as social and cultural, standards that had hitherto appeared firm.

Sensation fiction thus participated in, shaped, and was shaped by the political-legal debates of the era, the debates over what was real, what was legislatable. In a conversation between novelistic text and parliamentary debate, *The Woman in White* took up the tensions represented in the Divorce Act of 1857.[2] The novel re-marks the language of violence in the domestic space, anticipating and casting the frame of later debates, particularly the Married Women's Property Act (1870) and the early attempts to repeal the Contagious Diseases Acts (1857–70), which carried with them the same anxieties over gender, class, and violence as the Divorce Act had.[3] The impact of the mutually constitutive discourse of the novels and the debates on women's rights issues was certainly dubious. While providing opportunities for reenvisioning the cultural construction of issues such as violence and gender, they also made a range of behavior and understanding, which had previously remained outside the boundaries of polite social conversation and thus outside the boundaries of legislation, subject to prescription.

Despite their accessibility to a legal redefinition, the alternative representations in sensation novels[4] challenged the solidity and impermeability of the legal and cultural understanding of violence in the home, offering not the pleasing safety of morality in the ranks of the well-to-do, but a wealthy family in strife. By identifying these sites as vexed, the novels challenged the identification of the law as a coherent, seamless text that provided unity to social articulations of violence, gendered identity, and social control. They exposed the law as a scripted social text and contested the justifications of the law's articulation and functioning as natural, godly, and inherently true. Reducing the law to the level of myth threatened to confound its authority as well as that of its manufacturers. This development prompted a push for juristic control of the issues addressed, a desire that persisted and blossomed into a variety of legislation late into the century. The alternative representation in sensation novels and the ripples it produced in the legal system provide us—and provided the Victorians—with ways of reenvisioning violence in the domestic space.

### Violence and the Working Class

> *The dangerous wife-beater belongs almost exclusively to the artisan and labouring classes.*
>
> —Frances Power Cobbe, "Wife Torture in England"

The parliamentary debates surrounding the Divorce Act of 1857 lend insight into both the construction of the term "violence" and cruelty in the Victorian home. Divorce was previously only available as an act of Parliament and was a prohibitively costly affair. Couples were granted *a mensa et thoro* (what we now know as legal separation) and *a vinculo* (total dissolution of the union) in cases of a wife's adultery. Prior to seeking divorce proceedings in Parliament, a disgruntled husband was required to sue the alleged adulteress for criminal conversation in a court of law. If he won, he recovered damages and could proceed to Parliament. His wife, the alleged adulteress, could not speak on her own behalf, nor was she necessarily notified of these proceedings, but she could be, in the frequently invoked biblical phraseology, "cast off" if her husband was successful in court and Parliament. The Divorce Act was intended to rectify some of the injustices of these laws. A standard, reiterated argument in favor of divorce dealt with the responsibility of the legislative body to protect working-class women who were plagued by brutal, drunken husbands. Significantly, Parliament did not consider upper-class men a danger to their wives. Rather, only in "the humbler ranks of life [was] some prompt remedy" necessary. Only poor women were conceived of as sufferers of violence at the hands of their husbands[5] despite the convention of the upper classes' rakish decadence, reinforced by criticism (and contemptuous representations) of the aristocracy in the Regency period. Although upper-class men such as Caroline Norton's infamous husband committed widely publicized acts of brutality against their wives, even Norton identified herself in this condition as a member of the "helpless classes," invoking images of the poor, exploited, and working class (qtd. in Poovey, 65). Norton declined to identify herself as a victim of a degenerate aristocracy. This pattern holds true in *The Woman in White* as well. Parliament sought to prevent "unworthy husbands" from the lower ranks from "sweeping away their wives' earnings."[6] Dehumanized and marginalized, working-class men were perceived as "drunken, profligate husbands"[7] and working-class women as provocateurs whose infidelity or dissolution forced their husbands into drunkenness and abuse.[8] Ironically, when generosity overcame the Members of Parliament, their patronage was extended to other men who might require recourse to divorce, not women in like situations in the upper classes. "Remedy ought to be afforded to the poor as well as to the rich—to all husbands who could prove themselves free from any imputation of misconduct in the marriage state, and who had the calamity of having an unfaithful wife."[9] Further, in the case of a husband's adultery, even the most sympathetic of the debaters felt "divorce should not be granted to the wife on the ground of adultery, unless with such aggravation as would render it impossible for the parties to live together."[10] This aggravation, elsewhere called "extreme aggravation" or "brutal violence," was frequently perceived as the natural outcome of a woman's behavior, especially if her husband believed she had been unfaithful.[11]

*The Woman in White* draws upon all of these tensions, plaiting the threads of the debates—violence, gender indeterminacy, and class—within the narrative. A mercenary marriage between the poverty-stricken aristocrat Sir Percival Glyde and Laura Fairlie addresses violence in the home as well as the complexities of class identification. In fact, the initial depiction of the marriage between Sir Percival and Laura as a possible site for domestic violence relies upon her identification as an unfaithful woman, like the working-class women undeserving of legislative protection. Early in the novel, before their marriage, Laura decides to reveal that during her engagement to Percival she has fallen in love with her former drawing master, Walter Hartright, and can never love her fiancé. Without exposing Walter's identity, Laura remarks to Percival, "I have heard . . . and I believe it, that the fondest and truest of all affections is the affection which a woman ought to bear her husband. When our engagement began that affection was mine to give, if I could, and yours to win, if you could. Will you pardon me, and spare me, Sir Percival, if I acknowledge that it is not so any longer?" (191–92). Percival denies Laura's request and punishes her lack of devotion through precisely the kinds of violence that the debates claimed evolve from a woman's inconstancy: economic and physical brutality. Like the working-class men of Parliament's imagination, Percival attempts to extort Laura's money and harms her physically, eventually taking her life—metaphorically—in a scheme that replaces her identity with that of a dead woman's. Although overtly exonerating her, the undercurrent of the text emphasizes Laura's culpability. Percival attempts to borrow against her fortune—to which her legal settlement gives him direct access only at her death—by demanding that Laura sign a document. She refuses, insisting that she be allowed to read the text, a gesture that Percival interprets as "a wife . . . distrusting her husband" (267). Despite her denial of the charge, Percival wastes no time in linking her infidelity over the document to her love for the unnamed man: "It is rather late in the day for you to be scrupulous. I should have thought you had got over all weakness of that sort when you made a virtue of necessity by marrying *me*" (269). Scalded by his remarks, Laura falls silent, but neither her silence nor her continued refusal to sign the document can overwrite her "infidelity" with his crimes.

Percival's manipulations do not end with attempts at economic control, and physical brutality enters the equation. Although depicted in the frames of poverty and criminality in *Oliver Twist,* physical violence appears elevated far above the squalor of the East End and in a country estate in *The Woman in White.* Yet there is a catch. Percival's behavior, although encoded as a man's right, is also linked directly with the working-class subjectivity imagined in the parliamentary debates. A most dangerous identification for Percival, these tensions increasingly destabilize his upper-class identity as the novel progresses. We ultimately learn that Percival bears a purloined title, estate, and monies because he is an illegitimate child. His illegitimacy makes his class status so obscure, Percival must carefully guard against ambiguity at this site lest his secret be betrayed. However, his identity continues to degenerate, and rather than simply being identified as a decadent aristocrat whose inebriation led to adultery, absence, and cruelty, Percival remains predominately sober and insistently present in the domestic space, attempting to shore up a failing genteel identity that becomes more and more like that of the cruel working-class husbands of the Divorce Act. His performance as a "mean, cunning and brutal man" (274)—not a rake or a self-indulgent miscreant—defines him in the context of the debates as the only kind of violent man Parliament defined. A. James Hammerton notes that in their "preoccupation with the moral economy of the poorest marriages, contemporary critics and reformers themselves contributed to the myth that the problem of violent conflict was confined to the very poor. Violence became one of the touchstones here for distinguishing the 'rough' from the 'respectable'" (57). The tension inherent in Percival's shifting identity becomes a primary focus of the novel.

### Edge of the Domestic Precipice: Identification with "The Brutal Lower Orders"

Throughout *The Woman in White,* the narrative hints that Percival's anxiety over his secret identity precipitates his abusiveness. The reader and the other characters remain ignorant of Percival's secret until the close of the text, which perhaps leaves the reader to suspect bigamy or infidelity on Percival's part. However, once the secret is out, we have a new lens through which to analyze Percival's behavior. As a bastard son, he has no legal right to the title he bears, to the property on which he lives, or to the income that he draws. Percival's father had failed to protect his son with a will and died suddenly after landing the blow about his own deception: he and Percival's mother never married because she had been another man's wife. Percival's access to class status, income, and identity all result from his successful forgery of a marriage record, witnessed by Mrs. Catherick, mother of the half-mad woman in white, Anne. Percival's pilfered authority as a gentleman earns him the right to marriage with Laura Fairlie. Exposure of his treachery would lead to the loss of all he has gained and identify him as the most dangerous and eminently punishable of all Victorian figures—one who tampers with what Parliament called the "order of society."[12]

Despite, and indeed because of, his ambiguous status, Percival stages the most ostentatious betrayal of the domestic ideal in the novel. Although other women are abandoned by their partners (such as Mrs. Catherick), left childless (Mrs. Clements), or live with an adulterer (Mrs. Fairlie), Percival's ill treatment of his wife remains the only abuse thoroughly condemned in the text. A hot-tempered imposter, Percival promptly exposes his inherent lack of gentility following his mercenary marriage. He gradually becomes the unworthy husband described in the Divorce Act debates, exacting money from Laura, imprisoning her, and harming her physically. Rather than identifying the domestic realm of the titled classes as a possible site of violence, his violence plots the tensions in their relationship along the lines of class. The more violent he becomes, in fact, the more troubling his financial difficulties, the more he drinks, and the more he labors—not vice versa. This mechanism purges violence from the houses of lords, a process that is complicated further through Laura's slippage of identity along the class register through her identification with Anne Catherick, a poverty-stricken woman and a clearly degraded character. However, the text compels the reader to reconsider the potential production of violence in the upper-class home, especially because the revelation of Percival's identity is long delayed, and the exhibition of Percival's brutality urges us to examine the domestic environment and its inhabitants as well as its standards of representation. Simply by exhibiting the injury on Laura's body, the novel challenges the absence of the consequences of violence in the parliamentary debates. Thus, despite the fact that Percival becomes a grotesque caricature of the Parliamentarians' imagined failure of familial peace, his depiction calls for a reinspection of an overdetermined cultural text.

With only an animal-like cunning (another signifier of his debased class identity), Percival's behavior strikes at the vulnerable sites of the legal discourse. He brings to the surface formerly indescribable issues by using methods to control Laura that result in visible markers of his brutality. He leaves bruises on Laura's arm, an outcome of his attempts to restrain her and wring a response from her, and thus makes himself the key target of the novel's moral re-reading of the domestic scene. Count Fosco, Percival's comrade and guide, warns Percival that when he engages in such behavior he teeters on the "edge of the domestic precipice" (340). Unable to control his temper or manage his wife through Fosco's code of "propriety, patience, and peace" (307), Percival rages through the novel with the "clumsy violence" of a fool (334). Ultimately, this violence surfaces not only in Laura's bruises, but also in her imprisonment in their home and finally a "violence of manner" that Fosco claims leads to Percival's death.

The visibility of these acts leaves Percival open to attack on several fronts. Laura and her sister Marian threaten exposure, which they hope will "bring him to terms when nothing else will" (323). Bared to the public, Percival's behavior would surely call into question his identity. The publication of these private matters makes this reimagining of martial violence and of proprietous domestic identity a central effect of this text. Fosco urges Percival to recognize the implications of observable physical violence, a "method largely adopted by the brutal lower orders of the people, but utterly abhorrent to the refined and educated classes" (345). By behaving violently, Percival betrays his desperate anxieties about his own relationship to the public and commercial lives of the working class to which Fosco refers, marking himself as a member of a criminal class, a move he desperately wishes to avoid. Michel Foucault's *Discipline and Punish* examines the ways in which the move from torture to imprisonment created a class of criminals, camouflaging the crimes of other classes. The shift in the representation of marital violence mimics this pattern, remaining observable only in the working class. The destabilization of class in *The Woman in White,* however, disrupts the effort to isolate violence as a working-class phenomenon. Percival performs the violence Fosco describes, in spite of all warnings. Marian claims that Percival's conspicuous acts leave her recourse to the "laws [of] England that protect women from cruelty and outrage" (315). She insists that Laura show her the bruises on her arms so that she may testify against Percival if legal action is required: "That mark is a weapon to strike him with. Let me see it now—I may have to swear to it at some future time" (321). However, the ambiguity of the laws to which Marian refers and their identification of a brutal man as a working-class man become the tensions over which the text stumbles and lead to its closure. Further, Laura's bruises alone could not protect her, as Marian suggests. Still, Marian's reference to the bruises precipitates a shift in the pattern of legal expression. Those acts of violation that are exposed themselves expose and embody the violence, betraying linguistic limitations that formerly defined violence in nebulous terms such as "aggravation" or "harsh conduct." [13] Percival is reduced to a madman (322) for a betrayal of these standards coupled with preposterous hopes of securing financial gain in their wake.

Percival's degeneration in the narrative parallels his dwindling ability to control Anne Catherick, a woman who leaks information to Laura and Marian. Believing Anne's mother has told her the secret of his illegitimate birth, Percival has Anne committed to an asylum. Not only does this move contain Anne physically, but it also ensures her delegitimization on several fronts: as a woman, a poor woman, and a madwoman. Should she dare to speak Percival's secret, her language would be regarded as fallacious and therefore less threatening. Anne, however, doesn't require linguistic authority. She silently mirrors Percival's indeterminate social position, for she also is the illegitimate child of a married woman and an adulterous peer. She need not know the text of his secret; she embodies it and presents to him the threat of exposure, in the same manner as the bruises on Laura's arm. Her escape from the asylum—with the assistance of Walter Hartright, the man Laura professes to love—taunts Percival with her embodied knowledge. Her communication with those who already present a danger to him, including Walter, Laura (and through her, Marian), and Fosco, contaminates them with the text she carries and amplifies their strength in the fluctuating power relations that surround them all. She pens a damaging letter to Laura before Laura's wedding to Percival, describing her connubial future as nightmarish and soiled by a hidden evil. She trespasses on Percival's property, visiting his wife and making Laura an unconscious agent of her threat. Finally, Anne insistently remains out of Percival's reach, even after Fosco intervenes with his more successful management techniques.

Anne's complex lineage breeds dangers not only for Percival. Laura and Anne are mirror images of one another, and their identification blurs Laura's class position as well. Her continuous comparison to Anne puts Laura in jeopardy by removing the barriers that ostensibly protected upper-class women from ill treatment. Taking up the trope of "the greater sisterhood," as Dickens did with Rose Maylie and Nancy in *Oliver Twist,* Collins twists the tradition even further. Although Laura and Anne are separated by class, their virtually identical appearance calls into question the boundaries between them, their class positions, and the possibility for violence in their lives. Evidenced in Fosco's daring substitution of the two women, their interchangeability becomes the novel's crisis and forces Laura physically to take on Anne's amorphous lower-middle-class identity. We later learn that Anne is, in fact, Laura's half-sister, Mr. Fairlie's eldest, though illegitimate, daughter. Collins condemns this betrayal of propriety through adultery and illegitimate birth, writing Anne as the medium of Laura's debasement, madness, economic necessity, and life of fear and anonymity. The impact of these labyrinthine relations is twofold. By exposing the danger of this threat to the order of society, Collins rejects the parliamentarian notion that "dangerous" and "spurious offspring" can only attend from a woman's infidelity despite the widely accepted argument that a wife "might, without any loss of caste . . . condone an act of adultery on the part of the husband. No one would venture to suggest that a husband could possibly do the same."[14] Collins challenges the conviction that only women can endanger the order of society, crossing the boundaries of propriety himself, through the sensationalism of the novel, to generate a new notion of morality. In this move, he creates friction in the cultural understanding of who may perpetrate and who may be subject to violence.[15] On the other hand, the fluidity of Laura's identity, in its blurring with Anne's, suggests that Laura's abuse derives primarily from the uncertainty of her class status. The most severe beating she receives follows on the heels of her encounter with Anne, the evidence of the uncanny resemblance between the two reconfiguring Laura (a harbinger of the replacement that will follow) and marking Percival's aggressions as working-class violence yet again. What Laura perceives as Anne's greater freedom is a costly liberty, a sustained effort at escape (as Walter's first encounter with Anne demonstrates) that Laura comes to know intimately later.

The novel's equivocation on these issues, a complex rhythm of apertures opened then fused, is played out in the visible tensions of Percival and his (similarly vexed) relationship to authority in the form of a phallic metaphor of Victorian power, the walking stick.

> *In the plantation, Sir Percival strayed away from us. It seems to be a part of his restless disposition always to separate himself from his companions . . . and always to occupy himself when he is alone in cutting new walking-sticks for his own use. The mere act of cutting and lopping at hazard seems to please him. He has filled the house with walking-sticks of his own making, not one of which he ever takes up for a second time. When they have been once used his interest in them is all exhausted, and he thinks of nothing but going on and making more. (252)*

The walking stick serves as not only a cane to uphold the man who uses it, but also a weapon against his enemies.[16] Percival's activity with his canes, however, proves unsuccessful. He may shape and reshape the sticks, but they never function to his satisfaction. Those he carves are left behind when they prove to be useless, empty, ineffectual tools in all his endeavors, including siring progeny. Yet he remains obsessed with their manufacture, a skill that fails to advance him in his search for symbolic control over his wife and comrades. Once he has created them, he can only strike them "savagely on the sand, and [walk] away" (255), a mirror of his brutal yet ineffective attempts at coercing Laura. Further, when Walter Hartright contests Percival's position, in terms of his relationship to Laura and his identity as a peer, Percival must employ proxies to carry walking sticks of their own for him. Percival's fragile subjective stance as a patriarch would never stand the test of a beating. Mirroring Laura's temporary loss of legal, social, and moral identity, Percival's inherent taint denies him these permanently. His flaw fragments his identity and deprives him of his ability to engage in systems of power in which they all operate.

*The Deconstruction of the Law*

Percival's identity is not the only one at stake. Laura must take on an ambiguous identity when she becomes the victim of Percival's violence. This ambiguity reflects one of the greatest anxieties during the Divorce Act debates: the position of the woman in the event of her husband's failure to fulfill his role adequately. In fact, Parliament voiced this tension precisely along gender lines and in terms of subjectivity. Divorce, it was feared, would "give a wife all the distinct rights of citizenship. [The Member of Parliament] believed the measure [of divorce] to be a most mischievous one, and he proposed his Amendment [which would reduce the political authority granted to women] as going as far as was desirable, and so to prevent a greater evil." [17] The possibility that a woman might gain the status of British subject and thus the power to act on her own behalf threatened the subjectivity of British husbands, which was based in part on their ascendancy over their wives. To counterbalance this danger, women must be instead granted a "new status" [18] that would protect their property in the event that their husbands were unfit, but not allow them to remarry or become *femes soles*.[19] Situating only exceptional cases in this amorphous position would not damage the rights all husbands had over all wives, but would instead punish only those husbands (or wives) who behaved inappropriately. They would lose control over something that was still regarded by the law as theirs: their wives and their wives' money and property. The courts secured the power to decide who would retain or cast off the title and role of husband, but the woman's status would shift in a very different fashion. Even in this more favorable conceptualization of the marital relationship, one that imagined the possibility of a husband's failure along with his wife's, a woman would not have the renewal of a former status or the freedoms of her former spouse. She would become a "wife without a husband . . . not altogether free, nor altogether fettered." [20] This shift would have the effect of fixing her position as a wife, screening any violence present in the relationship, and forcing her to maintain the subservience and silence implied in her title. It would bind her to the same social contract, although it removed the authority of one specific man.

Inherent in the ambiguity of woman's status in this position was the potential for a shift that might constitute resistance. Once women were uncertainly bounded, unexpected, uncontrollable, and undesirable things might occur. The shift had already afforded one woman the power to retaliate against her husband in a public forum. In a tense moment in the debates, one M.P. drew attention to a "libelous" book his wife had written about him, pleading that "after a woman had been separated, she should not be permitted to make use of that situation, being a wife without a husband, to injure and asperse his character, and so to destroy his reputation." [21] It was precisely these perils to those who were British subjects that the law must attempt to control. "Danger," the catchword of the debates, represented the anxiety over that lack of control. [22]

A fear of collusion was a prominent way in which the fear of destabilized boundaries and lack of control was expressed. Several debates grew out of the desire to reduce the possibility of collusive adultery, in which a man and woman would work in concert to pretend the circumstances that would allow them to be freed from their marriage. That a man or a woman might stage the sexual acts necessary or assert falsehoods about them to secure divorce implies that the law is a script people may take up or reject, that all such behavior is essentially performative. [23] Many critics have read such a threat in Mary Elizabeth Braddon's *Lady Audley's Secret,* the most subversive of acts in the novel being Lady Audley's performance of a gentility formerly articulated as innate. By winning the hearts of a baronet and his community with sheer spectacle, she exposes the qualities of a "lady" as social construction, not birth. Emphasizing the flaccidity of the law and exposing it as a culture-wide narrative constructed by many voices, like Walter Hartright's chronicle that collects the testimony of many characters, would deny the power of Parliament to make the rules, pass judgment, and control the behavior of those in its realm. It would disintegrate the boundary between the real and the constructed, fiction and law, realism and sensation.

Instead, Parliament chose to frame divorce only as a condition of exception, refusing the right of individual choice—particularly for those external to the legislative powers of Parliament. It would be "dangerous to throw open the power of divorce to the whole country; it was one thing to grant relief in exceptional cases where there was the opportunity of instituting the fullest inquiry, than to grant relief in all cases, when the proceedings must necessarily assume a looser character." [24] Certainly it would be dangerous to shift the locus of control from Parliament to individual subject, which might allow individuals to make choices outside the boundaries of the law or to reveal its fabricated authority. The desire for absolute control (self-control, control of others) drives the myth that it can be attained, a myth the sensation novel cripples through its assaults on the law. *The Woman in White* represents and interrogates these attempts in the characters Count Fosco and Walter Hartright.

### "Propriety, Patience, Peace" and the Private Rod

Count Fosco represents the acceptable alternative to Percival's exhibitionist violence, far more effectively managing his wife, her behavior, and her money. Fosco converts his wife from a person interested in women's rights to a mechanical automaton. Mute and submissive, she plays the "civil, silent, unobtrusive woman, who is never in the way" (239). Fosco achieves this marvel of feminine decorum with the softest touch of sublimity: "He bows to her, he habitually addresses her as 'my angel,' . . . he kisses her hand . . . [and] presents her with sugar-plums . . . which he puts into her mouth playfully" (244). In contrast to Percival, who "beats his spaniels,"[25] Fosco has an "extraordinary fondness for pet animals" (242), and he rewards Madame Fosco in the same way he does his pets, with treats from his pocket when she has performed appropriately.

Fosco's seemingly gentle behavior, however, is underwritten by another kind of authority. Fosco covertly oversees his wife with the help of the infamous Victorian staff. "The rod of iron with which he rules her never appears in company—it is a private rod, and is always kept upstairs" (244).[26] The concealed rod remains outside the bounds of legislative and social authority, and indeed, its haunting presence amplifies its power. As Marian puts it, Fosco manages to "manage" them all (245). For example, when Percival becomes violent, Fosco subdues him like an animal tamer with the mere touch of a hand on his shoulder (268–69). The Count's civil and seemingly gentle suppression of Percival, however, reproduces the threat that lies beneath Madame Fosco's submission: his touch always insinuates violence. If we examine the language of the scene, we discern this tension manifesting itself in more subtle ways as well, embedded in the ambiguity of the language itself: "The Count took one of his hands out of his belt and laid it on Sir Percival's shoulder" (267). The two possibilities of the referent for "it," Fosco's hand and his belt, offer us a metaphor for Fosco's method—polite public gestures paired with the threat of private violence, a method contrasted to the direct threat Percival makes to lay his horsewhip on the shoulders of Walter. This subterranean violence echoes other scenes as well. Marian remarks that the manner with which Fosco controls Percival "ha[s] been the means he has resolutely and impenetrably used to get to his end ever since he set foot in this house" (334). Fosco accentuates this fear by allowing others to glimpse the power of his commanding hands. Domestic objects quiver under the force of his touch and signify his management of that realm. The Count seats himself at the piano to play for Marian "without waiting for a word of assent or dissent on [her] part, looking [her] hard in the face all the time." He plays, sings, and talks "fiercely," the piano "trembl[ing] under his powerful hands." As the piano quakes, so does Marian, recognizing the grip he has on her, the power he has over her movements, the dread he can create. "There was something horrible—something fierce and devilish—in the outburst of his delight at his own singing and playing, and in the triumph with which he watched its effect upon me as I shrank nearer and nearer to the door" (336–37).

This is not the only way in which Fosco demonstrates his power over Marian. Twice, he delves into the private recesses of her mind, metaphorically wielding his rod, evidence of his power over her. The first time, he responds to an unspoken question, and in another instance, he seems to supernaturally penetrate her secrets in a psychic "rape" that leaves her terrified. "His eyes seemed to reach my inmost soul through the thickening obscurity of the twilight. His voice trembled along every nerve in my body, and turned me hot and cold alternately" (310). Finally, in one of the most shocking scenes of the novel, Fosco pilfers Marian's private journal, while she lies on her sickbed, and reads it from cover to cover, writing his own addendum. Fosco's ability to penetrate Marian embodies the threat implied in the piano passage and bespeaks one of the central tensions the novel plays out and exposes about privacy and violence; indeed, these events are so private Marian can speak to no one of them. In *The Novel and the Police*, D. A. Miller calls this scene the accomplishment of the vague fear that plagues the text, "virtual rape. We might consider what is implied or at stake in the fact that the head game of suspicion is always implicitly transcoded by the novel into the body game of rape" (162). Fosco controls other written texts as well, battering

Marian's efforts representationally, a move underwritten by the threat of his private rod. As he has perused and altered the pages of her journal, he intercepts and reads Marian's letters to her lawyer and to Mr. Fairlie. He occasionally allows a missive to continue, safe in his knowledge of what it contains; another time he replaces the text with a black piece of paper through the intermediary of his wife. Easily substituting Marian's discourse with silence, the older woman becomes the model for womanly discourse, the blank text. Susan Gubar notes in her article " 'The Blank Page' and Issues of Female Creativity" that women's bodies become the only forum for expression and that their textuality is often identified with their sexuality. In this scene, then, Fosco's control of Madame Fosco and his appropriation of Marian's written texts and control of their content become other forms of sexual battery and mastery. The sexual implications are emphasized here by Madame Fosco's title. Never identified as "the Countess" in the text, she has indeed become a "madame" for her niece, supplying Marian's text/body for the Count's manipulation. The silent extension of her husband, Madame Fosco forces Marian into the same position: her movements are directed, what she speaks is controlled. Like a ventriloquist's dummy, Madame Fosco speaks only with "her husband's permission" (316).

The Count's violations and maneuvering serve as a metaphor for his theory of control. He philosophizes with Percival, pointing out that there are only "two ways to manage a woman": by beating her, which he marks as the province of the working classes alone, and by "never accept[ing] provocation at a woman's hands. It holds with animals, it holds with children, and it holds with women, who are nothing but children grown up. Quiet resolution is the one quality the animals, the children, and the women all fail in" (345). Women, then, must be trained that their desires, wishes, and concerns have no impact on their lives or the lives of the men around them. Fosco requires only the quiet resolution of a glacier and the constant threat of private violence to tame his pets and Madame Fosco. Fosco notes, as should we, that these two methods are not different in content and intent, but rather merely in design. By setting himself publicly at odds with the women in the novel, Percival merely provokes their ire, engages them in active resistance, and moves into the range of the law's reach, rather than forcing them to succumb.

In one of his most sustained monologues in the text, Fosco describes how this method of abuse/control serves to aid the husband and patriarch most effectively. Like the criminal whose acts society abhors only when he is captured, "[t]he fool's crime is the crime that is found out, and the wise man's crime is the crime that is *not* found out" (254). For Fosco, discretion (and in the case of marital violence, privacy) in the enactment of criminal violations—the maintenance of propriety, patience, and peace—alleviates the unlawfulness of those acts. Their blame becomes discursively impossible, unlegislatable. One may remain within the law, the standards of English culture, and commit a heinous act, provided that act falls outside the linguistic domain of the current cultural idioms or statutes. A man whose violence remains concealed behind two linguistic structures—middle- and upper-class men are not physically violent with women, and physical violence has observable public results—remains free from discipline. Fosco further explains that the invention of the moral epigram only abets the evildoer by salving the consciences of those who fear what might escape their detection.[27]

Significantly, then, English society itself becomes the accomplice of the crime, allowing the gaps through which a criminal might escape and offering material reward and social sanction for those who act in their own best interest. An awareness of what looks like working-class violence allows one to avoid the threat of punishment, yet achieves the same effects. This construct, however, is vexed. Like the dangers inherent in collusive adultery and the fears that the law would be treated as a fictional, constructed script, Fosco proposes this disturbing breach of concrete, immobile reality that rings through the novel. This disruption suggests that the wise (uncaptured) criminals, like the ones Fosco describes, are identifiable here, in the fictional space, outside the framework conceived of by the law. Indeed, Fosco and Percival themselves are punished, though not, perhaps, for the acts we would expect, as I will explain below.

Despite her condemnation of them, Fosco's words echo in the critique Marian offers of Percival's actions. Marian recognizes the threat and force in Percival's successful manipulation of Laura when he "releases" her from their engagement. By behaving like a gentleman, Percival earns the right to marry Laura in spite of any wrongdoing she might suspect. Further, frustrated by Percival's occasionally successful management of them both, Marian persists in condemning only the public, physical threat he offers. An articulation of the power that Fosco employs and

Percival intimates on these occasions only begins to create a fissure in discursivity in the space of this text. Marian can only say, "If you hurt a hair of Laura's head, if you dare to interfere with my freedom, come what may, to those [laws protecting women from cruelty and outrage] I will appeal" (315). She recognizes that in his wife's case, only the obvious physical harm, such as the bruises she (and Parliament) catalogs, may serve to denounce Percival for any wrongdoing. She mentions freedom only in reference to herself because her status as a single woman exempts her from his command, except regarding her economic dependence and her relationship to Laura. This calls into question the construction of genteel identity laid out in *Oliver Twist*. One can trick the system by being both a gentleman and violent, but this trick makes its own loopholes less effective, as Fosco discovers.

Thus Fosco articulates the ideal method of management as discursively inaccessible—linguistically subtle, yet threatening. This novel is part of what makes violence in a gentleman's home socially accessible and thus subject to critique and legislation. Miller argues the sensation novel may "'say' certain things for which our culture—at least at its popular levels—has yet to develop another language" (*Novel and the Police* 148). We understand this violence in the Count, for his mellifluous oration always rests on the threat of potential physical violence: "Mind, they say, rules the world. But what rules the mind? The body" (622). Coiled beneath the genteel diction lies the "rape" that Fosco enacts on Marian and the private rod that rules his wife. "Where in the history of the world," Fosco asks, "has a man of my order ever been found without a woman in the background immolated on the altar of his life?" (632). He need not conceal this mechanism, only temper its use, call it up carefully, and, literally, watch what he says.

In addition to Fosco's manifestation of the terror accruing to assault discursively, he exploits the visual plane. Collins employs the metaphor of the cane or walking stick with Fosco as well. Fosco is as clever at managing his sticks as Percival is ineffective. He appears at Marian's door, commanding attention with "his great size, his fine black clothes, and his large cane with a gold knob" (566). His cane complements his presence and authenticates his statements of authority and control to Marian. Later, when Walter sees him for the first time, Fosco is "swinging his big stick . . . with superb, smiling patronage . . . [and] paternal good humour"

(587). He has positioned himself with the manner in which he swings his stick about, its impressive size, and his seemingly indifferent comportment. Fosco's lack of attention to the stick he carries gives him the power to threaten with it. Were he obsessed with managing and mastering its privilege, continually testing and refashioning it as Percival does, it would lose the force that lies in the threat. It would become frail and impotent. For Jacques Lacan, it is precisely the ambiguity of the apparent presence, yet inertia, of the phallus that lends it its power. In *Ecrits* he writes, "All these propositions [concerning the marking of the phallus as the privileged signifier] merely conceal the fact that it can play its role only when veiled, that is to say, as itself a sign of the latency with which any signifiable is struck, when it is raised (*aufgehoben*) to the function of the signifier. The Phallus is the signifier of the *Aufhebung* itself, which inaugurates (initiates) by its disappearance" (288). Walter Hartright reproduces this pattern, demonstrating ways in which one may employ the phallic instrument successfully. However, for Walter, these tools are invested with imperial significance and authority, and the villains ultimately lose their rank and the power to enact violence themselves.

## The Empire Strikes Back

### *The Colonizing Cudgel and Middle-Class Authority*

Walter Hartright, the hero of *The Woman in White,* wields his share of sticks, and through various transitions in power, grounded in social and discursive formations that gave new authority to middle-class enterprises, appropriates Percival's position. Because he is a middle-class gentleman, Walter has no right to the affluent Laura's hand at the beginning of the tale. He can gain Laura only by demonstrating the efficacy of middle-class morality and the infidelity of the villains who have illegitimately ascended to their positions of power: Percival, whose title has been stolen from its rightful heir by his forgery, and Fosco, whose sham identity allows him to spy for his government and double-cross a group of political dissidents. *The Woman in White,* like its literary antecedents, establishes a framework in which middle-class morality (much like our rhetoric of "family values" today) serves as a central figure in structuring the culture's value system and distributing power, rationalizing the grid on which those complex power relations are laid out.

Lenore Davidoff and Catherine Hall describe one aspect of this value system as the "single greatest distinction between the aristocracy and middle class": the willingness "actively to seek an income," even if that income might be passively available in other ways (20).[28] Laura herself takes up these values when she asks Walter if she might contribute to the maintenance of their household after she has lost her position in society and her identity. Walter proposes that she make sketches, "and the same person will buy [them] who buys all that I do" (499). Though Walter never tries to sell Laura's sketches, her desire to produce them is the important issue: it indicates her ingestion of the value system that Walter represents. In this move, she is made appropriate to receive a new cultural inheritance in addition to her familial one, a growing social authority. Forging this inheritance, as *Oliver Twist* demonstrates, is often a violent act. Violence may sustain the economic imperatives that underlie the development of this cultural shift, but that violence must be authorized as vital to larger cultural concerns. Though the brutality of Percival and Fosco seems to dominate the tale (as does Bill's in *Oliver Twist*), it is simply the only violence that is presented as such. In the following sections, I demonstrate the ways in which an undercurrent of violence pervades the heroic characters as well, an analysis that suggests the connection between the rhetoric of imperialism (and the violence it implies) and the authority to engage in marital violence. I argue that the violence of the hero in all of these arenas is sanctioned and screened by a moral code based on the economic and social enfranchisement of the growing middle class.[29]

Walter seems to be innocent of any wrongdoing or violence, bristling at Mrs. Catherick's suggestion that he has punished Percival for his transgressions. But the scene in which Percival dies, when read in the framework my argument provides, offers a different means of interpretation, explaining Walter's anxiety over the letter and other landmarks in this series of events. Trapped in a burning church vestry while attempting to steal the documents that would expose his illegitimacy, Percival cries for help and Walter responds by launching a "rescue" that ensures Percival's consumption by the conflagration. Foregrounding the question of middle-class authority I point to here, three characters—Percival,

Walter, and Percival's servant—provide a dramatic conjunction of class markers in Percival's death. Walter demonstrates his superiority to the simple-minded servant below him (as well as to the paralyzed, incompetent working-class figures in the crowd) and to the tainted aristocrat above. Though Walter's ascendance over Percival—both literally (Walter conducts the rescue and climbs to the roof) and metaphorically (Walter's ethical high ground)—appears to be a product of Walter's own labor, the moral requirement Davidoff and Hall describe, his efforts are invisibly aided by the classes below. He ascends to the roof with the assistance of Percival's servant—commanding the man to "Stoop!" then literally climbing to his new position on the back of the man below him. Once on the roof, Walter claims that he must "give [Percival] some air!" (536) and cracks open the skylight with his walking stick. In a culture that used candle snuffers to extinguish flames, the humblest of Victorians must have understood the relationship between oxygen and fire and the implications of this act. Walter's "rescue" attempt feeds oxygen to the flames and encourages the fire that consumes Percival. Though Walter insists that he hopes to save Percival—and later remarks anxiously, "There is no doubt in my mind, there can be no doubt in the mind of any one, that he was a dead man before ever we [reached him]" (544)—there can instead be no doubt that Walter hastened, perhaps even caused, Percival's death. As if haunted by the tensions that resist containment in this scene, this is one of the only places in Walter's narrative in which the events slip out of the comfortable past (tense) and urge themselves into the present, demanding attention. His gestures toward ethics, his moral good will in seeking to "rescue" the man who has been his and Laura's bane, and the naturalization of class relations in the scene are still troubled by the violence so effectively obscured that it has, until now, never received comment. Peeling back these layers reveals important ideological information. In these moments we can begin to read one facet of middle-class ideology as this novel depicts it and see how violence was sanctioned in the "proper" hands. Through Percival's death, Walter paves his way to taking Laura's hand in marriage, and through his extortion of Fosco's confession (also marked by threats of grave violence), he makes accessible her great fortune. Though Walter disavows "base speculation on the future relations" of Laura and himself (475), he is rewarded with the wealth that both Percival and Fosco desired, desires for which they were condemned as brutal and violent. Walter, however, labors effectively and within the moral constructs of the novel, securing his right to the advantages he gains.

In Hartright ("heart right"—a none too subtle suggestion that he embodies this morality), we are presented a man whose fidelity to Victorian values[30] via an economic system increasingly linked to empire earns him the right to engage in violence that rivals Percival's and Fosco's, the men he displaces. Violence is not eliminated from the middle class, but rather translated through the frame of class and finance as a moral and worthy enterprise.[31] These three elements—violence, imperialism, and morality—are threaded together to define the outlines of the middle classes. Evidence of Walter's adherence to this code appears in Percival's death scene when Walter holds his newly purchased, homely, phallic "cudgel in [his] mouth" as he ascends (536), giving metaphoric homage to the authority his stick represents. Walter and Percival's "meeting" after the latter is dead is described as a "Visitation of God" (541), a preordination of events by the ultimate moral authority. Further, before Walter returns, Marian's vision of him in Central America exhibits an eighteenth-century use of capitalization to emphasize the sacred quality of the "Design" that will lead Walter back to Laura and Marian, the "unknown Retribution and the inevitable End." Walter urges that the "Pestilence that wastes, the Arrow that strikes, the Sea that drowns . . . take me nearer and nearer to the End" (296–97). These biblical afflictions—like the plagues of Egypt, the martyrdom of saints, the parting of the Red Sea, or the salvation of Noah—leave Walter unscathed and sanction his preordained "End," evidence that clearly indicates his priority, his morality, God's will.

The authority to act with violence does not just manifest itself in relation to Percival. As D. A. Miller has pointed out, the novel opens with Walter preparing to wield his stick in another situation. He grasps his cudgel, braced to pummel Anne Catherick, his eventual bride's half-sister and near twin. Miller reads this as the reaffirmation of masculine authority (152). I would supplement this notion by pointing to another aspect of the gendering and domestication of Walter's potential violence. Anne's resemblance to Laura and their later substitution for one another blur them in such a way that Walter's threatening posture may be read as an opening caveat concerning the role of violence in structuring gendered relations and, by extrapolation, the relations between "man and wife," not just masculinity. Further, this move is situated in the careful mapping of Walter's class identity. Just prior to this passage, we have been informed, in great detail, of his economic and social situation, and when Anne speaks to him of his rank and asks if he is titled, Walter responds, "a little bitterly," "Far from it. I am only a drawing master" (51). His discomfort with his position will be reframed in the course of the novel, however, when he learns (along with the readers) that the balance of the morality in his identity will outweigh the benefits of wealth and power, and indeed, those benefits will accrue to him because of his morality. His moral choices and the shifts from an "obsolete" ethic that they imply are foregrounded as well when he distinguishes himself from an "older, wiser, and colder" gentleman. To that end, he spends pages explaining his encounter with Anne, defending and justifying the ethics of his response to the woman, assuring us that he has behaved with propriety. The narrative vindicates his behavior when Anne becomes the key to revealing the villainy of the wicked titled men about whom she had questioned Walter. These elements suggest that a transition is taking place in which Walter's identity as a middle-class gentleman will not only be key to our understanding of the novel's events, but will be shaped by our reading of his ethics, ethics that might demand access to the stick around which his fingers tighten when Anne approaches him.

Indeed, the novel amplifies the power of the middle class in the face of the aristocracy, stripping the authority of Percival and Fosco and uplifting Walter, once he has gone through trials that prove his mettle more surely than the "older, wiser, and colder" gentleman to whom he compares himself in the novel's opening. Percival's degradation begins before Walter defeats him at the church when we learn that Percival has "no more claim to the baronetcy and to Blackwater Park than the poorest labourer who worked on the estate" (529). Baronet is reduced to laborer in one blow, in part because he was one who had not labored, but maneuvered to obtain his wealth. If we are in any doubt as to the significance of this flaw, Fosco, whose "life was one long assertion of the rights of the aristocracy and the sacred principles of Order" (644), dies with the mark of "Traitor" over his heart in the final pages of the novel. The novel does not suggest an elimination of rank altogether, but rather asserts a definition of rank that is based upon the values represented in Walter. When

Marian announces, at the novel's close, that Walter's son, "Mr. Walter Hartright," is the "heir to Limmeridge" and its great fortune, the naming effectively blurs Walter's economic and social success with that of his son, imbuing Walter with the credit of rank and his son with the credit of his value system. Surely, this child will have the values that will allow him to use that wealth wisely. And of Sir Percival's ancient estate? An East Indian officer, another man who has labored in appropriately moral ways, has all along been the rightful heir and inherits the title and Blackwater Park upon Percival's death (563).

This officer's means of "earning" Blackwater Park leads me to the third part of the triad of class, gender, and imperialist violence mentioned above. The necessity of the middle class's imposition of its values, evidenced by the revision of those held by the "older, wiser, and colder" gentleman, was developed at this point in the century through the colonial mission—not just in the colonies themselves but in the most domestic of spaces. Patrick Brantlinger argues that early Victorians were indeed imperial; though they "did not call themselves imperialists . . . they traversed the world as advocates of free trade, commerce and Christianity, and the benefits of being British" (*Rule of Darkness* 44). Morality becomes a central screen of imperial enthusiasm and also for the domestic acts for which it serves as a figuring metaphor, such as the aggressive growth of the middle class and marital violence, underpinning violence and marking it only as good business and good ethics. Imperial fervor becomes the means of justifying both violence and the morality of Walter's ventures in the field and in his home. We see evidence of these connections in Walter's description of the changing economic landscape, another transformation linked to the rise of the middle class: "Is there any wilderness of sand in the deserts of Arabia, is there any prospect of desolation among the ruins of Palestine, which can rival the repelling effect on the eye, and the depressing influence on the mind, of an English country town in the first stage of its existence, in the transition state of its prosperity? I asked myself that question as I passed through the clean desolation, the neat ugliness, the prim torpor of the streets of Wellingham [with] the tradesmen who stared after me from their lonely shops" (503). The explicitly foreign desolation present in Wellingham is the product of an evolving economy in its first stage of existence. In the transition to prosperity, these new sites of economic growth require the influence of the morality that Walter represents to "vivify" them, to breathe into them more than simply existence; they need purification. Just as the aristocracy would be cleansed and foreign nations would be civilized by the imposition of "superior" values, so these new primitive economic arenas and the domestic space upon which the economic depends would require the kind of experience that Walter (not only a moralist, but an imperialist who has made ventures to Central America) is especially skilled at providing. Wellingham, the home of Percival's forgery and Mrs. Catherick's "hardened shameless depravity," as Walter describes it (560), clearly needs moral purification. Mrs. Catherick plays out these dangers like the threatening women in Parliament's imagination, colluding with Sir Percival to make people believe she has engaged in an adulterous affair with him, just as the writers of the Divorce Act feared. Her "unnatural" desire for more than could be provided by her own and her husband's labor lead her astray and into conspiracy with Percival. It is precisely this behavior from both the working classes and the aristocracy that can be healed by the purifying influence of a character such as Walter. The novel urges that the middle classes might provide the moralizing force to heal the gaps in the legislation, even if the gaps must be violently cauterized.[32]

Through a series of narrative substitutions, the violence of both the colonial campaign and the economic and domestic relations of the middle class are obscured by what was abstractly conceived of as middle-class morality. These themes are united in the passage describing Walter's return to Limmeridge to visit Laura's grave, to find her alive and deprived of her name and fortune: "From thousands on thousands of miles away— through forest and wilderness, where companions stronger than I had fallen by my side, through perils of death thrice renewed, and thrice escaped, the Hand that leads men on the dark road to the future had led me to meet that time" (435). This trinity of dangers survived, the divine guiding Hand authorizes Walter's violence through the rhetoric of the references to the colonial expedition. Indeed, Walter's return is destined to make justice possible—a justice that could not exist under the law that has failed to meet the changing moral codes. Thus, Walter may rely on this code alone and require no explicit recourse to the law or the police to successfully complete his displacement of Percival. His identity as a proper policing figure in middle-class morality, shaped and authorized by his colonial expedition, screens the violence of his attack on those betraying the order he has learned to protect. Drawing upon what appears to be a transcendent moral law, like the morality offered in *Oliver Twist,* he participates in Percival's execution for betraying the boundaries of that which was entirely articulable, not transcendent at all. Percival's ambiguous class standing further distances the crime of domestic violence from Walter, marking it as outside the realm of gentlemanly behavior.

Walter, then, may brandish the stick he chooses and use it violently without being marked as violent. His stick derives authority from the imperialist project he has studied abroad and the class improprieties of his enemies. In a conflation of the purification of the familial domestic space and the domesticating function of colonial enterprise, Walter describes a new stick he purchases as "a stout, country cudgel, short, and heavy at the head. With this homely weapon, if any one man tried to stop me I was a match for him. . . . I had not wanted for practice since the latter time of my experience in Central America" (531). Walter uses descriptors that suggest his chosen tool is invested with nationalistic energy: it is a homely weapon, from his country. Further, he recalls his successful venture to Central America and labors among the savages, which the cudgel represents. As he dealt with the "primitive natives" he would deal with those who had become savages on his own soil.[33] He must expel invaders from the peerage and metaphorically cleanse the space they leave behind, once with fire, the second time with a wound over the heart and the mark of "Traitor." Walter succeeds in thwarting the attack on him (launched at Percival's behest), landing a blow "heavily on [the] head" of his assailant and demonstrating the power of his cudgel (531). Only a few paragraphs after eliminating Percival's hired assassins, Walter battles with Percival himself, dramatizing in the scene the outcome of these "moral" and socioeconomic power negotiations: Walter will become the valued patriarch and Laura's husband, effectively bearing the walking stick (and demonstrating his efficacy by impregnating Laura, as Percival failed to do) and putting Percival in his proper place; he is returned to his class, and his position is cleansed in a symbolic purification. Yet despite the ways in which this move in the novel undermines its message of violence in the upper ranks of society, its gestures of containment ultimately fail. The possibility of violence presented, even if reclaimed, becomes a free radical within the narrative, attacking the structure of the laws that Walter indicates are inadequate to address violence within the home. Still, the novel works to carefully position violence as a product of a lack of morality. These complexities are evident in Fosco's nearly successful attempt to escape punishment for his crimes.

## Imperial Debt

Fosco situates his crime outside the logical boundaries of the law and in the private room with his private rod, always cloaked with gestures of gentility, not the "brutality of the lower orders" we might expect. However, his defeat ultimately takes the same form as Percival's: debasement and death. Pesca, an old friend of Walter's, supplies Walter with the discursive link that enables him to interpret Fosco's behavior as a betrayal of the new "law" that ruins Percival. In a doubling of the colonial metaphor, Walter calls on the Italian Pesca to exterminate a savage foreigner. Pesca, unlike Fosco, has attempted to conform to English standards, making himself "a perfect Englishman" (39). Like the well-behaved, colonized man, he felt himself to be rescued by the English, and the "ruling idea of his life . . . [was to] show gratitude to the country." Grateful and obsequious, Pesca actually "appear[s] in the servant's place" when Walter visits home in the first moments of the novel (35). Significantly, Walter had saved Pesca from drowning in the prehistory of the tale, rather than being saved by the foreigner and owing a debt to him, as Percival had. This debt provides an indication of the proper functioning of colonial power and repositions violence to make it appear the product of the colonized, rather than the colonizer.[34] We learn that in Pesca's youthful allegiance to Italy, he joined a political brotherhood devoted to the people of Italy and demanding fierce loyalty. Once he matriculated, he was bound for life, despite the condemnation of his maturer and sufficiently British–ified judgment. Fosco, much altered from his youth and hiding under a false identity and title granted by the government for his work as a spy, had as a young man joined and forsaken the same brotherhood. Walter calls upon Pesca's services as a loyal British subject to overthrow Fosco. This forces Pesca to risk his life and virtually to take the life of one of his own countrymen, but this is precisely what Walter expects of Pesca's loyalty. Though it is Walter's demand, it is marked as a product of Pesca's and his country's savagery, not Walter's desire for revenge, that leads to Fosco's death. Confirming the goals of the imperialist project by playing on

Pesca's desire to achieve the status of the proprietous English middle-class family man, Pesca makes the sacrifice that becomes the linchpin in the scheme, freeing Walter from his dilemma, confirming Anne Catherick's death, and returning Laura's identity to her. Deeply intertwined and interdependent, the fervor for this genteel identity, violence, and the ideology of imperialism reposition Walter (as master of Limmeridge) as a middle-class man with the authority and wealth of an aristocrat.

### The Poison Pen

Textuality plays a significant role in Walter's battle for legal, social, and moral authority. The entire novel might be read as a tribute to the power of text to alter the seemingly unalterable, to rewrite other kinds of narrative, such as the existing moral code and the law. Through the narratives that Walter collects, he is able to piece together the evidence to achieve his ends where the law had failed. We expect this text—Walter's and more expansively Collins's—to have a corresponding effect on the text of the law, to reshape it by reshaping the ideologies that put it into place. As Walter sutures the lacunae in understanding in the novel's world in order to demand change, so too does Collins's novel in the world outside the text. We see Walter's use of text as a transformative force in the scene in which he captures Fosco. So powerful is Walter's text that it renders Fosco's gun impotent. Just like Percival, Fosco loses access to phallic power once his crime is framed with the moral structure that Walter provides. Though Fosco's hand "softly slip[s]" in and out of his drawer and onto his gun, he can't pull the trigger. Walter produces a letter written by Pesca that forces Fosco to act against his wishes, exemplifying his new discursive authority. This text, like the text Walter produces to make up the novel, makes up Walter as well. The transmission of letters, diaries, and wills serves to position Walter, to mark him as proper, to screen his violence and label the violence of others as illegitimate.

In addition, Walter's discursive authority becomes the overriding trope of the novel, superseding that of the police and the law whom he claims would have been ineffective in aiding his struggle to free Laura (640). His narrative holds the text together and presents us, he suggests, with "the truth[,] always in its most direct and most intelligible aspect" (33). His discourse provides the measure of reality, and the texts of the other contributors to the narrative are judged against his authority. However, despite the fact that Walter claims to transcend the governance of the police and the law by clinging to the truth, we learn as the novel nears its finale that Walter has been telling the "story under feigned names" (563). According to Pamela Perkins and Mary Donaghy,

> *This startling disclosure is significant, indicating as it does that Walter's aim is not simply to re-establish Laura's identity. Ironically, "Laura's" true identity only become increasingly confused when we learn that Walter, somewhat like the Count and Sir Percival, is deliberately concealing it. Far from being a paragon of chivalry, and protecting the woman he loves for her sake alone, Walter is also defending what he believes is a harmonious and enduring social order. It is not inconsequential that this orthodox social order serves him very well, leaving him at the novel's conclusion in possession of both Laura and Limmeridge House. (393)*

Although true to his words that he must extend his search beyond the apparent boundaries of the law in order to convict the villains, Walter bridges this gap with a new ideological ethic that allows the internal legal order to redefine them as villains. In this aggressive depiction of scenes outside the law, the gap is bridged by the very authority that seems to condemn it, middle-class morality. In this move beyond the boundaries of the law, the narrative exploits the excess of sensation, transgressing "reality" and "nature," to bring those treading beyond its confines into the range of punishment, to rethink and alter the law. For this service, Walter indeed reaps rewards.

### (Wo)manly Anger

Despite the explicit objective of the preamble, Walter's dedication to avoid hearsay evidence, every detail regarding Laura and Madame Fosco remains lodged in the narratives of others. These significant characters in the tale never speak directly of their own experience. Rather, the wives, the most directly and profoundly abused of the characters, remain overtly voiceless, as did the women of England in the parliamentary debates that touched their lives so intimately. In fact, Madame Fosco's access to only a blank page metaphorizes the women's complete textual muteness. Their imposed silence, however, divulges a danger that the novel does record in its interstices, particularly in its delineation of the female characters, a danger that offers a more disruptive critique than that offered by Walter and that in later novels becomes increasingly central as the source of sensation: the dangerous woman.

Throughout the novel, the silence of women reveals the threat of something their text might have produced, something that must be excluded from the novel. In these unspoken narratives lies an inarticulable menace. Marian suggests Madame Fosco's "present state of suppression may have sealed up something dangerous in her nature, which used to evaporate harmlessly in the freedom of her former life." Within her "suppressed tigerish jealousy" and the unknown that has "deteriorated in her secret self" (239), Madame Fosco's danger hovers near the surface, a persistent threat. Although silent, it offers a challenge to the Count's iron rod. Nor is Sir Percival's authority uncontested. Anne Catherick's "wild animal eyes" (127) and her incessant attacks on Percival mime her double's potential and represent an anxiety of what Laura might become. Finally, Laura and Madame Fosco "tremble violently" throughout the novel, evidence perhaps of the volatile tension contained within, the danger that may explode. I wish to counter the claim that the novel simply authorizes "as a cultural value . . . privacy, the determination of an integral, autonomous, 'secret' self" under constant surveillance (Miller 162). Rather, I would argue, the novel proliferates the exposure of the secret, making the private public, threatening to uncover the secrets that aren't always explicitly revealed, such as those of violence in the domestic space and the agency of the angry woman. Elizabeth Langland underlines the nineteenth-century logic that "demands the visibility of even private spaces" and the "continual scrutiny" to which the lady is subject ("Enclosure Acts" 8),[35] a phenomenon particularly evident in the "sensation of sensationalism" (3). Langland points to the ways that this visibility might become oppressive and confining. Yet visibility was also an exposure: what *The Woman in White* uncomfortably restrains, it cannot contain, and both the men's violence and women's frustration become visible. Later sensation novels address these tensions directly, granting voice to the dangerous woman and the lives of the women in abusive situations. *Lady Audley's Secret,* which many critics have read as a revision of *The Woman in White,* offers a heroine who attempts to murder her husband and nephew while maintaining the outward beauty and gentility of a Laura or Madame Fosco, fulfilling the possibility expressed in the cultural oxymoron of "women's violence."[36]

Fosco's description of the narrow delineation of womanhood in English law supports the contention that the current legal definition didn't allow for the identity of the abused middle- and upper-class woman: "I remember that I was married in England, and I ask if a woman's marriage obligations in this country provide for her private opinion of her husband's principles? No! They charge her unreservedly to love, honour, and obey him" (632). When a husband fills his role poorly in this formulation, a wife's dependent role is confounded. Her identity become confused, ambiguous, and inadequate to control and contain all the possibilities. Characters such as Laura and Madame Fosco become sites of unstable suppression—dangerous, violent. Marian's delineation serves as the novel's attempt to manage that fear, shrouding her in a "masculine" identity and interpreting her anger and explicit desire for retributive violence as male identified—a desire she cannot fulfill as a woman.

Described throughout the text as shockingly masculine in the face (moustache and all) though feminine in body (an indicator of her limitations), Marian carries a "manly umbrella," a substitute for the phallic cane. She has masculine foresight and resolution, and is by virtue of this the only female character in the text who regularly expresses a desire to behave violently. When she and Laura are insulted by Percival, she remarks, "I started to my feet as suddenly as if he had struck me. If I had been a man, I would have knocked him down on the threshold of his own door, and have left his house. . . . But I was only a woman—and I loved his wife so dearly!" (268). Again, when Fosco appears at her door, she remarks, "My hands tingled to strike him, as if I had been a man" (566). Marian's "masculine mind" allows her to imagine an aggressive response, but her words remind us of her gendered weaknesses: "I was only a woman." Her woman's subjectivity seems to hold the possibility of enacting physical retribution. Her relationship to textuality demonstrates this potential as well. Her narrative becomes swallowed up and framed by Walter's in the text. She serves simply as a conduit for his desires while he stays in Central America, temporarily substituting for his place in the text. When she takes up the thread of his narrative with her diary entries, this performance of memory and writing is praised by

Fosco and Walter as a marvelous exhibition of manly attributes. Marian recalls details in her mother's letters that initiate the mystery and reproduces lengthy conversations after the fact in her journal. Marian also becomes a channel into the narrative for Walter's activity when he is overseas, experiencing a trance in which she has a vision informing her of Walter's movements and inserting them into the text (295–97).

Another marker of Marian's representation of Walter lies in the intensity of her passion for Laura. When Laura informs Marian that she plans to tell Percival she loves another, Laura demonstrates her love for Walter, threaded through a markedly romantic love for Marian, blurring the identity of the lover she plans to reveal. "She put her lips to mine, and kissed me. 'My own love,' she said softly, 'you are so much too fond of me'" (186). Further, Laura begs Marian: "promise you will never marry, and leave me. It is selfish to say so, but you are so much better off as a single woman—unless—unless you are very fond of your husband—but you won't be very fond of anybody but me, will you?" (235). Marian serves as a proxy for Walter while he is absent, and the focus returns to the domestic family unit once he becomes directly involved in the tale again. Despite the fact that Walter's first suggestion of marriage to Laura leaves Marian pale and fills her with "a sad, hesitating interest" (571), Marian cedes her position to him. Touching Laura only through her child, identifying herself no longer as Laura's sister but as an aunt, she holds the couple's son in her arms as the novel draws to its close.

In spite of Marian's shifting representation—her manly resolution, anger, and love—she may not enact the violence she desires to express. However, her fantasies represent the potential for violence in the other women characters as a response to the violence enacted on them, and her temporary replacement of Walter hints at the possibility of usurpation. Marian embodies and bespeaks the excess that remains suppressed in characters such as Laura and Madame Fosco, and as the containment of violence in the home cannot be fully ensured by Walter's presence, the response of a woman cannot be contained by Marian. Indeed, the sensation novel as a genre proliferates this excess, representing both an undeniable sense of realism and the sensation that the legislature would condemn and attempt to control. By exposing the threat of women's access to power in the circulating power dynamic, sensation novels eventually formulated alternative ways of enacting and responding to violence in the home, providing representations of increasingly dangerous women. However, they also made alternative formulations intellectually accessible to the culture at large and accessible to legislation. The mass consumption of sensation novels ensured the transmission of new possible formulations of womanhood to the public. The marginalia of the sensation novel— precisely that which makes it sensational— open up new subjectivities for women, a discursive shift in the face of the legislative surveillance the novels introduced.

# III

# The Dangerous Woman: Mary Elizabeth Braddon's Sensational (En)gendering of Domestic Law in *Aurora Floyd*

*The sensation novel of our time, however extravagant and unnatural, yet is a sign of the times—the evidence of a certain turn of thought and action, of an impatience of old restraints, and a craving for some fundamental change in the workings of society . . . [that] devote themselves to destroying conventional moralities. . . .*

*It is in the existence of the real with the impossible that [Braddon's] power lies.*

—"Our Female Sensation Novelists"

## Mary Elizabeth Braddon and the Sensation Novel

*Aurora Floyd* (1863), the successor to Mary Elizabeth Braddon's widely read *Lady Audley's Secret* (1862), mobilizes many of the same challenges to legal and social questions as did the sensation novels that preceded it. Braddon's novels reinvent the conventions laid out in Wilkie Collins's *The Woman in White* and in the relationship between women, violence, and sensation. Leaping from the possibilities hinted at in Collins's fiction, female characters in Braddon's novels conspicuously enact or are associated with violence against men as retribution for cruel behavior on the part of their husbands or fiancés. They become unauthorized disciplinarians, or more disruptively, murderesses or suspected murderesses.[1]

As Homi Bhabha argues, the imperial figure must constantly re-form itself to prevent the kind of mimetic disruption that may occur in the colonized Other (168); we might read sensation as a mimetic reformation of the master text of realism and Braddon's novel as the same to *The Woman in White,* continuing to disturb the notions that had been laid out in the previous model. Here, Bhabha's argument becomes particularly apt, because *Aurora Floyd* deals with violence and the Other, explicitly invoking the imperial metaphor to lay out its themes. Although the violence of the heroine as murderess, particularly when she embodies the features of the colonial object, might seem to be a formula that would repel the middle-class Victorian reader, Braddon's novels were astoundingly popular. However, they also provoked a firestorm of controversy. This tension suggests that the novels were effectively upending received knowledge, but doing so at a site in which there was already enough disruption to make such images palatable. The terms in which Braddon's fiction was critiqued lend insight into the kinds of "truths" they called into question. The "depraved" behavior exhibited by her heroines seemed to some contemporary critics to delineate unseemliness and impropriety in new, even moralistic, terms. Reverend Henry Longeville Mansel noted in his critique of sensation that it "usurp[ed] 'a portion of the preacher's office, moulding the minds and forming the habits and tastes of its generation' " (251). Sensation novels threatened, in this way, to refigure what was moral.

Yet the notion that sanctified authority could be replaced by the discourse of sensation did not dampen enthusiasm for the genre or for Braddon's novels in particular. The questions of morality seemed to revolve around two primary issues: gender-codified behavior and class. Thus, W. Fraser Rae lamented, in a caustic critique of the "low type of female character" who could enact the violence depicted in *Aurora Floyd,* that Braddon might still "boast, without fear of contradiction, of having temporarily succeeded in making the literature of the Kitchen the favourite reading of the Drawing room" (Wolff 196–97). The invasion of the drawing room and disruption of angelic femininity offer an inversion of proprieties Victorian scholars have come to associate with middle-class notions of identity. The sheer materiality of bodies and their processes was implied by the portion of the domestic space to which they seemed banished, the kitchen, along with the primarily working-class people who inhabited that space. Unlike earlier fictions, which had preserved the bodilessness of the middle-class heroine, Braddon's novels evoked not only labor, consumption (of food and bodies), and carnality, but also physical dangers, including exhaustion, filth, sickness—indeed, violence.[2] Further, these feminized bodies materialized desires, dangers, and sexuality. Rather than "subordinat[ing] the body to a set of mental processes that guaranteed domesticity," as Nancy Armstrong argues of domestic fiction ("Rise of the Domestic Woman" 907), the sensation novel draws attention to the bodies of the figures inhabiting the drawing room.

The sensation in Braddon's sensation novels lies in the substance of the heroines and those around them and resists the dominant novelistic and social discourse of the mid-century that operated to manage women's identities in terms of the domestic ideal.[3] Braddon's *Aurora Floyd,* in its abundance of carnality, death, violence, and conspicuous eroticism, particularly as they surround the women in the novel, offers a resignification of not only middle-class women's identity, but also the material circumstances of Victorian women's lives and the law that articulated them. As Judith Butler suggests in *Bodies That Matter,* the link between bodies and politics is constitutive, resulting from the "citational accumulation of and dissimulation of the law that produces material effects" (12). Yet, these citations are fraught with instability, and the seemingly secure production of the domestic woman and the idealization of the domestic space may be contested—along with the notion that violence and danger are confined to this realm—even while they are deployed. *Aurora Floyd,* even in its parody of realism, serves as a performance of these terms whose hyperbolic nature "disrupt[s] the closeting distinction between public and private space" (233).[4] It publicizes the functioning of even middle-class bodies, highlighting the management of gender and sex that casts women as the bodiless victims of impossible crimes. Physical abuse must be enacted on a body; and Aurora's body, along with the bodies of those who are beaten or murdered, materializes despite the powerful pressures that Armstrong notes domesticate women and keep their bodies invisible. *Aurora Floyd* goes even further by demonstrating the ways in which the violence played out on women's bodies is obscured in many narratives through the employment of the discourse of the colonized Other, which defines and insulates her, authorizing a violent reshaping of her identity and eventually attempting to rehabilitate conceptually the British domestic scene. Like Pandora's box, however, once Braddon's novels release the contagion of resistance and reconsideration, here manifested in women's refusal to tolerate violent domestication, it cannot be contained.

*Aurora Floyd,* in particular, seemed to many critics a Pandora's box. Though Lady Audley, the heroine of Braddon's first best-seller, had been wicked, she had been punished as well.[5] Aurora, as horrified critics pointed out, was returned to the center of the domestic space. The furor over this novel points up its importance to the Victorians and compels us to carefully examine the text and its context. One critic claimed that "half the world" knew Aurora Floyd ("Miss Braddon" 593), and another remarked that "no novelists, with the exception of Mr. Charles Dickens, [had] so completely gained and so indisputably held the public attention" as Braddon, calling *Aurora Floyd* "an event in literature" in which "everyone" participated ("Miss Braddon's Novels" 436–37). Though Braddon had her champions—one essay called *Aurora Floyd* a sign of her genius ("Miss Braddon's Novels" 436–38)—her reviewers often were exceedingly hostile, an indication of the novel's challenge to cultural norms. They lamented the immorality of the "unnatural" heroine, a creature possible only in a sensation novel (Rae 93–101), and argued that this fiction had a "deteriorating effect on the mind" ("Our Novels" 424). One suggested that "the injury that these ill-toned, ill-wrought productions work on dispositions the least qualified to resist baneful influence [girls and young women] is incalculable" ("Novels in Relation to Female Education" 516–17). In the year of *Aurora Floyd's* publication, an essay that excoriated Aurora's identity as a violent, unnatural, and dangerous creature condemned sensation novels for their dangerous heroines and effects: "There is nothing more violently opposed to our moral sense, in all the contradictions to custom which they present us, than the utter unrestraint in which heroines of this order are allowed to expatriate and develop their impulsive, stormy, passionate characters. We believe it is one chief among their many dangers to youthful readers" ("Our Female Sensation Novelists" 353). The eponymous heroine was perceived to be a "dangerous woman" to those inside the text and to the novel's readers— a concern that was evident not just in the literary or social criticism of the day, but the law as well.

At roughly the time of *Aurora Floyd's* publication in 1863, Parliament was generating a vision of the dangerous woman in the Contagious

Diseases Acts (C.D. Acts), and the similarities between the rhetoric of the novel and the debates surrounding the repeal of the acts are stunning. In these acts, the prostitute, like Aurora, was marked as a murderess and the moral and social bane of the respectable family. Furthermore, both the laws and the novel erected their figure of the dangerous woman on the grounds of colonial rhetoric, Orientalizing her and providing a context for her recuperation. The intensity of the response to both the C.D. Acts and the novel indicates that they figured prominently in the cultural conversation, and the parallel patterns in these texts suggest that they not only spoke to their culture, but to one another. The commentaries on the sensational qualities of the novel echo concerns about the C.D. Acts debates inside and outside of Parliament. Parliament believed that the acts had spawned "sensation literature" marked by "the grossest exaggeration,"[6] precisely the terms with which critics characterized Braddon's novels and identified them as dangerous. Indeed, Parliament expressed the same concern as the critics about the texts falling into the hands of women and children, complaining that activists regularly delivered them into the hands of virginal women and likening the textual threat to an assault on chastity. Just as sensation fiction seemed to compromise the respectability of those women who read it, so too did the literature surrounding the C.D. Acts, and even the acts themselves, seem to create a sullying effect, disrupting the domestic purity of the M.P.s' houses.[7] Ultimately, this conversation produced such social upheaval and bitter conflict that the acts were repealed. Both texts served as pivots around which fierce debates about propriety, the family, and womanhood circulated, and each was persistently and pervasively present in the Victorian social framework.

The correspondence of the specific concerns in both the criticism of the texts and the texts themselves begs analysis.[8] It indicates that both texts were products of a circulating debate that pervaded the culture, but they are more than simply products of social tensions; they participated in the production of these cultural debates, as well. The debates surrounding the Contagious Diseases Acts, which appeared only after *Aurora Floyd* had been widely circulated and digested, suggest that Braddon's contentious, exploratory fiction engaged in the revisioning of the language that created law, playing out and exposing the complex network of cultural tensions that generated the construction of the dangerous woman. Braddon's novel challenged the often unspoken beliefs that produced both the domestic angel and her dangerous Other, and more significantly for my argument, resisted the containment of violence in the home, culture, and the letter of the law within the body of this figure, anticipating and supplying a framework for the sensational anti-C.D. Acts literature and debates.

### Paternal Terror

*Aurora Floyd's* first words in the novel are "He is [dead]." By the novel's climax, the police, her servants, her friends, and even her jovial, warm-hearted husband suspect her of shooting her first husband at point-blank range. Aurora is a bigamist, the near ruin of her second husband's respected family name, and, most disturbingly, a suspected murderess. No one escapes the threat of death that hovers around her; both of the men to whom she later becomes engaged contemplate suicide during their courtship. Her doting father and all her lovers suffer or perish—all, seemingly, because of her presence. Though we might be tempted to dismiss Aurora's threatening demeanor as a trope of the sensation novel, it reveals much more about a culture in transition than a cursory examination might suggest.

The men with whom Aurora becomes intimate view her with escalating fear over the course of the novel. She seems, after all, increasingly dangerous. Aurora becomes the repository of anxieties surrounding dangerous women and their potential to respond to marital abuse. The "terror" of these men, a key term in the discursive structure of the narrative, is not a diffuse anxiety. Rather, it specifically signifies men's fear for their lives. The first tremors of fear are associated with Aurora's unmanageability. We learn early in the novel that Aurora's father, Archibald, has failed to domesticate her: "If he could have governed or directed that impetuous nature, he would have had her the most refined and elegant, the most perfect and accomplished of her sex; but he could not do this" (I 34). Archy attempts to tame her by boarding her at a Parisian finishing school, but Aurora leaves the school and returns months later more unmanageable than ever. Further, she reappears with a damaging secret, whose appearance coincides with the first eruption of terror in the narrative. Her father's comportment is dominated by erratic, nervous behavior when she arrives, conduct that culminates in "a gesture almost of terror." He concretizes his agitation with a question: "That person—he is dead?" Aurora replies only, "He is" (I 41). Aurora's ominous words address themselves to the anxiety that the novel develops as it progresses: that a woman might respond to her husband's abuse with murder.

Aurora's secret concerns James Conyers, the man she claims is dead. A deceitful groom employed at the Floyd stables, James had beguiled Aurora into marriage, hoping to gain access to her wealth. He behaved cruelly[9] once they were wed, even staining their socially disproportionate union with infidelity. Ashamed of their marriage, Aurora leaves James and reports him dead to her father. In effect, she does kill him—by linguistically obliterating him for herself, her father, and the social circles in which she moves. After her disposal of James, her beauty and wealth draw suitors, and she is not long hindered in selecting another husband. Only a few months after Aurora arrives home, an inaccurate newspaper account informs her that James has been killed in a riding accident, and she assumes that she is free to marry again. This faulty record of James's death literally lies at Aurora's feet while her next suitor pledges his undying love. It is this account that inspires her affianced lover's terror. Concerned about Aurora's past, Talbot Bulstrode, a proud Englishman of fine family, fixates on the narrative of her former husband's death. Despite his ignorance of her previous marriage, he feels overcome with a fear he cannot name and "shudder[s] in spite of himself" (I 139). Talbot's terror of Aurora, however, begins much earlier when he contemplates the position of a man affianced to Aurora: "[W]ould there not always be a shuddering terror mingled with [his] love,—a horrible dread" (I 118). Once bound to her, Talbot becomes subject to precisely the fears he had prophesied, and he begins to fantasize about his own death. Significantly, his vision foreshadows a murder that will later be linked to Aurora—her first husband's death by gunshot at the side of a pool: "He had a vague fear that he was too happy; too much bound up heart and soul in the dark-eyed woman by his side. If she were to die! If she were to be false to him! He turned sick and dizzy at the thought; and even in that sacred temple [of the church] the Devil whispered to him that there were still pools, loaded pistols, and other certain remedies for such calamities as those" (I 187).

Immediately following this scene, Aurora learns that Talbot's cousin, a woman with whom she was to have attended the Parisian finishing school, is visiting Bulstrode Castle. Aurora fears her lengthy absence during her clandestine marriage with James Conyers will be betrayed. She flees and refuses to speak to Talbot. In his ignorance, Talbot articulates the danger that haunts his relationship with Aurora as "a brooding shadow, with a veiled face, ghastly and undefined; but . . . *there*" (I 194). Although indistinct, his fear haunts him like a veiled woman, a dangerous, half-concealed aspect of Aurora's identity. His mother and cousin compound his suspicions with hints concerning Aurora's secret. When he confronts her for full disclosure, Aurora remarks, "This is my secret, which I cannot tell you" (I 201). He breaks his engagement with her, and not surprisingly, the terror resurfaces in Talbot and the discourse of the novel: "[S]he rose from her chair, and, tottering towards him, fell upon her knees at his feet. No other action could have struck such terror to his heart. It seemed to him a confession of guilt. But what guilt? what guilt? What was the dark secret of this young creature's brief life?" (I 202). This secret, although ostensibly only her marriage to a man below her station, becomes more and more explicitly associated with the threat of death that hangs about the men who court Aurora. Despite her innocence, James Conyers's murder assigns guilt to Aurora, a guilt that terrifies rather than offends the lofty and disdainful Talbot Bulstrode, the guilt of the homicidal wife.

Aurora's own rhetoric seems to position her as a guilty murderess. She alludes to Macbeth's assassination of his king and master to describe what she calls her incurable illness: "My foolish Talbot . . . do you remember what Macbeth said to *his* doctor? There are diseases that cannot be ministered to" (I 190). In addition, when Aurora bickers with Talbot over her philanthropy, she tells him, "If I told [my petitioners] that I had committed half a dozen murders . . . they would [still] take my money and thank me as kindly for it as that man did just now" (I 168). Talbot later reevaluates his relationship with Aurora and comes to describe her as one of that breed of "creatures, who speak out fearlessly, and tell you that they love or hate you—flinging their arms round your neck or throwing the carving-knife at you, as the case may be" (II 14). Aurora's ability to speak out fearlessly and her brazen aptitude for wielding the carving knife threaten Talbot's position of domestic mastery and—at least in his imagination—endanger his life.

John Mellish, Aurora's next suitor, experiences the same fantasy of death in his relationship with Aurora. Significantly, this apparition arises just before John proposes marriage to Aurora. He simultaneously contemplates matrimony and suicide on the edge of a seaside cliff. Aurora's self-examination reveals the drive to locate in her the failure implied in this essential Englishman's despair. She wonders, "What was this? What had she done? More wrong, more mischief? Was her life to be one of perpetual wrong-doing? . . . Was this John Mellish to be another sufferer by her folly?" (I 243). Indeed, the threat of her potential for violence is communicable among all her suitors. After Aurora reveals to John the existence of her secret (never, however, alluding to its substance), he confirms her characterization as a dangerous woman with his telling colloquial diction: "The murder is out now" (I 247). There is a telling shift, however, in the undercurrent of the narrative's depiction of violence and threat at this moment. As Aurora agrees to marry John, she is the one who experiences terror.

### A Husband and a Servant

Once installed in Mellish Park as John's bride, Aurora encounters the character who will serve as the novel's embodiment of the violence within the domestic space. Effectively shifting the focus and anxieties from Aurora's new husband and the couple's genteel marriage, Softy, a stable hand who's a "bit touched in the upper story" (I 266), becomes the site of danger. The narrator remarks of their encounter: "Reader, when any creature inspires you with this instinctive unreasoning abhorrence, avoid that creature. He is dangerous. . . . Nature cannot lie; and it is nature which has planted that shuddering terror in your breast; an instinct of self-preservation . . . tells you plainly, 'That man is my enemy!' Had Aurora suffered herself to be guided by this instinct . . . what bitter misery, what cruel anguish, might have been spared to herself and others!" (I 269–70). Despite the fact that Softy is the source of the threat to Aurora, she must bear the brunt of the tensions surrounding the intrusion of this menace into the domestic space, a pattern that pervades the novel. Aurora has no positive choice. She must either obey her "instinct of self-preservation" (Softy's threat in this premonition is lethal) and offend the husband who has urged her to accept Softy's presence, or fail her instincts, eschewing the path of "nature" that will become the cause of "bitter misery." Aurora's unnaturalness not only leaves her vulnerable to critique but marks the ways in which the novel resists and reconsiders the very notions of naturalness in relation to violence. Speaking directly to the reader, offering a pointedly direct consideration, the narrator suggests that naturalness counters the will of the husband and disrupts the naturalized domestic scene. Aurora's unsettling response to Softy's "instinctive unreasoning" danger disrupts normative notions of the family narrative. Rather than serving as the veneer that screens these dangers from sight, Aurora fails to passively obscure Softy's danger, responding violently to violence—the source of anguish that accrues to others as well as herself. This is evidenced shortly after their introduction, when Aurora discovers Softy brutally kicking her beloved mastiff, Bow-wow. In a stunning scene that appeared again and again in contemporary reviews criticizing the novel, Aurora's attack on Softy serves as a turning point in the narrative.

> *Aurora sprang upon him like a beautiful tigress. . . . Taller than the stable-man by a foot and a half, she towered above him, her cheeks white with rage, her eyes flashing fury, her hat fallen off and her black hair tumbling about her shoulders, sublime in her passion. . . . She disengaged her right hand from his collar and rained a shower of blows upon his clumsy shoulders with her slender whip; a mere toy, with emeralds set in its golden head, but stinging like a rod of flexible steel in that little hand. . . . Her tangled hair had fallen to her waist . . . and the whip was broken in a half a dozen places. (I 273–74)*

John Mellish stumbles upon this scene and stares in horror at Aurora, whose propriety, sexuality, and hair have all come undone in her passion. He immediately takes her whip, which had been intended as a "mere toy" for a woman until Aurora transformed it into a weapon. Feeling "bitter shame" at her conduct, he returns her to the confines of the domestic space, abashedly bringing her through the back entrance. John recognizes that this display radically deviates from the accepted standards of womanly behavior and acknowledges that in this manner Aurora might "bring disgrace, or even ridicule, upon herself," and certainly him as well. He ponders the situation and cannot even bring himself to acknowledge what she has done, thinking brokenly, "He would have stripped off his coat and fought with half a dozen coal-heavers,[10] and thought nothing of it; but that she—!" (I 274). Aurora's beating of Softy, however, is the unspeakable (yet palpably present) text of his vision, lost in the dash that represents what John fails to articulate. Softy's violence remains utterly absent in John's concerns, an absence that is telling.

John's response to Softy is equally revealing. He selects a whip of his own "from a stand of formidable implements," commandeering Aurora's and stowing it safely in his pocket (I 275). He symbolically reappropriates the authority Aurora had demonstrated with the whip by the production of his much larger one and the assimilation of Aurora's—significantly storing this overtly phallic weapon in his pants. He then returns to Softy supposedly to administer his own punishment, but instead he focuses on Aurora's improprietous behavior—never mentioning Softy's attack on the dog at all. "[I]t wasn't Mrs. Mellish's business to horsewhip you, but it was her duty to let me do it for her" (I 276). Despite his assurance that he will see to the punishment of the stable hand, tensions running through the novel implicate John in Softy's behavior, suggesting an implicit authorization of Softy's violence. John not only refrains from administering a beating with the whip he has displayed, implying that its exhibition was not for Softy but Aurora, he simply banishes Softy from Mellish Park, an injunction they both later ignore. Further, he literally pays Softy an extravagant sum, as if rewarding him for his services: "He took a handful of money from his waistcoat-pocket and threw it on the ground, sovereigns and half-crowns rolling hither and thither on the gravel-path. . . . [Softy's] white face relapsed into a grin: John Mellish had given him gold and silver amounting to upwards of two years of his ordinary wages" (I 277). John's endorsement of the happily grinning Softy makes them tacit confederates, linking their behavior and identity. Thus, when the narrator warns us that "Aurora had two enemies, one without and one within her pleasant home," although she ostensibly refers to two servants who bear Aurora a grudge, John is linked with these enemies as well. Significantly, the narrator marks the province of this danger as the "pleasant home," that which has been called into question in the preceding scene.

John's subsequent remarks on the contest between Aurora and Softy draw out further indications of the erasure of Softy's violence and Aurora's responsibility to provide a screen for it. John comments gravely to Aurora, "I'd never wish to see you do anything that didn't square—that wasn't compatible . . . with the manners of the noblest lady, and the duties of the truest wife in England" (II 97). Softy's behavior, although an un-motivated and cruel assault on an already wounded animal, remains un-questioned. Aurora's behavior provides the greater social challenge. A woman's violence threatens to collapse the distinctions between gendered behaviors and unsettle the domestic space and John's identity as a man, husband, and sovereign. Only he, in this position of authority, has the right to enact violence. When John discusses the event later, he cannot even articulate Aurora's aggression and instead couches her behavior in the rubric of mental illness: "Don't you remember the day [Softy] flogged her dog, you know, and Lolly [Aurora] horse—had hysterics?" (II 234). The word "horsewhipped" evaporates even as John begins to speak it, and he replaces it with an acceptable explanation for Aurora's unspeakable behavior. Women's madness, a less threatening phenomenon,[11] becomes the source of the dilemma. John contains Softy's impropriety in the body of his wife. Yet the continued threat of Aurora's desire and ability to trans-gress the boundaries he demarcates when she feels compromised repro-duces the terror of death John felt during their engagement.

Aurora's attack on Softy and John's response to it may be illuminated by examining two other elements embedded in the scene. The first of these, the attack on the dog that prompts Aurora's assault, becomes in-creasingly significant when we attend to the association between Aurora and Bow-wow. The narrative grafts the dog to Aurora throughout the text. He is introduced in the scene in which Talbot first calls upon Au-rora, and the narrator describes Aurora and the dog simultaneously. The dog's depiction physically borders Aurora's description, and he is men-tioned in nearly every paragraph of Aurora's portrayal, even intruding upon it with a bark. The two have grown up alongside each other and together represent the "marvellous . . . sympathy which exists between some people and the brute creation" (I 90). Bow-wow reappears in the text when John begins to woo Aurora, and as Talbot before him, John must court the dog as he courts his future bride. In Aurora's married life, Bow-wow, like Aurora, becomes a "privileged creature" at Mellish Park, "spen[ding] his declining days in luxurious repose" (I 271). Based on these associations, we may read Softy's attack on Bow-wow as an attack on Aurora, something Softy fantasizes about throughout the novel.

We also may examine the identification of John and Softy. Although at first glance their characterizations seem antithetical, they are delineated in strikingly similar terms. The "big, empty-headed Yorkshireman [who] babble[s] about his stud" (I 106) parallels the "soft" stable hand. Softy's size, with his gladiator-like features and "sinews of iron" (I 268), correlates to the athletic John Mellish, who weighs in two stones heavier than average. John considers business and scholarly thought "terrible bugbear[s]" (I 285) but talks of horses with comfort and authority. Similarly, Softy, "although a little 'fond' upon common matters, [is] a very acute judge of horse-flesh" (I 285). Both characters have also been lifelong residents of Mellish Park and were favorites of John's father. The similarity between them resonates when placed in the context of the novel's tensions. The slippage between their identities invests the threat of Aurora's potential for violence with even greater significance for John, but it also marks Softy's violence in several complex ways as well. The narrative not only depicts Aurora's presence as a deadly threat to John (and to James, her first husband)—the enactment of this threat on the body of John's double underscoring the anxiety concerning her potential for violence against her partner—it metonymically depicts an initial assault by John that precedes Aurora's socially inappropriate behavior.

Ultimately, Softy's attack on Bow-wow becomes an encoded performance of marital violence, dramatizing the potentially menacing side of the domestic space—a husband's assault on his wife—as well as Aurora's response to this danger.[12] An assault that Softy might have imaginatively enacted on Aurora (and which he later explicitly visualizes) becomes redirected to her pet, deflecting the anxieties of such a direct representation and allowing John and Aurora's union to remain within the bounds of the normative marriage this text critiques. Softy becomes the embodiment of male violence within the home, a specter who sustains the violence we are reluctant to identify with John. Softy reaps a significant reward for his performance from John (while Aurora is punished and chastised by her husband), and he serves as a scapegoat for Aurora's anger as well. In fact, although the text characterizes Aurora's fury as aggressive, it is always responsive, provoked by potential or enacted male violence. John and Softy's extraordinary strength and their potential for and demonstration of physical assault are the catalysts that incite Aurora's wrath.

Following Aurora's assault on Softy, the narrative articulates John's relationship to Aurora differently. Despite his physical power, John seems to acquiesce to Aurora's rule: "who could ever convince a fellow of six foot two in his stockings that he was afraid of his wife? He submits to the pretty tyrant with a quiet smile of resignation." However, the narrator's remarks demonstrate the tensions in two arenas: first, that John clearly has the strength and power to abuse Aurora, a capacity that traditionally would be veiled by his identity as a gentleman, and second, that Aurora has the faculty to respond to this violence. The narrative graphically matches her violence to and against his ability to physically abuse her. The narrator remarks that John could "break [her] tiny wrist with one twist of his big thumb and finger" because "[s]he is so little, so fragile." However, until "such measures *become necessary* . . . [he] let[s] her have her own way" (emphasis added). These passages indicate both John's potential for violence, a tacit acceptance of a husband's battering in the home,[13] and that which seems to hold him at bay: that he is "afraid of his wife['s]" response (I 283), something defined in the text as John's childishness and Aurora's immorality.

Others respond to Aurora's violence as John does: with not only fear, but also, as John's characterization indicates, with a bilateral demonstration of and concealment of force. The space of the sensation novel allows Aurora to strike back with fury against this violence; indeed, this was the element that made the novel sensational. In the imagination of the narrative, as in Softy's imagination, Aurora becomes powerful enough to squelch this clandestine, domesticized violence—even when it threatens murder. Softy, despite his "horny hands" and "big clasp-knife," sees her grow larger and more powerful as his fantasies of violation grow more barbarous: "I've seen her in my dreams sometimes, with her beautiful white thro-at [*sic*] laid open, and streaming oceans of blood; but for all that, she's always had the broken whip in her hand, and she's always laughed at me. I've had many a dream about her; but I've never seen her dead or quiet; and I've never seen her without the whip" (II 79). Softy's fear in this account—and the terror of all the male characters in this text—distills into the danger embodied in Aurora's potential to respond to male violence with violence of her own. The novel unmasks the seemingly oxymoronic Victorian representation of a woman's desire/ability to return the abuse circulating within the domestic scene, making that abuse visible and enacting a response proportionally impressive to the threat she experiences. The auditor of Softy's tale, James Conyers, experiences the same fear as Softy, knowing that his presence at Mellish Park threatens Aurora. Recently hired as the horse trainer, James contemptuously ignores Softy until a "revelation" of Aurora's threatening ability to respond to violence produces in James a "darkly thoughtful expression, which overshadow[s] the whole of his face" (II 80). As her legal husband, and the man has heaped a wealth of abuse upon her shoulders, James feels the special impact of Aurora's potential for reciprocal violence. Indeed, Aurora has already participated in his symbolic death twice, once when she obliterated him verbally and again when she responded to the false announcement of his death. In fact, she will be the closest bystander in his death, the prime suspect in his murder, and will be the conduit for the real murderer's motive and weapon.

Although James calls Softy a coward for fearing visits to Aurora—bitterly asking, "Do you think Mrs. Mellish will eat you?" (II 208)—his remarks are immediately followed by a lengthy meditation on Tennyson's "Lady Clara Vere de Vere," [14] the tale of a woman's "murder" of her lover, Laurence. The juxtaposition of James's comment and the poem rebuts his flippant dismissal of her threat and, by paralleling Lady Clara and Aurora, virtually insists upon Aurora's participation in the young man's death. Emphasizing the class tensions in the poem and novel, Laurence's death relates to his status as a "foolish yeoman" and Lady Clara's as a woman of noble birth, evoking the rash union between Aurora and her father's groom. Further, the narrator's evaluation of the poem accents "[t]he ugly gash across young Laurence's throat, to say nothing of the cruel slanders circulated after the inquest" (II 210). Like Lady Clara, Aurora will become the prime suspect in her first husband's murder, distrusted by the community, the servants, and even her husband.

### The Specter of Murder

Aurora's long-lost uncle, Captain Samuel Prodder, cements the link between Aurora and James's murder. When Aurora and James meet for the last time—Aurora hoping to expel him from her domestic space—Samuel eavesdrops on the couple's conversation. Aurora describes James as the "primary cause of every sorrow [she has] ever known, of every tear [she has] ever shed, of every humiliation [she has] endured." She explains that his "presence poisons [her] home" and that his "abhorred shadow haunts [her] sleep" (II 264).[15] James's defects, those of the prototypical working-class, abusive husband (described by Parliament in the Divorce Acts) who callously mistreats his wife and violates the sanctity of the home with adultery and alcohol, bleed over into Aurora's current domestic situation. James and his violence haunt her home, a specter of the abuse she suffered in her first marriage and that continues to haunt her second. As we have seen in the novel's correlation of Softy's violence and John, the unspeakable taint in Aurora's marriage with John surfaces in James, yet is cloaked by the working-class man's presence. James appears as soon as the couple is married, and when he is gone, a much more direct representation of John's anger and violence emerges at the site of James's absence. Aurora attempts to exterminate the violence James represents by compelling him to leave and offering him a bribe. Samuel notes the lethal intensity of Aurora's passion by observing that if it endured, "coroner's juries might have to sit even oftener than they do" (II 264). He also overhears her remark that she would like to "stab [James] or shoot [him], or strangle [him]" (II 267).

Throughout their conversation, James suspects surveillance and continually pokes the bushes with his ever present cane. Aurora repeatedly suggests that her dog must have followed her; James, however, believes it is Softy. The phantasmatic presence of both Softy and Bow-wow in this scene evokes the beating Softy gave the dog and leaves the image of domestic violence lurking about the perimeter. Samuel suspects that James and Aurora are man and wife; their squabble, even with its persistent threats of death, "seemed natural enough . . . while he looked at it in a matrimonial light; but seen from another aspect it struck sudden terror to his sturdy heart" (II 272). Although violence is naturalized in Samuel's conception of working-class marriages, the manifold possibilities that the "other aspect" reveals haunt Samuel and the novel: Aurora's bigamous marriages, her potential for violence, and the contamination of the middle- or upper-class home with the violence of a working-class marriage. All of these elements play at the heart of the tensions that immediately follow.

A gunshot rings out over the park, and Samuel hears the howl of a dog, a sound "doubly terrible" in the wake of the interview he witnessed between Aurora and James (II 275). The howl of the dog, echoing the abuse earlier in the novel, does not mark Samuel's recognition that

Aurora might be in danger. Rather, he is concerned about James's fate, underscoring the terror of a woman's responsive violence and obscuring the threat that James posed to Aurora. Samuel carries this fear along with his unvoiced suspicions into the domestic space when he reports to the main house that a man has been "shot through the heart" (II 285). Significantly, this report follows on the heels of the household's recognition that, in spite of the late hour, Aurora is absent. When Aurora returns to the scene, her manner "present[s] a singular contrast to the terror and agitation of the assembly in the hall" (II 287) until she too learns of the man's death. This revelation ignites in her the emotions the others feel. The descriptor "terror" appears twice in the brief mention of Aurora, emphasizing her association with the murder by invoking the narrative economy's signifier for her violence and the threat she poses.

Samuel Prodder circulates, as do his beliefs, among the common people of Mellish and the village who remain out of the range of Aurora's husband and friends. Samuel reinforces Aurora's guilt and blameworthiness, channeling this notion through the narrative, despite his claims to protect her. He lies in wait to eavesdrop again,[16] this time in a local pub, and is rewarded when he hears one of James's former associates describe Aurora as "a stunner . . . one of your regular spitfires, that'll knock you into the middle of next week if you so much as asks her how she does in a manner she don't approve of" (III 162). Softy, another of the bar patrons, exponentially compounds tensions when he hints at Aurora's responsibility for the murder by detailing her involvement in the events. Significantly, Softy points to her abandonment of the domestic space, remarking that she "ran away from her own home and hid herself . . . afraid to stop in her own house . . . run[ning] away to London without leaving word where she was gone" (III 168). Aurora's fears of her home, another suggestion that this is where the danger lies, do not become an issue to her uncle, however. Instead, he becomes angry at the public implication of Aurora in James's death, opening up the question of marital violence to social inquiry—precisely what the novel overall accomplishes.

At this point, Aurora's mother, the captain's sister, becomes another complicating factor in Aurora's delineation. Samuel's silence, indicative of his belief that Aurora has indeed murdered James, derives in part from his reminiscence about Eliza. He describes Eliza in much the same way that Talbot has characterized Aurora. Like Talbot's fantasy of the violent woman who embraces and then assaults her lover, Samuel remembers Eliza as an aficionado of affective extreme, a girl who could cry for the slaughtered lamb and box his ears with equal proficiency, marks of her class identity (III 147). Aurora issues from a working-class woman whose heavily criticized penchant for "sawdust and spangles" is believed to have been transmitted to Aurora along with her other failings. In the heated investigation conducted by Scotland Yard detective Joseph Grimstone and his assistant, Tom Chivers, the narrative invokes the presence of Aurora's actress-mother in their search for James's murderer. Positioned above the men who have just lost Softy's trail hangs a poster with "glowing announcements of dramatic performances that had long ago taken place; and above the mud stained relics of the past, in bold lettering, appeared the record of a drama as terrible as any that had ever been enacted in that provincial theatre[,]" like the drama of this murder (III 274). An ominous banner over the investigation, this montage reveals that Aurora's identity is inflected by her mother's past and the "mud stained relics." This heritage of sawdust and spangles introduces another vector of condensed signification, Aurora's working-class origins, and the marginalization of Aurora through class and imperialist rhetoric in order to contain and reappropriate her capacity to respond to violence.

### An Actress and an Empress

*Wandering Vagabonds and Learned Pigs*

Two elements in the text inflect our understanding of Aurora's identity, justifying and naturalizing the abuse heaped on Aurora as well as the marginalization of her responsive violence. One of these elements, her mother's working-class identity, suggests an inherited taint that flaws Aurora's character, making her an appropriate target and perpetrator of abuse. The first chapter, entitled "How A Rich Banker Married An Actress," underscores the impropriety of Aurora's parentage. Over and over the refrain "she was an actress" appears as an explanation, a motivation, a distinction, a description of Eliza's identity. Furthermore, Eliza was not simply an actress: "nay, lower still, she was some poor performer, decked in dirty white muslin, red-cotton velvet, and spangles, who acted in a canvas booth, with a pityful set of wandering vagabonds and a learned pig" (I 8). The narrative insists upon Eliza's humble origins, setting out at length the oddity, indeed the transgression, inherent in Eliza and Archy's union. From the first, we are informed that relatives and friends considered instituting a commission of lunacy for Archy over his marriage to the penniless performer and "shut[ting] their crazy relative in the madhouse[.] He deserved it" (I 9–10). The community around her perceived Eliza as a "base intruder" (I 23), a "daring, disreputable creature" (I 9), a mere "factory-girl" (I 8). The community's evaluation of Eliza seems to be reinforced by her relationship to the poor. She attends to their needs in a way that only one who identifies with them can. She becomes "sacred" to them, repairing their lives with gifts from her material wealth and clever bribes, not the orthodox but failed benefaction of tracts and blankets. Aurora inherits all these traits, from the penchant for sawdust and spangles to the intuitive service to the poor.

The narrative voice corroborates the community's criticisms of Eliza's working-class identity and links this identity to a taint of violence. Foreshadowing John's comment about Aurora's secrets, the narrator juxtaposes the colloquial mention of murder to Eliza's socioeconomic identity: "Yes, the murder must out; the malicious were not altogether wrong in their conjectures: Eliza Prodder was an actress; and it was on the dirty boards of a second-rate theatre in Lancashire that the wealthy banker had first beheld her" (I 13). Further, Archy and Eliza's marital relationship is compared to that of Nancy and Bill Sikes: "Such a love as this may appear a low and despicable thing when compared to the noble sentiment entertained by the Nancys of modern romance for the Bill Sykeses [*sic*] of their choice" (I 24–25). Sikes, the Dickensian antihero who murders his lover, becomes a referent for the lethal violence in the working-class home and more radically, for its concealed presence in the home of the wealthy middle-class banker and his son(s)-in-law as well. Eliza seems to introduce this threat into the upper ranks through her marital invasion. Aurora, the daughter of a banker and actress, repeats this offense by marrying above her station as well.

Talbot Bulstrode, the voice of English moralism, also relates Aurora's working-class heritage to the violence that surrounds her. After John discovers Aurora's secret marriage, she flees to Talbot and her cousin Lucy and calls upon Talbot to guide her next steps. Talbot reinforces the connection between Aurora's dilemma and her class origins by pondering his notion of the working-class formula of interrelations at this vital moment in the narrative: "The simple Cornish miner who uses his pickaxe in the region of his friend's skull, when he wishes to enforce an argument, does so because he knows no other species of emphasis" (III 105). Talbot further sees "knavery and vice and violence" as uniquely working-class modes of communication and conflict resolution. Thus, Aurora's working-class heritage becomes one means of categorizing and dismissing her violence. Despite the evocation of her origins, however, Aurora issues from a middle-class home and with a great deal of wealth. Braddon significantly refigures the pattern laid out in earlier fiction of applying middle-class morality as a poultice for all social ills when she presents the violence within the middle-class home. Braddon adheres to and disrupts this signifier of violence; she parodies and thus remarks it. The savagery of the foreign Other receives the same treatment in the novel.

### A Cup of Bang

Aurora's Orientalization also sets her apart. It marks her with a "touch of native fire" (I 31), a notion that resonates through her representation as the imperialist object.[17] Significantly, this characterization identifies her as an appropriate target for correction.[18] Mirroring the justification for British colonial invasion, the Orientalization of Aurora inverts the sequence of violation-categorization and identifies her "savage and primitive nature" as the origin rather than the casualty of the imperial hero's violence;[19] she must be contained and civilized, even if great violence is required to complete the task. Positioning Aurora as an object to be colonized and controlled by the men in the novel—a feat eventually accomplished by her husband and ex-fiancé—provides a rather fragile closure to the danger Aurora embodies.[20] Further, this identification marginalizes her responsive anger in such a way that it becomes an economic and social anomaly, safely jettisoned to the outer boundaries of class and culture.

Aurora's aberrant subjectivity revolves exclusively around her relationship to the men in the novel. She creates in Talbot the sensation of drinking bang, an East Indian drink "which made the men who drank it half mad; and he could not help fancying that the beauty of [Aurora] was like the strength of that alcoholic preparation; barbarous, intoxicating, dangerous and maddening" (I 59). She contaminates him with the poison of her Otherness, an effect that distorts his judgment, alters his native Englishness, and both demonizes and eroticizes Aurora. This impression intensifies as Aurora draws Talbot's attention away from her "pale, prim, and saint[-like]" cousin, Lucy (I 73). Aurora surpasses and suppresses Lucy's image with divine black hair "crown[ing] her an Eastern Empress" and "wonderful black eyes . . . in themselves constituting royalty" (I 76). Talbot felt "himself to be bewitched by this black-eyed siren; freely drinking of the cup of bang which she presented to him, and rapidly becoming intoxicated" (I 87). Talbot constructs Aurora as a seducer, bewitching him, offering him her mortal potion. This depiction implies Aurora's toxic threat as well as her active role in endangering Talbot.

However, the novel exposes the construction as Talbot's fantasy. Aurora is not a seductress—even Talbot himself notes her distraction and lack of attention to his company, a "listless indifference, half weariness, half disdain" (I 80). He claims that her wiles affect him against his will, against his desire to fall in love with the more suitable English gentlewoman, Lucy. He implies that he has been compelled by some mystical attraction, even a death drive, to comply with Aurora's sirenlike desire. He describes Aurora as Cleopatra, Mrs. Nisbitt, Nell Gwynne, Lola Montes, and Charlotte Corday, a battery of exotic, erotic, and treacherous women. He perceives her as "everything that is beautiful and strange, and wicked and unwomanly, and bewitching" (I 87). Yet the notion that she has pursued him is a clear transposition of the desire's source.[21] When Talbot plans to propose to Aurora, he describes her as Semiramide, a great conquering, imperialist Assyrian queen. He imputes the responsibility of the seduction and colonization, the control of his mind and body, to Aurora—yet she stifles a yawn in their first moments alone together (I 128).

Although Aurora refuses his proposal, Talbot later learns that she has also refused John Mellish and begins again to fantasize about possessing her. He pictures her in a conflation of Cairo and Bulstrode Castle, "clad in imperial purple, with hieroglyphics on the hem of her robe, and wearing a white clown's jacket of white satin and scarlet spots" (I 136). Talbot desires Aurora to bring the spice of the alien and exotic into his ancestral British home, yet he clearly wishes to maintain the power to control her as he does his fantasy. His status as an officer in the Crimean War and his skill at taming "refractory Sepoys" in India (a skill that involves a tremendous capacity for violence) ensure his ability—and authorization—to accomplish the task of domesticating Aurora at any cost (III 308). Aurora's wavering middle-class status and native identity allow for the inversion of the invasion of the colonies, marking it instead as the invasion of the British aristocracy by the native influence and duplicating the "base intru[sion]" Eliza had accomplished. Talbot's fantasies and colonial self-assurance inspire him to return to Aurora just after she has read the bogus account of her first husband's death. Swooning from the shock, she consents to marry him. Once she has agreed, the narrator remarks, "[Talbot] had accepted the cup of *bang* which the siren had offered, and had drained the very dregs thereof, and was drunken" (I 139). Despite Talbot's beleaguering persistence and Aurora's nearly etherized acceptance, Talbot describes himself as the one who has succumbed. Consonant with the fantasy of her deadliness, her sirenlike characterization justifies Talbot's manipulation of her and all of the violence enacted against her.

When their engagement fails, the pattern of Aurora's Orientalization continues in her engagement to John Mellish. John imagines himself in the role of an Eastern potentate. Unlike Talbot, who has the experience of the imperial veteran, "the glittering orders on the breast of his uniform [telling] deeds of prowess lately done" (I 58), John has no medals to ensure his proper management of Aurora's violence. Over the course of the novel, he must learn from Talbot the finer points of taming Aurora. However, John is not without the power to inflict violence upon Aurora to gain submission. Like the hunter who displays his catch on the walls of his den, John adorns his India room with Aurora, displaying her among the arsenal of weapons he stores there. Thus, although Aurora's Orientalized identity provides the narrative explanation for her seeming ascendancy within the Mellish household, John's management appears in the barter for Aurora-as-possession. Her vexed subject position, as an "unwomanly" woman (I 87), a seemingly non-British woman, permits her defeminization and marks her as a product for Oriental object of exchange. Aurora represents the delectable yield of British labor, the mysteriously Assyrian fruit of a "Scotch banker and his Lancashire wife" (I 128). She becomes an item of marketable merchandise to be bought and sold by her father. Emphasizing the economic value of Aurora's identity, Archy denotes her happiness in terms of material exchange: "Like the Eastern potentate in the fairy tale, who always offers half his kingdom and his daughter's hand to any one who can cure the princess of her bilious headache or extract her carious tooth, Archibald would have opened a banking account in Lombard Street, with a fabulous sum to start with, for any one who could give pleasure to this black-eyed girl" (I 228).

John Mellish employs all of his authority to gain possession of Aurora. Aware of the connection between wealth and Aurora's hand, John initially fears his resources are inadequate and defines his inability to lure Aurora in terms of material possessions: "What was the use of his money, or his dogs, or his horses, or his broad acres? All these put together would not purchase Aurora Floyd" (I 171). However, "the spoiled child" knows that eventually all such desires can be satisfied, that he cannot long be "cheated out of that toy above all other toys, upon the possession of which he had set his foolish heart" (I 177). Indeed, Archy affirms John's courtship with a businesslike handshake on the deal after being informed that foremost among John's qualifications is "one of the finest estates in Yorkshire" (I 234). John's purchase of Aurora does not preclude his exploitation of the same tactics other suitors had used when proposing to Aurora. Persisting as Talbot did before him, despite Aurora's rejection and her father's warning that she may never love him as more than a brother, John follows Aurora on a trip meant for her convalescence. Recovering from Talbot's brutal rejection of her, Aurora remains insensible to John's intentions. However, John manipulates her into accepting his proposal by claiming that she would be responsible for his grief and death: "You would never have suffered me to stay with you so long, and to be so happy if you had meant to drive me away at the last! You never could have been so cruel. . . . I lay my life at your feet" (I 243–44). Like Talbot's appeal, John's takes "the form of an accusation rather than a prayer, and he . . . duly impress[es] upon this poor girl the responsibility she would incur in refusing him" (I 244–45).

Despite the fact that John seems to have been mastered once they are married, the invocation of Aurora's Eastern identity makes John's authority over her more entrenched, lending irony to the rhetoric that marks him as her slave: "John followed his mistress about like some big slave, who only lived to do her bidding; Aurora accepted his devotion with a Sultana-like grace, which became her amazingly" (I 254–55). This slavery, although implying a complete surrender to Aurora, mirrors Talbot's identification of Aurora as the active figure in his seduction. In John's case, this appears more suggestively depicted within the domestic space: "He was so proud of his Cleopatra-like bride . . . that he fancied he could not build a shrine rich enough for his treasure. So the house in which honest country squires and their sensible motherly wives had lived contentedly for nearly three centuries was almost pulled to pieces, before John thought it worthy of the banker's daughter" (I 259).[22] Aurora bears the responsibility for the destruction of the Englishness of John's home, for an infiltration and reconstruction of the domestic scene, despite her absence and inactivity during the remodeling of both.[23] In a recapitulation of the self-seduction that becomes Talbot's excuse for vilifying Aurora, the "violence" Aurora does to the English home articulates her as an appropriate target of a domestically conceived violence.

The appearance of James Conyers after Aurora's marriage to John renders visible the presence of marital violence that haunts Aurora's Orientalized identity. In the chapter entitled "On The Threshold of Darker Miseries," Aurora's identity becomes the supposed source of all the couple's difficulties. John and Mrs. Powell (Aurora's household manager and former governess) perceive Aurora as an alien and mystical figure of male destruction, a Medusa and a Hecate, rather than inquiring into the cause of the anxiety that makes her aloof. When John first learns that Aurora has some relationship with James, Mrs. Powell informs John of messages that pass between the two, insinuating Aurora's betrayal. John seeks Aurora out and finds her in her room, "her masses of ebon hair uncoiled and falling about her shoulders in serpentine tresses, that looked like shining blue-black snakes released from poor Medusa's head to make their escape amid the folds of her garments" (II 241–42). Aurora becomes villainized, and like the Medusa of myth, she immobilizes John, freezing him into a supplicating position, as he falls into a deep sleep in her shadow.

Finally, the narrative accents the homicidal potential of the colonized rather than the colonizer by linking the weapon that kills James and its cache to Aurora rather than John. The gun Softy uses to execute James originates in the room John "reserved to himself" (II 22), the India room decorated with matting, basketwork chairs, and a wide variety of weapons. In this Eastern setting, Softy finds not only Aurora, but a gun that is "as pretty as a 'lady's toy,' and small enough to be carried in a lady's pocket, but [a] hammer [that] snapped upon the nipple . . . with a sound that evidently meant mischief" (II 221). The narrative, through its Orientalization and feminization of the murder weapon, connects the gun to Aurora. Further, the text ascribes to Aurora culpability for its presence despite the fact that it is John's weapon and that this "lady's" weapon seems not to be owned by a lady, but to land its blow on a nipple, evoking an assault on the body of the sexualized woman.

The circulating tensions of murder, femininity, and Otherness ultimately attribute violence to Aurora through the imperial project. Aurora must be incorporated, her violence quelled, with the aid of constant surveillance, a panopticon that includes the ever watchful eyes of the servants. Aurora's complete colonization authorizes the violence enacted against her and renders her fully British and purified of that native influence that makes her so uncontrollable and threatening.

"Listeners in the Corners": The Surveillance of the Upper Class

Talbot and John assure Aurora that working-class and lower middle-class characters (or anomalously classed ones, such as the governess[24]) scrutinize, investigate, and evaluate her conduct and language. They become "the household spies, we call servants," a "lurking audience" who seem to exercise a great deal of power over their socioeconomic "betters."[25] Middle-class morality here is guarded by Talbot and John's insistence that a defective or uncontrollable character be returned in her proper form to the domestic circle. Although lower-classed characters do indeed observe Aurora, their surveillance urging and expediting her reformation from the exotic, Orientalized woman to the dutiful wife and mother depicted in the conclusion, Talbot and John use this surveillance to negate their responsibility in her domestication.

After Aurora and Softy's conflict, John urges Aurora inside and informs her that her inappropriate behavior is the object of scrutiny: "The servants are peeping and prying about" (I 275). When she visits her father, she begs him for a private consultation, saying, "I always fancy there are listeners in the corners" (II 150). John and Aurora's attention to these details escalates when they return to Mellish Park. Agonized by the circulating accusations, "[t]hey were very silent at dinner, for the presence of the servants sealed their lips upon the topic that was uppermost in their minds" (III 186). Aurora's countenance must be regulated as well, and she leaps up as a butler enters the room and walks to one of the windows "in order to conceal her face from the man" (III 188). The text of her facial expressions may be just as damaging as that which she speaks.

However, as Talbot schools John in the manner of colonial authorization, he also teaches him to sacrifice Aurora to this network of surveillance. Before John has learned his lesson, he secrets the murder weapon, found days after the murder, and his efforts are exposed as fruitless: "John had hidden the rusty pistol in one of the locked drawers of his Davenport; but it was not to be supposed that the fact of its discovery could be locked up or hidden away. *That* had been fully discussed in the servants' hall; and who shall doubt that it had traveled further, percolating through some of those sinuous channels which lead away from every household" (III 207–8).

Talbot urges John to provide all the information he has—even that which might appear to implicate Aurora in the murder—to Scotland Yard, the newspapers, and the public at large. Concealment, Talbot warns, would "inevitably [fix] a most fearful suspicion on [Aurora]." Talbot indicates, in essence, that the intricate and pervasive system of public surveillance must be fed any available information about Aurora's improprieties—a move that distances John and Talbot from the act, making Aurora's punishment a function of the social system as a whole:[26] "Any reticence, any attempt at keeping back suspicious facts, or hushing up awkward coincidences would be fatal to us" (III 223). The danger in silence threatens Talbot and John, not Aurora, who might face the death penalty. Instead Talbot focuses on a fatality, which like the other threats of death in the narrative seems to originate in Aurora, to derive from her improprieties and endanger them. Talbot exposes Aurora's threat to the police but conceals John's questionable and damaging behavior: "John exhibited himself altogether in such an imbecile light that Talbot Bulstrode was compelled to keep the servants out of the room" (III 116). Aurora is scrutinized by, and John protected from, that gaze. No other characters, including the murderer himself, are suffered to take responsibility for the couple's predicament. Only Aurora's threat remains visible— Talbot's, John's, and even Softy's violence are screened by Aurora's seemingly pervasive violence. She alone embodies the menace and is defined so by the surveillance that constitutes her identity, a reading of the text that lends another vector to Foucault's notions of surveillance. Significantly, however, the publicity the novel provides about the presence of domestic violence also opens the door to scrutinize these procedures, to examine the functioning of violence, which is shown by the novel's end to have been Softy's, James's, John's, and Talbot's, never Aurora's.

Those who are marked as Aurora's observers become the explicit villains of the novel, despite the fact that they function in Talbot and John's best interest. Talbot and John's domestication of Aurora becomes lost in the working-class violence, articulated by them as violence in toto. Like Talbot and John, Softy and Mrs. Powell carefully observe Aurora for signs of weakness. Mrs. Powell fulfills this task as an exemplum of feminine decorum, dogging Aurora's footsteps with polished grace. Painted as an unattractive and bitter woman whose economic dependence on Aurora fires her resentment, Mrs. Powell embodies the chastising voice of the moral code in the text, mirroring and anticipating Talbot's comments, aligning the two characters. When she learns with Softy of Aurora's former marriage and urges her discovery upon John, the narrative represents her motivation as solely malice, yet Talbot draws the same conclusion and in fact later encourages the rigorous observation and interrogation that Mrs. Powell represents.

The morality that had in other novels been offered as an antidote is here exposed as part of the problem. From her introduction, Mrs. Powell is portrayed as a "grim, pale-faced watchdog" for Aurora (I 96). After Aurora's indiscretion with James, Archy and his sister-in-law select Mrs. Powell to be the agent of Aurora's pruning. The young girl would "be trimmed and clipped and fastened primly to the stony wall of society with cruel nails and galling strips of cloth" (I 93). The violence of Mrs. Powell's pruning is apparent, yet there seems to be no trimming and clipping enacted by Talbot or John. It appears that only Mrs. Powell employs these devices and that only she attempts "actually as well as figuratively, to see a great deal farther than most people" (I 228). She judiciously reports her findings to John, seeming to alleviate his participation in the use of the "cruel nails." She "watches [Aurora's] every movement" (II 93), and as the novel progresses, she is identified as the "pale watcher," lurking about where Aurora's secrets might be found, "with her pale face close against the window-pane" (II 107). Her middle-class morality,

rather than being unequivocally lofted as the salvation of the law, becomes instead the site of an unattractive and clearly aggressive delineation
that disturbs the self-congratulatory comfort with which much of the
middle-class saw itself. (Still, John and Talbot seem free from such manipulation.) Mrs. Powell adheres to all the social codes. She appears outside her empire of the domestic space, and without some womanly task
such as embroidering or ordering a meal, only when she follows Aurora
to James's lodgings at a crucial point in the narrative. When Aurora leaves
the heart of Mellish Park to meet James, "Mrs. Powell paused, almost
terrified by her unlooked-for discovery. What, in the name of all that was
darkly mysterious, could Mrs. Mellish have to do between nine and ten
o'clock on the north side of the park—the wildly kept, deserted north
side, in which, from year's end to year's end, no one but the keepers ever
walked?" (II 104). Aurora's transgression of the civilized boundary of
the park foreshadows both the threat of contamination that she poses
upon her return and the danger inherent in her "untrimmed" identity.
She becomes the untamed native on the primitive landscape. Aurora's
free movement across the boundary between these two worlds terrifies
Mrs. Powell. Aurora enters a space inhabited exclusively by the working
class, the wild darkness of the uncivilized realm, where only keepers,
colonizers of the darkness, can enter.

Mrs. Powell, even as one of the keepers, only hesitatingly crosses
this boundary to probe and punish Aurora's behavior. When Mrs. Powell
arrives at James Conyers's lodgings and peers in, the appearance of Softy
links their behavior, implicating her as the medium of violence for John
as Softy had been. Softy evokes this violence by clutching Mrs. Powell's
arm and physically detaining her: "With her wrist still pinioned in his
strong grasp, he motioned her to be silent, and bent his pale face forward; every feature rigid, in the listening expectancy of his hungry gaze"
(II 111). The properly pale-faced duo remains silent, rigid. A striking
contrast to the dark, exotic foreignness of Aurora, they devour the increasingly long list of social infractions that empower John and Talbot
with justifications for Aurora's punishment.

At the close of the scene, Mrs. Powell returns quickly to the house
before a rainstorm begins and institutes the first in a series of punishments
for Aurora. Significantly, she orders other servants to lock the house before Aurora returns, keeping her from reentering the domestic space,

metaphorically implying her unfitness for the home, and making insinuations about Aurora's relationship with the stable man to John. When Aurora arrives at the house soaking wet, she appears as drenched in impropriety as she is by the rain. She is forced to beg for admission to her own home by pounding at one of the shutters for entry. Aurora can only blame Mrs. Powell, remarking sarcastically, "I did not know that you had done me the honor of watching my actions," a remark that becomes even more significant when "the colour fade[s] out of John Mellish's face," identifying him with the pale watchers who critique and observe Aurora's behavior (II 122).

When John "chastises" Mrs. Powell (as he had Softy), he identifies Aurora only as "Mrs. Mellish" and his "wife," both positions unsuitable targets for critique. "Whatever Mrs. Mellish does, she does with my full consent, my perfect approbation. Caesar's wife must not be suspected, and by Jove, ma'am!—you'll pardon the expression,—John Mellish's wife must not be watched" (II 239). Calpurnia can only be acquitted when she fits properly into the appellation "Caesar's wife"; likewise, Aurora must be pacified, her identity replaced and renamed as wife in order to secret the violence of murder invoked by the reference to Caesar and underlying the tensions that abound in John's assessment of the domestic space. Thus, John asserts a relationship between husband and wife that must be reconstituted before the novel draws to its close. Aurora must be defined by silence and submission, the violence that threatens her veiled by her surveillance and her identification as a dangerous woman. However, the text, in its representation of this phenomenon, rends this veil and is flooded with disclosures of the tensions that lie at the heart of the domestic space. Although providing authorization for the violent redefinition of Aurora, male abuse fails to be cloaked by the anxious observance and correction of her behavior. Despite the focus on Aurora's responsibility, accounts of male homicidal rage proliferate in the narrative, providing another perspective on the landscape of violence as it is plotted within the domestic space.

### The Fantasy of the Murdered Wife

The threat of female violence serves to screen the presence of marital abuse, both of which are ultimately subsumed in the intersecting trajectories of male marital authority and imperial colonization. Although Aurora has been characterized as a figure with lethal power, the text reveals that it is not she who poses the threat, but the men in her life who threaten her. John and Talbot both imaginatively construct Aurora's death over the course of the narrative. When Talbot breaks his engagement with her he thinks to himself as he leaves the room "that he would rather have left Aurora lying rigidly beautiful in her coffin than as he was leaving her today" (I 206). Further, when Talbot learns that Aurora has fallen ill after their separation, he angrily ponders her situation as he stands alone in the fields of Bulstrode Castle: "What did it matter to him if she were well or ill? The grave could never separate them more utterly than they had been separated. . . . Was it his fault if she were ill? Were his days to be misery, and his nights a burden because of her? He struck the stock of his gun violently upon the ground at the thought, and thrust the ramrod down the barrel, and loaded his fowling-piece furiously with nothing" (I 219–20). Before Aurora's first act of violence, we see Talbot fantasizing her death and all but enacting an assault on her, violently and furiously performing a symbolic rape with the ramrod of his gun. The mere thought of a woman nearly his wife—not in a powerful or threatening position but in the utter debilitation of infirmity—prompts Talbot's behavior. The novel exposes Talbot's violence as integral to the relationship he desires between a man and woman, the violence that lies beneath the proper English couple. Aurora's failure to fill the role of passive fowling-piece, however, leaves her unworthy to be his wife.

John also participates in the imaginative murder of Aurora. The arrival of James Conyers, one embodiment of marital abuse, evokes a scene of violence from John equal in fury to Talbot's frustrated imaginings in the field. John tells Aurora: "I would rather see your coffin laid in the empty niche beside my mother's in the vault yonder . . . than I would part with you thus. I would rather know you to be dead and happy that I would endure any doubt about your fate. Oh, my darling, why do you speak of these things? I couldn't part with you—I couldn't! I would rather take you in my arms and plunge with you into the pond in the wood; I would rather send a bullet into your heart, and see you lying murdered at my feet" (II 91). Ironically, it is John who appears frightened after his graphic fabrications of murder schemes; Aurora responds with, "Why you foolish John, how frightened you look! . . . Haven't you discovered yet that I like to torment you now and then with such questions as these, just to see your big blue eyes open to their widest extent?" (II 92). Although Aurora labels her inappropriate behavior as that which inflames John's verbal assault, her provocative behavior has simply consisted of "looking pale and tired" because she fears James Conyers's arrival. Like Talbot, John's most violent language follows on the heels of Aurora's passivity and weakness. The domestic ideology that manages this space, an ideology Aurora invokes in her ensuing reference to Mrs. Powell's management of the home, defines her behavior as the cause of John's violence.

The Victorian husband and the shape of the domestic space depend in part upon the husband's access to the power of violent action and the invisibility or camouflage of its manifestation as wife abuse. In Braddon's novel, these patterns are exposed and, in that exposure and the final revelation of Aurora's innocence, contested. Emblems of this power, evident in the emergence of phallic weapons, are always accessible to Talbot and John. Sticks and guns materialize from the blank space within the narrative and disappear almost seamlessly into the text after they have been deployed.[27] The presence of the weapons, though ultimately shown to be unnecessary, is so naturalized in the narrative that, despite the head-to-toe detailing of male characters' attire, their mention is unnecessary. This drama is performed during Aurora's engagement to Talbot, when Aurora encounters Matthew Harrison, a dog fancier and friend of James Conyers's. As Matthew attempts to stop Aurora's carriage, Talbot's weapon suddenly appears: "'Let go that bridle!' he cried, lifting his cane" (I 156). Matthew's identity as a dog fancier (he literally sells dogs, the metonym for the abused wife in the novel's economy) and an intimate of James's evokes images of abusive violence in marriage. Thus, when Talbot becomes angry, he inflicts his assault not on Matthew—the supposed source of the tension—but upon Matthew's dog. Echoing the scene in which Softy beats Bow-wow, Talbot exercises violent authority over Aurora in this situation, frustrated at his inability to control her behavior: he "whirl[s] round his cane and inflict[s] such chastisement upon the snub nose of the animal as [to] sen[d] him into temporary retirement, howling dismally" (I 156). The narrative underscores the identification between the dog and Aurora, culminating in a scene in which the dog "burst[s] into a joyous bark, frisking and capering about Miss Floyd's silk dress, and imprinting dusty impressions of his fore paws upon the rich fabric"

(I 163). Significantly, the impressions his paws leave mirror the diaphanous impressions of the marital violence that haunt the narrative. These marks of violence allow us the means of rereading this scene. The dog becomes to Talbot a "vulgar rivalry" that he must control. It is not a rivalry between Talbot and Matthew or even Talbot and James; rather, Talbot responds here to Aurora's desire to manage her own affairs—an intolerable domestic situation that results in a series of assaults that focus his aggression on Aurora. Thus, the dog receives the blow that Aurora might have, bearing the representation of the unspeakable violence between marital partners. Aurora stands "pale and breathless" in this passage, yet continues to be showered with assaults.

Other gestures of aggression follow the dog's beating: Talbot's scrutiny of Aurora with his "darkest expression . . . [and] a sulky silence" (I 164), his "cross-question[ing]" of her behavior (I 169), and a posture of hostility so prominent that Aurora is described as "Marie Antoinette going to face her plebeian accusers" (I 165). Further, Talbot abandons Aurora in a scene he himself later describes as agonizingly cruel: "He had grievously wronged, insulted and humiliated [her]" (III 194). He breaks their engagement while she lies at his feet in a "half kneeling, half crouching attitude, her face buried in her hands," begging him for pity and trust (I 205). In the wake of this cruelty, another metaphoric demonstration of Talbot's cane and its power appears as he engages himself to another woman. While discussing Aurora with Lucy, he "whisked the end of his cane across a group of anemones, and decapitated the tremulous blossoms. He was thinking, rather savagely, what a shame it was that Aurora could be happy with [John]" (II 11–12). When his performance leaves Lucy in subdued silence, he happily proposes marriage to her instead.

## Colonial Authority

Not surprisingly, scenes of Talbot's violence are often accompanied by markers of his imperial training, which authorizes displays of even the most violent gestures to control Aurora and reduce Lucy to silence. Lacking this preparation and authority, both James's and John's violence are less effective. However, neither of them lacks the physical power to use the canes at their disposal to metaphorically express their displeasure with Aurora. As before, these sticks remain unseen by the reader, invisible in

the text, until they are employed. When James recalls the loss of Aurora
and her fortune, he "growl[s] something like an oath between his set
teeth, [and] he [strikes] his stick with angry violence into the soft grass"
(II 195). John responds with the same vigor when he learns that Aurora
has been sending messages to James: "'A message for *him*?' roared John,
stopping suddenly and planting his stick upon the ground in a movement
of unconcealed passion" (II 235). Their sticks and this narrative reveal
what other cultural markers hope to obliterate, the presence of marital
violence. John's equipage for this is clear. He even dedicates one entire room in his house (appropriately fitted with Indian furnishings) to
"whips, canes, foils, single-sticks, boxing-gloves, spurs, guns, pistols . . .
[where] many happy mornings were spent by the master of Mellish Park
in the pleasing occupation of polishing, repairing, inspecting, and otherwise setting in order, these possessions" (II 23). We also learn that he
keeps "a stout leather-thonged hunting-whip" among other "formidable
implements" (I 275).

John, however, remains childlike throughout most of the novel, incapable of adult employment of these tools of phallic power. Not only
does he have difficulty taming Aurora's responsive violence, but he does
not sire a child either. Softy must fill his place to tame Aurora, performing
the paid services John has yet to master until Talbot intervenes and offers
the training John lacks. The narrative informs us that John's "greatest
follies were no worse than those of a big school-boy who errs from very
exuberance. . . . [T]here had been none to restrain his actions" and none
to direct his use of the implements he has at his fingertips (I 112). Once
he is schooled by Talbot in the proper domestication of the Eastern figure, John will silence Aurora the way Lucy has been silenced.[28] James,
Aurora's first husband, has the same difficulty. Despite the fact that he has
a physical disability that mirrors Talbot's lame leg, the differing sources of
the injuries betoken the basis of James's difficulty and Talbot's success.
Talbot's leg injury, earned during the Crimean War, "added to the distinction of his appearance, and, coupled with the glittering orders on the
breast of his uniform, told of deeds of prowess lately done" (I 58). Their
bodies both bear indicators of their class and ideology. Talbot's wounds,
acquired in the suppression of the conquered Orientalized Other, serve
as a marker of his colonial mastery. James's injury, a maiming in a near
fatal racing fall, identifies him as a working-class man—a man without

the authority to use the force of deadly violence against one outside of his own class. The novel can easily condemn James's normative working-class abuse of Aurora, leaving him dead at the end of the narrative. However, Talbot's managed, socially legitimized violence becomes the tool that ultimately restores Aurora to her proper position as a disenfranchised and socially palatable woman.

Talbot's authorization as a soldier of the troops in India becomes a pivotal factor in John's conversion as well as Aurora's eventual transformation. Initially, John's troubles reduce him to a "sorrowing woman" (III 212), but Talbot transforms John into more than a man; he makes him a soldier. Talbot becomes "a keeper to watch over a hearty young jungle-tiger . . . bidden to prevent the noble animal from committing any imprudence" (III 285). Like the keepers who watch over the dark side of Mellish Park, Talbot participates in the system of power that oversees all their behavior. When John accepts Talbot as his new master, he submits with complete compliance, uttering, "I will do what you like, Talbot" (III 225). John's submission to Talbot's form of authority channels their "savage and wild Indian-like fury" into an efficient form of violence, eradicating Aurora's attempts to respond.

John becomes "pitifully dependent" upon Talbot's "superior wisdom" (III 225), and he refers to his past behavior as "madness." After he marks out his new manner, Talbot must stop the expression of these sentiments and remarks on Aurora's fear:

> *"[A]nd it was only when Talbot—"*
>
> *Aurora lifted her head from her husband's breast and looked wonderingly into his face, utterly unable to guess at the meaning of these broken sentences.*
>
> *Talbot laid his hand upon his friend's shoulder. "You will frighten your wife if you go on in this manner, John," he said quietly. "You mustn't take any notice of his agitation, my dear Mrs. Mellish. There is no cause, believe me, for all this outcry." (III 227)*

Elided in the dash is John's imperial training, a process that Talbot immediately begins to cloak. He orders Aurora to ignore its presence and, in fact, attempts to erase the origin of the change in John's behavior: "There is no cause, believe me, for all this outcry." By the end of the passage Aurora has become "Mrs. Mellish"—John's wife—despite the fact that Talbot has referred to her as Aurora throughout the novel. Talbot rescued, trained, and led John to realign his identity, and along with John, manages the incorporation of Aurora as well. It is through the operation of a morally sanitized colonial authority that John and Talbot suppress Aurora's violent response.[29] As Susan Jeffords indicates in "Performative Masculinities," Talbot and John's colonially authorized violence is a performance that claims to protect women, eliding their own violence. She notes that while a character poses as one who opposes violence—as John and Talbot do with the unknown murderer—he is not violent himself. Jeffords provides the apt example of the Gulf War to illustrate her point: "While [George] Bush [was] filling media screens with warfare against [Saddam] Hussein, he [was] not attacking another country. Because they are not raping [beating, brutalizing] now, the logic of performative masculinities would ask us to believe they are not rapists [or batterers], not the enemy" (115).

In order to cleanse the presence of marital violence from the novel, this colonial purgation must be administered at one other site, James's murderer, Softy. Talbot, along with the police, must overcome Softy to free Aurora from the suspicion of murder and to expunge unauthorized violence from the novel. Further, Softy's violence must then be displaced onto a working-class man who bears no association to the family. In the final scenes during Softy's capture, Talbot invokes his power as a colonizer again and again. The narrative emphasizes his identity as "the man who had done battle with bloodthirsty Sikhs, and ridden against the black mouth of the Russian cannon at Balaclava" (III 309). As they grapple, Talbot authorizes and aggrandizes his power by claiming, "I've been accustomed to deal with refractory Sepoys in India, and I've had a struggle with a tiger before now" (III 308–9). The Scotland Yard detective, who first ascertained a series of remarkable facts related to the case, justifies the legality of Talbot's violence along with his suspicions of Softy. In addition, Samuel Prodder, Aurora's working-class uncle, concludes the struggle between the brawling characters in order to reinforce the identification of all violence as a working-class phenomenon, screening the violence that Talbot himself uses. Like the other characters who engage in surveillance, Samuel's lurking and spying more than saves Talbot's life; it restores order to a system in chaos. Samuel's reappropriation of violence and Softy's repression must be a part of Aurora's reclamation. Without their management, the visibility of domestic violence within the novel cannot be expunged. Further, Softy must be hung at the novel's close, a symbolic execution of the visible presence of martial violence and its return to the silence of domestic privacy.

### The Inward, Semi-whispering Voice

Softy becomes the target of assault for more than the murder of James Conyers; he represents precisely what the male characters must shroud. From his initial appearance in the text, the narrative identifies Softy as the "inward, semi-whispering voice" (I 268). The word "instinctive" appears five times in Softy's introduction, matched with other cues such as "inward," "involuntary," and "unreasoning" (II 266–70). Softy's appearance also hints at a preternatural identity; his face is as "white as a sheet of writing paper"; his specterlike "ghastly pallor" and "queer temper" make him eerily unmanageable at the stables. The trainer remarks of Softy, "[N]one of us has ever been able to get the upper hand of him, as the master knows" (I 267). Significantly, this web of associations casts Softy as a figure of the unconscious and, more particularly, the British social unconscious. He speaks in "reduced . . . half-whisper[ing]" tones, voicing that which the other characters attempt to suppress: the submerged threat of domestic violence. Softy becomes the dichotomous site of the unspeakable domestic ills in the social system and the corporeal representation of the violence that appears in his assault on Bow-wow and Aurora's horse-whipping: the perpetrator and the victim, enacting the drama of marital violence. Alternately materialized and disembodied, Softy batters and murders, yet crumbles under Aurora's hands despite the strength of his massive body. Additionally, his soft voice articulates the understanding that domestic dangers are exposed in Aurora. He acknowledges that she represents a cultural rift, not an individualized occurrence—a rift so profound that it won't be erased by her absence. Despite the fact that Softy murders her in his dreams, "she's always had the broken whip in her hand, and she's always laughed at me" (II 79).

Against the grain of the novel's teleological resolution of the threat of marital violence and the danger of a woman who would respond just as violently, Softy recognizes this threat as a social constant, a repetition that defies the death he imagines. Although the narrative describes him as a malevolent character, Softy merely defines a cultural system whose machinations are as repulsive as the character he represents, a character who "seem[s] made to crush and destroy whatever comes in [his] way" (I 266). His voice seems whispered only because he embodies what should remain unutterable. The other characters desire to see Softy silenced in order to eradicate the voice that speaks through him. This becomes evident in the narrative's progressive and increasing mutilation of Softy's body. Softy's physical form serves as the site of detailed examination, distortion, and deconstruction. Initially, thick muscles are the only signifiers that characterize Softy, but moments before his defeat, Talbot describes Softy's shadow as "even more weird and ungainly than such things are;—the shadow of a man with a hump-back!" (III 304). The lengthy and detailed description of Softy earlier in the narrative neglects to mention a hump back, which suggests that its addition is related to his increasingly threatening presence. Many other defects follow this one. Softy becomes not only animal-like, but "more repulsive than the ugliest of the lower animals" (III 307). In the closing passages he becomes incapable of speech and produces only a "savage yell of rage" and "gnaw[s] savagely at his bonds" (III 314, 315). Softy's savage body, and his savage embodiment, contain the fears and anxieties of a culture that must be eradicated. Accomplished with a death sentence in the last passages of the novel, Softy's erasure attempts to contain two fears: the abuse of a wife and the threat that she might respond with equal violence. However, the exposure of these tensions disturbs the stability of the discourse that makes them possible, unsettling the cultural truths and pointing up uneasy tensions. That disruption makes change possible: change in attitudes, change in the law.

### The Containment of Dangerous Women: The Contagious Diseases Acts and Their Repeal

Anxieties about the dangerous woman were available to resignification because they were tensions circulating in the culture as well, tensions that the law sought to explain and contain. The Contagious Diseases Acts were central in the effort to identify and remedy the problem of the dangerous woman. Although the acts provoked profound controversy in the attempts for repeal, they were passed almost entirely without debate in

1864 and extended in the same fashion in 1866 and 1869, around the time of *Aurora Floyd*'s publication. The initial uncomplicated acceptance of the acts (in their passage and extension) indicates a drive to constitute the dangerous/contaminating woman and her behavior as the sole threat and, thus, as a vessel to contain cultural contradictions.

Concerned primarily with the registration and treatment of prostitutes infected with venereal disease, the C.D. Acts were designed to prevent the spread of syphilis and gonorrhea, especially among the troops of her majesty's navy. Leading to madness and death in its tertiary stage, syphilis was without a cure and was a particularly dangerous disease for the Victorians. Physicians and legislators believed the increasing numbers of infected soldiers arose from "women spread[ing] physical poison through [the] troops." [30] Suspected prostitutes were seized on the streets, examined by an official physician with a new medical device, the speculum, and forcibly detained in "lock hospitals" until their caretakers felt the danger to be over. The community explicitly identified these dangerous women as a life-threatening peril to the men with whom they came in contact, eliding the men's participation in prostitution and their active solicitation of the danger. Similarly, Aurora bears the onus of danger within the home. Identified as the sole contaminant, Aurora is mastered and managed through a markedly violent colonization. In the same way, the prostitutes were controlled and contained, their bodies subject not only to the intrusion of medical instruments, but to imposition of a middle-class moral reconditioning as well. Like the characters in *Aurora Floyd* who justify their violence as a desire to reform a homicidal and dangerous woman, one Member of Parliament claimed that "the [C.D.] Act was, in point of fact, a law to prevent murder—to prevent the murder of the unfortunate children who died through the most horrible malady every week, and to prevent the murder of those who died later in life from a thousand other diseases springing from that one." [31] Aurora, like the prostitutes, became the target of reformation, the M.P.s (both fictional, such as Talbot, and historical) ignoring the matrix of cultural contradictions that lay at the source of the difficulties Aurora and the prostitutes came to represent. These difficulties revolved around the notion of the domestic space as an untainted safe haven of gentility and fidelity, a notion sensation fiction exploded.

The lack of public and published exchange during the C.D. Acts' initial passage suggests that no mainstream forums were fit to tackle the tensions in the acts. So utterly naturalized that it was discursively invisible, the containment and reformation of dangerous women surfaced in the debates only after the publication of novels such as *Aurora Floyd*. Sensation fiction was conceived of as lying outside the boundaries of mainstream texts and charted the configuration of the dangerous woman, depicting her chastisement and improvement as a way to ensure domestic purity and in that depiction calling into question the violent means by which domestic purity was attained. Sensation novels in this period parodied and exposed patterns of containment and opened the cultural possibility of critique. One may gain insight, then, by examining the ways in which the discourse of *Aurora Floyd* anticipates the language of the public outcry and the parliamentary debates, beginning in 1869 and raging until the acts' repeal in 1883. The sustained conflict indicates a gradual change in cultural attitudes, and the date of the debates' appearance suggests that the sensation novel may have participated in a shift in ideology that suddenly made it possible to reevaluate a five-year-old law. Connections between the debates and the fiction is supplied, first, in the language of the debates, which mirrors the tensions and language of the sensation novel, and second, in the invocation of the concept of sensation literature to describe the nature of the debates.

The C.D. Acts and the debates surrounding them clearly identified prostitutes as the site of contamination. As Judith Walkowitz notes in her ground-breaking study on Victorian prostitution, "[D]efenders of the patriarchal family . . . regarded prostitutes as a source of pollution and a constant temptation to middle-class sons" (34). The legislation reinforced this analysis. One M.P. noted that syphilis, and indeed prostitution itself, was "a frightful disease . . . ravaging the country—affecting not only those who had brought it on themselves, but numbers of innocent persons, and, from its hereditary character, undermining the health of future generations." [32] Similar to the danger posed by women who threatened to expose another cultural infirmity, marital violence, the taint of syphilis might become a fountainhead infecting the empire's subjects throughout the age. The subjects in danger were definitively marked by the legislators as men and their offspring: "Many a poor man suffered and died,—many a poor child was born to a life of misery and premature death." [33] That women were the perpetrators and men the victims of this disease was a foundational assumption. It went almost without saying that this danger was gendered, devolving solely through women and curable only by their reappropriation to the norm. In fact, disease in prostitutes was often thought to be the result of a dissolute life, rather than an infection passed on through a client (Walkowitz, *Prostitution* 56). Women alone were examined under these acts—clearly an ineffective means of eliminating a disease that was frequently transmitted through heterosexual intercourse, but a very effective way of isolating women as the cause and source of the disease. Legislators assured one another and the community through exhaustive study of the towns in which the acts were in operation that the taint would be eradicated with this method. Endless tables and graphs as well as countless laudatory speeches filled the fissures of the debates. By themselves, these consolatory texts betray the tension surrounding the need for reaffirmation of the acts' effectiveness and the ideology that had made them possible. The external pressure from opposition within and outside the House began to break apart the acts, exposing the conventional assumptions upon which they were based and demanding extensive reconstructive surgery.

M.P. after M.P. urged the legislation's power to reform the source of contamination, the prostitutes themselves. The House of Commons was assured that although "[m]any of the women formerly looked bloated from drink [and] others were greatly emaciated and looked haggard through disease[,] [t]heir language and habits [were] greatly altered. Swearing, drunkenness, and indecency of behavior have become quite exceptional. The women now look fresh and healthy and are most respectful in their manner and behavior."[34] The laws attempted to control the women's language and their bodies, two sites at which the contaminant might become visible. The M.P.s imposed middle-class moral standards and assured themselves that their treatment created new bodies: ones that participated in and respected the disciplinary regime the laws represented. However, the urgency of the argument itself and the fear of the "exceptional" women who failed to conform indicate a profound anxiety over the laws' function. The connection between the C.D. Acts and the law defining the boundaries of gender makes clear the goal of reshaping the woman's body and mind: "The girls came into the hospital turbulent, lawless, and godless, and it is astonishing the change that a few weeks produces in them. . . . [T]he poor creatures are apparently perfectly contented and happy." [35] The lock hospitals disciplined women by erasing their lawlessness and contained them within the range of the cultural economy by placing them physically and sociomorally under control. These "happy" women, according to Walkowitz, were "trained in deference and subordination [through strict chores, prayers, lessons, and so on]. The social world of the hospital reproduced [or attempted to reproduce] the patriarchal and class order of Victorian society" (*Prostitution* 221–22). The normalized behavior and appearance of these prostitutes became the linchpin of the acts' success. Women were praised for bodily control, for maintaining standards of Victorian womanhood—silence and sobriety: "The conduct of the prostitutes in and about the town of Aldershot is less indecent, and their habits are more quiet and sober than before its establishment. . . . The conduct of the girls . . . has been very satisfactory." [36] Even in the "poor creatures who still continued in their pitiful career there was a marked improvement in their general habits." [37] However, as Walkowitz notes, the utopia about which Parliament fantasized never materialized (*Prostitution* 222). The conformity that the legislators and physicians sought from the women also threatened to destroy the acts by exposing the fragility of the borders between the dangerous prostitutes and the "safe" classes of women. In her campaign against the C.D. Acts, Josephine Butler pointed out the difficulty in establishing distinctions between prostitutes and respectables "among the poor—the classes dealt with by the Contagious Diseases Acts—[because] the boundary lines between the virtuous and vicious is so gradually and imperceptibly shaded off, that there is no one part which it would be possible to affix a distinct name or infallibly assign a class" (Walkowitz, *Prostitution* 185).

More complicating, as Walkowitz reports in *City of Dreadful Delight,* even middle-class women shopping in the West End of London, a district frequented by prostitutes, were sometimes mistaken for their fallen sisters by police and the prostitutes' clientele (55, 129). These glitches obviously upset the functioning of the acts in the districts of their operation. More significantly, they revealed the inability of the law to obliterate potentially dangerous women; the profusion of social contradictions in the acts and in the constructed identity of dangerous women made it impossible to identify those they sought to reform, women such as Aurora, who is dangerous and not, a murderess and not, a heroine and not. This friction would ultimately undermine the aim of the acts. If one cannot mark the differences between those who embody the threat and those who do not, the threat becomes dispersed and unfocused; it cannot be aligned with one stigmatized group. The legislators recognized the damage that this blurring could cause. Some M.P.s detailed specific cases of middle-class women who had been brought under the operation of the acts; others denied the accusation but agreed that "if true, [it] would be a horrible thing to be avoided at any price." [38] The evidence mounted, and soon many M.P.s were compelled to agree that the acts granted the power to the police of "designating any woman they [chose] as a common prostitute." [39] It was even feared that once prostitutes were identified and apprehended, physicians would be incapable of identifying the disease. The "doctor may be entirely unable to prove or disprove" contamination or communicability, and the "evidence [examination] affords is uncertain," [40] which again suggests that the threat was ideological, rather than simply biological. However, this disorder only served to provide greater impetus to clarify and contain prostitutes, and the British employed a time-honored, eminently Victorian method to achieve the nearly literal colonization of women's bodies and behavior.

In the same way that the empire subdued the Eastern Other, it would reclaim the uncivilized woman, retraining and purifying her. As Aurora becomes an imperial object, so did the prostitutes, in an attempt to imitate the imperial procedure of incorporation. As Lillian Nayder notes, the rhetoric of English resolve generated by the Indian Mutiny of 1857 was deployed in the discussion of the "war" against prostitution ("Rebellious Sepoys" 31).[41] One legislator commented that the prostitutes "should be redeemed from a state of savagery to something approaching civilization." [42] Another noted that the bishops who had supported the C.D. Acts were themselves "a smartish lot to go into an affair of this kind, some of them colonial." [43] Although this commendation might appear nebulous, it signifies the relationship between the techniques of reclamation and the colonial agenda. Not surprisingly, then, the acts included threats of legislative disciplinary action. The process of defining the women as criminal [44] authorized violent redefinition of their bodies. The police enforced the acts by forcibly apprehending and detaining women they believed should be examined; the physicians enforced them through the exams themselves.

One legislator remarked on "the cruelty of these examinations. The doctors say there is no pain. For my part, I would rather take the evidence of the patient than the doctor on this point."[45] Criticism like this began to question, as Braddon's novel had, who was being victimized and who was dangerous. The analysis of the pain was centered on the speculum. A physician-critic of the C.D. Acts argued that the use of the speculum could cause "great pain, and even permanent injury . . . [to] the person examined."[46] The speculum was perceived as indecent, intensifying the already sexual nature of a male doctor's examination of a woman. Mary Poovey points to one Victorian critique of speculum use as "a violent attack against chastity . . . produc[tive of] an internal blush [which] is a real prostitution" even in respectable women (39). Marked out discursively as the rape of a prostitute, this multilayered reading contentiously correlates the exam with an expression of the doctor's power over the women. Certainly consonant with Poovey's analysis, this was an environment in which obstetric and gynecological physicians were attempting to gain authority and control, "to adjudicate women's social role" and their bodies (26), an authority and control that involved complete mastery over a woman's pain.[47] This new aspect of the legislators' understanding of the acts suggests a marked shift in ideology had taken place since their passage, one that made seeing the dangerous woman as endangered herself possible.

Significantly, the counterargument to these claims urged that the menace of constant observation and punishment was eliminated when a woman conformed to social standards of respectable women. An M.P. noted that those "who gave security that [they] would give up their unfortunate avocation, or leave the district [were] immediately released from surveillance."[48] Their conformity to Victorian standards of womanhood, the internalization of the norms or exile, granted them amnesty from police observation. This promise, however, failed from its inception at several levels. First, amnesty from surveillance is impossible. One cannot distinguish the single figure exempt from surveillance. Second, this promise implied the power of minute discrimination between classes and types of women, something the Ladies National Association (LNA) denied was possible or appropriate. In their campaign opposing the C.D. Acts, members of the LNA aligned themselves with the women they saw dominated by the acts, describing the plight of their fallen sisters as a threat to their own safety and freedom. Echoing this critique, legislators pronounced that the "insecurity of every woman results from the prerogatives granted" in the operation of the acts.[49]

The predicament of male ownership when (suspected) prostitutes were married further problematized their identification and punishment, as well as the staging of legal control. Clandestine prostitution, a constant concern of the Parliamentarians, also posed a complication. All of these tensions betrayed one of the primary motivating factors of the C.D. Acts. As with the Divorce Act, the desire for legislative control stimulated the institution of the C.D. Acts and was a primary tension in their administration. However, many feared that "the forced examination of women tend[ed] directly to increase clandestine prostitution and to increase the amount and the intensity of the disease."[50] Clearly, this comment metonymically evokes the uncontrolled/uncontrollable women themselves, as well as the biological virus the acts were designed to suppress. Despite counterarguments that clandestine prostitution had diminished, the anxiety that prompted the consistent allusions to its increase demonstrates the inability of the law to contain the threat of dangerous women.

The excess implied in the inability to contain provides another significant link between prostitution (and its control) and the sensation novel. The construction of arguments against the impingement of the diseased prostitute on the domestic space mirrors the condemnation of sensation fiction. In the same terminology that had been invented to contain, often debase, and categorize the sensation novel, one M.P. remarked, "From the unattractive sensational literature, which has been, with more zeal than discretion, put upon our tables for the last few months, one would be inclined to believe that the hospitals under these Acts are prisons and places of torture."[51] Indeed, it is the interior spaces, spaces of violence, that the sensation novel addresses. Further, "discretion," diametrically opposed to "sensation," marked not only the appropriate method of suppressing prostitution, but also described the vein of realism in fiction lauded by science and reason. Contrary to realist fiction, sensation exposed the underlying assumptions of cultural operation. Indiscrete, it peered into the private, and unbounded by the restraints of logic, it addressed issues that seemed to be cultural impossibilities, such as the presence of marital violence and the potential for an outraged response from an abused woman. It challenged the legislators and the culture to reconsider the modes of analyzing gender, gendered violence, and women's subjectivity that had reigned throughout the century. The M.P.s felt that sensation literature had been produced by critics of the acts, and was, like venereal disease, uncontrollable and limitlessly contaminating.[52] Not only did it fall within the reach of women and children—activists regularly delivered it to "the drawing-rooms and breakfast-tables of the wives and even the maiden sisters of the most respectable families"—but it was conceived of as an "invasion" and a "deluge."[53] Parliament had hoped that elevating the issues in the C.D. Acts to the level of legislative debate would mean "a cessation of this agitation and a stoppage of that stream of offensive literature which [had] flooded [the M.P.s'] houses for the several months past."[54] Rather, it widened the seam that had been opened, increasing the outpouring of anxious discourse along with the possibility for an alteration in attitudes. In fact, this literature had been distributed to precisely those whom the legislation had attempted to control, (potentially dangerous) women: "[P]rinted papers had been circulated calling on women in the most inflammatory language to resist the Acts."[55] Ultimately, the sensation of the anti–C.D. Acts literature and the anti- and pro-acts debates served the same purpose as the sensation novels that anticipated the issues they addressed: to work through the anxieties surrounding marital violence by managing the paradoxical process of establishing an identity for women that would screen this violence and containing the woman who became dangerous.

Because women, as a class, were considered to be "as much outside legislative interference, as their virtue and goodness [were] outside and far removed from the sins of the fallen of their sex,"[56] there was a drive to identify and categorize women as British subjects to position them within the range of the law. Simultaneously, however, there was a drive to maintain the ideology that disenfranchised women, conserving the differentiation of "civil and female, [between which] there is as broad a distinction as between any two words in the English language."[57] Signatures on petitions opposing the C.D. Acts were considered invalid when they belonged to women, and women who opposed the acts through activism such as public speaking walked a thin line between self-degradation and ensuring their status as gentlewomen. This ideal of an unadulterated woman was depicted as an alternative and secure identity (although it was dependent upon and defined against that of the fallen woman). This "pure" woman remained free from diseases social or biological, and *Aurora Floyd* renders an example of her as faithfully as it does Aurora. She is the converse of Aurora's corruption; she embodies utter purity and passivity. The independence of prostitution, a *feme sole* status, is washed away, and she depends entirely upon her caretaker for direction, guidance, and identity.

## The Unblemished Page

Lucy, Aurora's cousin, serves as the novel's alternative to the tainted woman. Presented in the narrative as the pale British angel, Lucy is Talbot Bulstrode's ideal of a woman, a "gentle and feminine creature crowned with an aureole of pale auburn hair; some timid soul with downcast eyes, fringed with golden-tinted lashes; some shrinking being, as pale and prim as the mediaeval saints in his pre-Raphaelite engravings, spotless as her own white robes, excelling in all womanly graces and accomplishments, but only exhibiting them in the narrow circle of home" (I 73). Confined to the domestic space, white and without mark, exclusively English in her purity, Lucy provides the perfect complement to Talbot's masculine authority. As silent as a proper Victorian child, she needs none of the pruning Aurora requires, for Lucy has been "watched over and hemmed in from her cradle" (I 89). Lucy resembles a statue who remains as deaf to the unseemly as she is mute about it; she is a "simple womanly martyr" (I 104) whose life has prepared her to impale herself— or be impaled—on the love and honor of her patron mate.

The "pale saint with the halo of golden hair" serves as a foil for Aurora's alluring "witch's dance" (I 121). She is in fact the "white unblemished page, which all the world may be free to read" (I 204). Lucy has no sign on the text of her presence, and further, as Talbot notes, "these gentle creatures love, and make no sign" either (II 14). Lucy signifies nothing. Only in absence can she create meaning.[58] Her whiteness, her blankness, becomes her only means of representation. She fills the space of the wife with absolute malleability. Lucy can commit no act of violence; she cannot even speak. When Talbot proposes marriage, "she made no reply to the captain's appeal, until at last, taking her hand in his, he won from her a low-consenting murmur which meant Yes" (I 14). Talbot literally shapes her replies with a touch of his hand, controlling the text of her speech and the contour of her identity. This submission does not guarantee her safety, however. In fact, even an unknowing offense to this standard of perfection authorizes violent correction. Poovey highlights a passage in an 1859 article from the *Saturday Review*, "The Intellect of Women," in which the writer asserts that

> *No woman can or ought to know very much of the mass of meanness and wickedness and misery that is loose in the wide world. She could not learn about it without losing the bloom and freshness which it is her mission in life to preserve. Her position is somewhat peculiar, and to her unsophisticated eyes may seem partly unintelligible. In order to protect itself, society is compelled to punish a woman's failings and transgressions more severely than it punishes the failings of the stronger sex; and yet it is necessary that the very sex which is to be so disproportionately punished should be left in ignorance of the dangers and characteristic features of transgression.*" (155)

John notes this when he wonders "whether solemn Talbot beats [Lucy] in the silence of the matrimonial chamber" (II 95). Although marked as a jest, this commentary exposes the sham that fulfilling the wifely ideal would protect a woman from violence. Even Sarah Stickney Ellis worries, in *Wives of England,* about the possibility of an "unreasonable class" of men who might behave improprietously, even when a wife performs all of her moral and social duties (72).

    Thus, in the final pages of the novel, when Aurora seems to conform to this model of behavior, becoming a gentle wife and mother, the conclusion is not as simple as it seems. The novel begins with a woman who hates England because she is forced to "stop forever in one place, chained to one set of ideas, fettered to one narrow circle of people, seeing and hearing the persons [she hates] forever and ever, and unable to get away from the odious sound of their names. [She] would like to turn female missionary, and go to the centre of Africa with Dr. Livingstone and his family" (I 98). No longer the empress who desires a life of independence and freedom in Africa, Aurora is transformed by a system of power deployed to secure her domestication. Deirdre David makes a persuasive argument about the way many Victorian texts operated to generate Victoria as a maternal figure "who so securely cradles her colonies that any rocking from restless natives and feminist women gets slapped down by a firm maternal hand." She argues that the "moral and biological fecundity" of women served to manage the empire (181), and here, one might read Aurora's return from the "Africa" of her imagination to the maternal cradle as the suppression of her feminist desires by the very discourse through which her liberation is depicted. Imperialism serves as the social structure that screens marital violence and disdains Aurora's power, and a legal system that acts against the threat of women such as Aurora makes her resignification possible. Thus, she ultimately appears "a little changed, a shade less defiantly bright, perhaps, but unspeakably beautiful and tender, bending over the cradle of her first-born" (III 318). Her beauty derives now from her gentility, not the Eastern splendor that had previously made her defiantly bright and encoded her violence. Her maternity ensures her presence in the domestic space, distilling her identity into the function of mother. Most significantly, her mental processes come into line with those expected of a Victorian woman: "I doubt if my heroine will ever care so much for horseflesh, or take quite so keen an interest in weight-for-age races as compared to handicaps, as she has done in the days that are gone" (III 319). These statements link Aurora's atypical behavior with the unacceptable identity embodied before. Once redeemed through moral and social correction and motherhood, Aurora erases the crimes of her past, cleansing not only the text of her life to fabricate a blank page for her identity, but the violence of the men as well. In its denouement, Aurora's "future belongs to [her] husband" (III 115), and for the last three chapters—nearly eighty pages of the narrative—we hear her voice in the text no more.

### The Dangerous Woman Revisited

Braddon's sensationalism allowed her to tap into multivoiced anxieties in her culture surrounding violence in the domestic space, particularly the violence that threatened women and the cultural disbelief in women's ability to retaliate. The legislative debates surrounding the C.D. Acts foreground the tensions that Braddon often indirectly exposes in *Aurora Floyd*. Braddon's novels are also of interest because the sensation genre offered a license for experimentation that others disallowed; it may have granted Braddon the opportunity to explore issues only cresting the Vic-

torian consciousness. The novel thus articulates the complexity and confusion concerning what species of violence are naturalized, and what
must be censured or safely encoded into respectability.

In Aurora's characterization, just as that of prostitutes, much of the
malevolence discursively woven into her identity is a fantasy authorizing
the use of extensive violence for her containment and subjective/discur-
sive reconstruction. A woman's identity must be debased—she must be
in some respect fallen—for the reading public to accept not only that she
is violent, but that her partner might be violent with her as well. Maintaining an identity as a lady (which was as dependent upon not being
violent as not being violated) could save a woman in the face of over-
whelming evidence that she had been a dangerous woman. In 1857,
Madeleine Smith, a young middle-class woman, was taken to trial for the
death of her working-class lover (a suspicion similar to the one that hovers
around Aurora). Significant evidence had been assembled against Smith,
including her (occasionally titillating) letters to the man. The case was,
however, found not proven, a Scottish verdict that did not absolve Smith
of guilt, but did not convict her. The courtroom erupted into "loud
cheers" at the announcement of the verdict. "Everyone, or nearly everyone, seemed to want to believe Madeleine" was innocent (Hartman 54).
Perhaps if there had been some glitch in her middle-class identity, perhaps
if her lover had not been perceived as an ambitious working-class villain,
this crime would not have seemed so intolerable to the horrified Victorian audience who fiercely defended her innocence against all evidence.

Braddon takes the terms of this case, a working-class man and
wealthy young woman, and draws them into the comfortable domestic
scene of Aurora's (second and) middle-class/gentrified marriage, ex-
trapolating the dangers of one marriage into the other. In this manner,
the implication of violence bleeds across the boundaries of gender, class,
and British identity. No longer is the middle-class home the safe haven
from and screen for violence. Braddon details Talbot's and John's aggression, and charges Softy with an unsettling role and Aurora with an
equally disturbing response. Although many have argued that Braddon's
novels simply capitulate to social expectations, I would contend that
they betray social contradictions. Even Braddon's use of Aurora Floyd's
maiden name as the title in spite of her two marriages, one of which we

are to regard finally as a moral and social success, renders visible the discomfort the text produces over the shape of marriage, over Aurora's identity as "Mrs. Mellish." Despite the eventual gesture toward normative middle-class morality and the magnification of Aurora's danger for the sake of its suppression, the eruptions of alternative readings throughout the novel and their implications for intimate relationships cannot be ignored. Jeni Curtis finds the same tensions present in Lucy's "infinitely replaceab[ility]," uncovering in her unspoken but narratively available thoughts and feelings a disruption of the domestic ideal. Even in the "espaliered" Lucy there are secrets, the possibility of resistance and contradictions. Thus, the closure offered cannot suture the tensions, the violence, and the critique of the middle-class family that pervade the novel. Perhaps, in the novel's economy, revoking Aurora's status as a dangerous woman is an even more radical move than allowing her to maintain such an identity. Making her a wife and mother without her flaws threatens to expose the violence she initially serves to screen. Overall, these tensions provide us with a method of understanding, and perhaps reconceiving, the shift in a discourse of domestic violence during the period.

# 3

# REALISM RECONSIDERED

# IV

## Sensational Violations:
## Betraying Boundaries in
## Margaret Oliphant's *Salem Chapel*

*[Romance writers know nothing] of marriage; and the*
*false pictures they give of those subjects cannot be too*
*strongly condemned. They are not like reality: they*
*show you only the green tempting surface of the*
*marsh, and give not one faithful or truthful hint of the*
*slough underneath.*

—Charlotte
Brontë,
*Shirley*

### Margaret Oliphant and Anti–sensationalism

Rachel Hilyard, the "heroine" of the prolific Margaret Oliphant's most
popular novel, *Salem Chapel* (1863), shoots her estranged husband, Colonel Mildmay, in the head at point-blank range to "end his horrid career," but her bullet blows apart much more than his body; it assaults an
entire corpus of ideological assumptions as well. The reverberations of
this gunshot and other transgressions in the novel shatter the middle–class
vision of domestic peace and propriety, a vision embodied by the novel's
decorous leading family, the Vincents. Answering Mrs. Pryor's call in
*Shirley* for a non–Romantic depiction of marriage, *Salem Chapel* supplies
another vision of reality that calls into question even the domestic security of the Vincents' home. Despite the contentiousness of the narrative,
however, Oliphant has been most often read as a defender of classical
virtues and ideologies. She was the staid Queen Victoria's favorite
novelist[1] and has been regarded as conservative by her contemporaries
and modern critics.[2] She condemned sensation fiction, describing it

as potentially "dangerous," particularly when serially published, a circumstance that might excessively stimulate an unsuspecting reader and lead her into moral turpitude.[3] She objected to Mrs. Henry Wood's *East Lynne* and Wilkie Collins's *The Woman in White* on the grounds that they drew the reader into a sympathetic relationship with a "Magdalen" or a villain ("Sensation Novels" 567).

Yet *Salem Chapel* defies her own admonitions. Noted for its debt to *The Woman in White,* it not only employs the tactic of "startling incident" in serial publication, but draws the reader into a sympathetic relationship with a character who commits villainous acts and even calls into question the nobility of the hero. Though a novel in the Chronicles of Carlingford, a series noted as a hallmark to Oliphant's rigorous standards of "reproducing nature," *Salem Chapel* is frequently regarded by modern critics as a descent into the sensational, bifurcating the text's plot into two narratives. The first, considered a realist plot, relates the story of Arthur Vincent, a Dissenting minister who falls in love with a woman above his socioeconomic reach and becomes disenchanted with his profession in a lower middle-class community. The second, a sensational plot, includes many stereotypically sensational elements: threats of violence, a kidnapping, a possible rape, and attempted murder.

The tensions in Oliphant's self-representation, in the divided critical reaction to the novel, and in the dual plot lines point to a complexity in Oliphant's work that has been, for the most part, overlooked. In these tensions, I discover a novel that subtly exposes the way violence is elided in representations of the middle class and therefore draws sensation into the real, providing evidence of the disintegrating border between sensation and realism. The fantastic elements in *Salem Chapel* derive from one man's abuse of his wife, an issue central to questions circulating in the culture and thus to tensions in the novel. Its portrayal of abuse offers a narrative so contrary to the established rhetoric of marital violence that in spite of Oliphant's avowed distaste for the mode, her narrative seems to undermine all attempts to restore the novel's domestic harmony and realism. This subject matter—marital violence, and attendant upon it, vexed gender and class identity—created a type of narrative that stood out in the body of Oliphant's ninety-two novels, vexing the narrative with the contrary drives outlined in preceding chapters and marking that which Oliphant desired to make most real with the characteristics of sensation. In evoking marginal notions, she wrote in a marginal form; perhaps more important, the apparent contradictions that riddle the novel and its critical reception call attention to the increasing instability of the boundaries between realism and sensation. *Salem Chapel* betrays many sacred social and political boundaries, defying the limits placed on body, speech, and, ultimately, ideology. I read the contradictions here against one another and contend that sensationalism may be employed to reconsider real social and civic politics, countering the notion that sensation inevitably recuperates the dominant discourse and that Oliphant's fiction simply reproduces and reinforces the conservative power dynamics in the period.

At the outset of the novel, the wealthy, upper-class protagonist, who should be a beautiful heroine, is utterly debased. She sequesters herself in dire poverty, taking the alias "Rachel Hilyard" and surviving as a needlewoman in Back Grove Street, a life style reserved for the wretchedly deprived. Her should-be heroic husband, Colonel Mildmay, has cruelly abused her, kidnaps their daughter to make a mercenary marriage for her, and repeatedly threatens Rachel's life. The Dissenting minister, Arthur Vincent, who should be the confessor and protector of this desolate woman, forsakes her and threatens her life in the same manner as her husband, all the while passionately pursuing a highly inappropriate object of affection, Mildmay's wealthy, high-church Anglican half-sister, Lady Western. Between these seemingly disparate plot lines, the realist narrative dedicated to the minister's struggles and the sensational narrative focused on the horrors of the Mildmays' lives, the generic boundaries slip, sensation and realism becoming blurred. Boundary betrayals expose the anxieties surrounding the normative middle-class family—the moral paragon and hero of the novel, Arthur Vincent, and his sister, Susan, "a straightforward, simple-minded English girl"—revealing the Mildmays' familial violence as an inherent feature in the seeming domestic peace and propriety of the Vincents' lives and of the Victorian middle class.

Faced with the contradictions inherent in a culture that denies domestic violence where it clearly exists, the characters (and the novel) are forced outside the normative cultural discourse—into the space labeled sensationalized by modern and contemporary critics—to narrativize their experience. Through a process of mimesis and performance,[4] the novel's two violated women, Rachel and Susan, exploit the rifts created

by the emergence of language, situations, and identities that realism cannot contain. Their sensationalized identities then distort phallogocentric
norms in a way that reframes female identity, rescripts the natural absence
of sexual violence in the domestic space, and makes them an enduring
threat to the structure from which Arthur and Mildmay derive their
power. I investigate three markers to explore the novel's transgressions
of boundaries and sensational revision of middle-class culture and understanding: speech, madness, and the woman's body, examining the presentation in fiction of the "unspeakable" and the ways its sensational depiction reframes our understanding of the sociopolitical system in which
the Victorians operated. In giving voice to an issue that would ordinarily
remain in silence, in citing social institutions and expectations to corrupt the social norms, *Salem Chapel*—and indeed sensation as a generic
mode—questions the confinement of sexual violence to the working
class and to fiction, as well as the passivity of women's response and power
relations between the genders. Thus, in the realist fiction of one of Britain's most prolific writers, a plot that has been identified as sensational
irrevocably marks the realism of the narrative, and the recognition of
this provides modern critics a means of uncovering an alternative social
discourse.

The alternative voice, spoken by Rachel, becomes "mad" speech
and her own bodily boundaries seem to dissolve, leaving her with social
fluidity but also lodged in the abject. In *Powers of Horror,* Julia Kristeva
describes boundarilessness as abjection, a site of vital creative (socially,
culturally, and personally) power, capable of "craftily rul[ing] social institutions" (169). Yet for Kristeva, this site, defined by its "oppos[ition] to
*I*" (1), is fraught with tremendous pain and (self-)revulsion as well. By its
very definition, abjection is a place of horror, but a place whose powers
may be "unveiled" in literature (208). Rachel both exists in and provides
these functions in the novel, unveiling the power of her speech and lack
of identity, but being threatened with obliteration as well. Her "madness," however, cannot be contained; her speech not only defies social
boundaries, but itself becomes boundariless, pervading the narrative and
disrupting the myth of middle-class domestic bliss. Rachel's unsustainable
and painful identity does not offer a satisfying response to familial violence, but through Susan, Arthur's sister, the novel suggests another and
less self-destructive response to the social impossibility of family violence

in the middle class. Also a victim of Rachel's abusive husband, Susan becomes the silent, intransigent "marble woman." Her marbleization encloses her within the bounds of social propriety, yet her rigid, prostrate body becomes an overdetermined site, implying the same cultural impossibility that Rachel's speech explicitly expresses. Thus, Susan also embodies and exposes the contradictions inherent in her culture—the potential for the seemingly impossible presence of violence in the middle class.

### Crossing Class Lines, Redefining Morality

When we are introduced to Rachel, this upper-class woman has already left her violent and calculating husband and put her daughter into hiding to protect the girl from her father. She refuses the support of her friends and abandons her former life. Meanwhile, her husband searches for his beautiful but mentally deficient daughter in hopes of marrying her well—while maintaining the life style of a gentleman. Rachel's life in grinding poverty remains unresolved by the narrative. Although hiding her daughter is costly, her ability to regain her lofty social position and wealth at any time is demonstrated when she easily does so later in the novel. Her banishment from the world of the elite, her deprivation in the face of her wealth, is the first gesture to rationally define Rachel's experience as an abused woman. Positioning her as a working-class woman makes her status as a victim of abuse conceivable. This move, however, fails to contain Rachel and instead leaves her the site of contradiction and tension.

When Arthur Vincent becomes the new minister of Salem Chapel, he immediately notes Rachel's enigmatic identity, which leaves him immersed in a "curious mixture of feelings" (I 36). He remarks, "[I]t surprises me more than I can explain, to find, . . . to find—," to which Rachel replies, "Such a person as I am in Back Grove Street . . . yes—and thereby hangs a tale. But I did not send for you to tell it" (I 33). The novel becomes a means of obsessively telling Rachel's tale, however, in the space of her vexed identity and the impact her identity has on others. Arthur conceives of Rachel in a way that provides a key to reading the novel overall (along with the various fictional patterns present) when he notes her "extreme thinness of outline" (I 29). He perceives that a mysterious force had "worn to so thin a tissue the outer garment of this keen and sharp-edged soul" (I 31). Rachel seems uncertainly bounded, only loosely framed by social reality. Her identity is so enmeshed with contradiction that the lady/working woman's outline fades, her soul's outer garment becomes translucent. Rachel serves as the novel's preeminent marker of broken boundaries and the link between all its seemingly disparate elements. In this scene, and others that follow, Rachel is described metaphorically and literally as bleeding. She spends her days "intent upon the rough work which [Arthur] could not help observing sometimes made her scarred fingers bleed as [her needle] passed rapidly through" the coarse blue fabric (I 32). She "work[ed] at those 'slops' till the colour came off upon her hands, and her poor thin fingers bled" (I 36). The reiterative references to the exchange of blood and dye emphasize a twofold result of Rachel's mixed identity as a gentlewoman and a working-class woman. On the one hand, they reveal the rupture of her boundaries and the seepage of the inside out, metaphorically representing both her abasement and her ability to resist norms in transgressing the social body as her fractured identity implies she does. She is repositioned on the margins of social reality, and her abject poverty is not only the price she pays for her abandonment of her husband and defiance of the legal and social system in which she lives, it becomes an avenue for her increasing transgressions of social norms. Thus, her bleeding, although painful, grants her the power of resistance.[5] Her physical embodiment of abjection allows her the authority to speak transgressive language and perform transgressive acts. However, it is a benefaction this character must pay for with her blood.

Sensation fiction as a genre, like Rachel in *Salem Chapel,* was expelled to the margins of polite discourse. Conceived of by many as growing from the models of working-class fiction, sensation was often read as déclassé. Further, it was defined, in large part, by the fact that it spoke to issues that realist fiction did not, such as bigamy, sexuality, and, as I argue here, feigned identities and violence. Because the novel takes up what seems unreal, Rachel's character becomes unreal—delegitimized and debased—but like Rachel's character, sensation cannot be safely contained in the margins of the text.

In exposing these contradictions, *Salem Chapel* renders visible the discrepancies in the domestic ideology and its relationship to the material circumstances of and dangers in women's lives. Despite the fact that Arthur attempts to elide the elements that suggest contradiction, like Rachel's strange poverty, his efforts fail.[6] He tells the beautiful and wealthy young dowager Lady Western that Rachel's existence "makes one feel how insignificant are the circumstances of life" (I 99). Lady Western, though eternally claiming inferior education and aptitude, remarks, "I think, when I see her, oh, how important [circumstances] are! . . . I think those circumstances which you speak of so disrespectfully are everything!" (I 99–100). Lady Western's resistance, conduct radically dissonant with the rest of her behavior, highlights not only the horrors of Rachel's position but the tensions in Arthur's assertions. Voicing this resistance through Lady Western, one of the novel's paragons of social propriety, renders visible the incongruity of Arthur's statements.

## Infiltrating the Domestic Ideal

### Class and the Odor of Cheese

Arthur's attempts to repress the improprietous violence that Rachel evokes grow increasingly violent themselves. Although Arthur's genteel education and identity as a gentleman should provide the alternative to the Mildmays' disruption,[7] he becomes implicated in their violence. Emphasizing the tensions in the boundaries between the sensational and the real, the moral and the depraved, Arthur actually forms the avenue through which middle-class propriety is contaminated by the danger Rachel represents. The novel shapes the domestic scene of Carlingford, but not by alienating this dangerous woman and her story from the realist plot line, as some critics have suggested. Instead, the domestic space is defined through the juxtaposition of the seemingly serene Vincent family and the chaotic mélange of betrayal and bitterness in the Mildmay family.

We see the breakdown of Arthur's middle-class morals from the time he appears in Carlingford, in spite of the fact that he comes from a family that epitomizes respectable middle-class economy, propriety, and purity. Arthur "[r]emember[s] the dainty little household which it took [Mrs. Vincent] so much pains and pinching to maintain. . . . He could fancy her trim little figure in that traditionary black silk gown, which never wore out, and the whitest of caps" (I 23–24). Though the domestic space provides security against violence in many fictional models, it no longer offers such safety in *Salem Chapel,* as evidenced by its ultimate contamination. Further, Arthur's judgmental hostility towards the members of Salem Chapel undermines his status as a representative of the expansive moral structure that guarantees this middle-class domestic safety. In spite of the crudeness of his congregation, he seems exacting and unkind, repulsing their affable gestures. The Tozers arouse his displeasure because they allow the odor of their business to waft through the doors that should properly separate shop and home, the smell of cheeses permeating their drawing room and constantly reminding genteel visitors of the family's dependence upon trade.[8]

The doors between the domestic space and economic enterprise, middle and working class, propriety and indiscretion cannot prevent the cross-pollination of these terms, betraying the fluidity of the boundaries that seem to separate them. A wide array of theoretical work supports the contention that play around the boundaries that separate dichotomies exposes them as insubstantial. Mimesis, in this case of middle-class customs such as the tea the Tozers have in Arthur's honor, uncovers the artificial nature of these cultural delineations. Judith Butler discusses a similar notion in *Gender Trouble* through which we may perceive the Tozers' performance of middle-class-ness in their parlor, at their tea parties, and through their relative wealth as a suggestion of the purely performative nature of the boundary between working and middle class. In this way, the novel questions the confinement of sexual violence to the working class, the passivity of women's response, and power relations between the genders. The collapse of these boundaries disturbs Arthur's comfort in part because it reveals the absence of a firm distinction between him and his "flock" and also because it is upon this distinction that his value system depends. His disappointment with the laboring people in his parish is thus explicitly linked with a collapse of his value system, represented in his abandonment of his religious convictions. The disruption of these values calls into question the exclusive association of decorum and the middle class and even middle-class values themselves. Though Arthur fights to preserve these boundaries, the novel illustrates that they are thoroughly permeable. The trembling barricades between the model domestic scene of the Vincents and the violence of the Mildmays are defined as equally fragile, ultimately exposing the artificial boundaries that maintain the mid-Victorian domestic ideal.

*Sullied Unions*

Oliphant marries her tale of the disenchanted Dissenting minister and his proper middle-class family to that of Rachel Hilyard and her abusive husband, Colonel Mildmay. The Mildmays represent the antithesis of the normative domestic scene: a broken marriage, a stolen child, physical and mental turmoil, and dispute. Arthur cannot remain aloof from the taint of the Mildmays any more than he can that of his parishioners. Instead, the Mildmays' turbulent relationship impinges upon and reveals the tensions in the Vincent home, thrusting forward the possibility of an alternative domestic setting, one that, like the Vincents', falls within the contemporary understanding of domestic propriety and yet is tremendously dangerous and predicated on violence.

Thus, the Vincents' home crumbles at its social and moral foundations, rewriting the institutionalized middle-class space. The violence of the Mildmays bleeds into Arthur's identity, the sensationalism into the real, as the slops bleed onto Rachel's fingers, revealing a gendered violence that, on the surface, seems to lie only within Rachel and uncovering the sensational within the center of the real. The first element of these families' coalescence is the relationship between Arthur and Rachel. Arthur's first assignment in Carlingford is to attend to her needs as a penitent in his chapel. Despite her dissociation with the community and her construction as an outsider, she and Arthur become so intimately connected that, later in the novel, Mrs. Vincent believes Rachel to be Arthur's lover. And indeed, Arthur becomes enraptured with Rachel. He makes special visits to her when he cannot bear to see the other people of Salem Chapel; he finds himself thinking about her regularly; he develops an uncanny ability to "instinctively recognize" her (I 138), his feet wandering to her door as often as his mind.

It is not long, however, before this entanglement increases to include another woman who draws him deeper into the circumstances of the Mildmays. Arthur falls in love with the young, wealthy (and high-church Anglican) dowager Lady Western. Although he is initially ignorant of their relationship, Lady Western is Colonel Mildmay's half-sister and Rachel Hilyard's sister-in-law. Arthur even meets Lady Western in Rachel's degraded apartment, confirming their near relationship. Arthur serves as the conduit between these two women and Colonel Mildmay across the axis of his seemingly docile family life. In the crowded Salem Chapel, "[h]e knew but of that fair creature in all her sweet bloom and blush of beauty [Lady Western]—the man who accompanied her [Colonel Mildmay]—Mrs Hilyard, a thin, dark, eager shadow in the distance—and himself standing, as it were, between them, connecting them all together" (I 127). Further, from Arthur's first meeting with Lady Western, whom he longs to marry, the violence and callousness he purports to despise—and that his identity as a minister and a middle-class gentleman demands he reject—become apparent in his behavior. Even the poor he has dedicated himself to serving, subjugating his will to theirs "without irony," become his target. When a small boy blocks Lady Western's path, Arthur, "[s]carcely aware what he was doing, as much beauty-struck as his *victim* . . . [and] with a certain unconscious fury, seized the boy by the collar, and swung him impatiently off the pavement, with a feeling of positive resentment against the imp, whose rags were actually touching those sacred splendid draperies" (I 53; emphasis added). His affection for Lady Western seems to elide his middle-class morality, transforming him into a violent and callous man. Later in the novel, when Arthur's sister, Susan, is kidnapped, his love of Lady Western serves as the means by which he justifies his inattention to Susan's dire situation as well as his obsession with Herbert Fordham, Lady Western's former lover. The more Arthur considers marriage, the closer he becomes to the Mildmays and the more cruel he seems.

Finally, the Vincents become associated with the dangers and impropriety of the Mildmays' lives on another level when Colonel Mildmay, posing as Herbert Fordham, proposes marriage to Susan and then kidnaps her from their home. The physical withdrawal of Susan from the domestic scene and her return to it a changed woman mark the alteration of the domestic ideal and revision of one of its primary sources: marriage. Mildmay's abuse of his wife, Rachel, his attempt to create a bigamous marriage with a "pure English girl," and Arthur's futile desire for marriage with Lady Western draw attention to the tensions at the site of marriage—particularly the ways in which this institution, even in the most proper middle-class home, may foster an environment of violence. However, the shift in this ideal image is more than an uncomplicated contamination of the Vincents' home. The text forces us to see the Vincents against the backdrop of the Mildmays, collapsing the boundaries between them. In articulating Colonel Mildmay's behavior as heinous, the novel exposes Arthur's behavior as a performance of the same kind: violence thought possible only in the most degraded working-class households.

### Rereading Marriage: "A Fine Organisation Capable of Pleasures and Cruelties"

Oliphant reveals Colonel Mildmay through Arthur and Arthur through Mildmay. The reader's first encounter with the Colonel comes when Arthur unabashedly eavesdrops on a conversation between Rachel and her husband from the window of the chapel vestry (a betrayal of decorum that hints at Arthur's impropriety). It is here that the reader and Arthur first learn about the violent character of the Mildmays' relationship, a violence that is distinctly defined by its matrimonial and domestic nature. Standing in the churchyard among the graves of Salem, Colonel Mildmay remarks to Rachel, "By Jove, it looks dangerous!—what do you mean to suggest by this sweet rendezvous—murder?" (I 164). Rachel identifies this rage, as well as Mildmay's homicidal intent, with their marital relationship: "This is too conjugal . . . it reminds me of former experiences" (I 165). Mildmay continues to threaten her, commenting, "[D]o you know how much it would be to my advantage if you never left this lonely spot you have brought me to? By Jove, I have the greatest mind—" (I 167). Although unspoken, Mildmay's intention is clear. His desire to physically manage Rachel, even murder her, a pattern represented in sensation novels such as *Aurora Floyd,* is offered here explicitly, rather than under cover. This violence, distinctly associated with Mildmay and Rachel's relationship as "man and wife," ultimately serves as a model for evaluating Arthur's relationship to women in the text as well. In fact, Arthur mimics Mildmay's violence, becoming more and more like him as the narrative progresses, even "making a desperate gesture of rage" as he sits alone (I 166). Only Rachel's slippery identity protects her from death at her husband's hands, as it later does with Arthur: "[Colonel Mildmay] lift[ed] up his stick and clench[ed] it in his hand as she turned away from him those keen eyes. . . . But even Mrs Hilyard herself never knew how near, how very near, she was at that moment to the unseen world. Had her step been less habitually firm and rapid,—had she lingered on her way—the temptation might have been too strong for the man, maddened by many memories. He made one stride after her, clenching the stick. . . . She might have been stunned in a moment and left there to die" (I 170). It is precisely Mildmay's reflection on their marital relationship that nearly leads him to exercise the most decisive power his stick embodies, the power to kill. In one of the most insistent representations of the man's walking stick under examination here,[9] the reader is reminded of its presence four times in two pages. We even see it through the eyes of the people of Salem, who incorporate Mildmay's stick into their vision of him as a powerful upper-class gentleman when they wonder what "had brought the Colonel and his stick to such a place" (I 171). The two are perceived together, an indivisible figuration, aligning Colonel Mildmay with a gendered form of power and, as we have seen, a power to kill. Rachel recognizes the connection of these terms as well. As she walks away she remarks, "I suppose, before leaving you, I should thank you for having spared my life" (I 169). Rachel, however, does not remain passive in response to Mildmay's caveats. Unbounded by the land-marks that held characters such as Marian Halcombe in *The Woman in White* to mere fantasies of violence, and demonstrating the evolution of the discourses I examine here, Rachel returns Mildmay's death threats. She warns, "[S]hould [you] ever be able to snatch [my daughter] from me—then confess your sins, and say your last prayers, for as sure as I live you shall die in a week" (I 168). Rachel's threat of murder is not the only gesture that identifies her behavior as outside the standards of social pro-priety. Her remarks draw together what would have been several distinct lines of rebellion for the Victorian woman.

One of these is Rachel's threat to Victorian legal and social notions of child custody, which defined men, not women, as the natural and proper custodians of children. A father was deemed by governmental leg-islation, not just social law, the best fit to care for his children, particularly those over the age of seven. A mother retained custody only of a child born out of wedlock, simply because "such a child was supposedly *filius nulli,* the child of no (known) father" (Shanley 132). Rulings in custody battles fell in favor of the father so frequently and "with such force and vigor that it had the effect of creating new paternal rights, the existence of which had only been vaguely hinted at" before the nineteenth century (Zainaldin in Shanley, 134). These paternal rights were particularly evident in the cases of women who had obtained separation for cruelty (a term used in legal debates and documents to describe physical abuse). One justice explained that although the wife and mother might be permitted to leave her abusive husband, her children must remain in the "protection" of their father's custody: "'To leave his wife with the defender [not offender!] [was] to subject him to an influence exciting and tempting him to violence towards her. To leave his little child in his house [was], or [might] well be, to introduce a soothing influence to cheer the darkness and mitigate the bitterness of his lot, and bring out the better part of his nature.' It did not seem to occur to Lord Ardmillan [the ruling justice] that a man who beat his wife might also abuse his daughter" (Shanley 141). In another case of child custody, a woman who left her husband, charging cruelty, had her child returned to the father by the courts. Even when the judge openly acknowledged the husband's violent abuse, he contended that the father should retain possession unless he intended to "abuse" or "sacrifice" the child (Shanley 134). Trollope's 1865 novel *He Knew He Was Right* details the failure of a mother's attempts to regain her child, even after her husband is widely acknowledged to be cruel and mad, one of the "unreasonable and dictatorial" men of whom Sarah Stickney Ellis feared to speak in her *Wives of England* (593). The miserable wife laments after her son is kidnapped, "If I could begin life again, I do not think that any temptation would induce me to place myself in a man's power" (655), and her father admits, "Here was a man married to his daughter, in possession of his daughter's child, manifestly mad,—and yet he could do nothing to him" (737). The novel illustrates the legal and social impossibility of rescuing a child from a father, except under extreme circumstances, and then only until the child was seven years of age.

However, Rachel's mixed identity as a working-class/upper-class woman may have made it possible for her to slip along the middle-class perception of working-class mores, aiding her in retaining control over her daughter. Although the working class certainly was not a violence-free nor matriarchal structure (as the voluminous cases of domestic violence in the working class show[10]), a working-class woman who defied paternal rights might be tolerated by her middle- and upper-class counterparts because they simply believed that the paterfamilias "was nowhere to be found" in the laboring classes (Barrett-Durocq 24). In fact, the father was often perceived as nomadic, "wander[ing] about from family circle to family circle" (Sims in Barrett-Durocq, 26), invalidating his role as familial provider, caretaker, and master of his children. (Interestingly, Arthur doesn't attempt to prevent Rachel from concealing Alice, a manifestly illegal act. It is only when she assaults her husband that the tone of his relationship to her changes.) It wasn't until roughly the 1880s that feminists began to use tactics we frequently hear in custody cases today, arguing that a woman's biological functions such as childbirth and lactation made her a naturally superior parent. However, working-class women who were the victims of physical violence were often perceived as instigators of abuse, and although standards surrounding middle- to upper-class women failed to regard them as potential victims of abuse, they did mark them as the only possible flaw in the domestic space. A man's misbehavior was often perceived as a product of his wife's deficiencies. Thus, the Mildmays' domestic dilemma sometimes marked Rachel as the murderous threat, like the dangerous woman in *Aurora Floyd*. However, *Salem Chapel,* through its conflicted representation of Rachel, also clearly portrays the danger Mildmay represents, in spite of the couple's upper-class origins.

Rachel moves outside the spectrum of appropriate womanly behavior not only because she reserves control of her daughter and dares to threaten violence, but because her violence fails to conceal her husband's. These tensions pose contrapuntal readings of the familiar terms of domesticity, class, and gendered identity. Rachel's identity, the one "possible" site of defect, contorts under the pressure of these contradictions, exposing them as the principles upon which her identity is based. When Rachel is in conflict with Mildmay on both of these fronts, she becomes increasingly "unwomanly." The narrative voice dubs her a "wild creature." Mildmay responds to her threats by denying her identity as a woman, labeling her a "She-devil" (I 168). However, Rachel refuses to take responsibility for these flaws and identifies Mildmay as the source of her altered identity. He had "poisoned" her mind and inflicted "so much torture and misery" on her body (II 251) that she became an outsider, living outside the social world into which she was born and outside the legal definitions by which Parliament had conceived of its laws.

Although Rachel's identity has been fragmented, Mildmay's identity remains within the normative marital role. In a suggestive passage in which Rachel defines the marital bond, she explains that her spouse lost his identity as a man, though, to be sure, his relationship to her as husband remains: "I am a woman that was once young and had friends. They married me to a man, who was not a man, but a fine organisation capable of pleasures and cruelties" (II 251). This "organisation" can easily commit Mildmay's crimes. His identity as a husband sufficiently extends the range of his activity to include acts of conjugal cruelty, and as this novel would suggest, without reprimand. Further, these cruelties, a term used throughout the century to refer to physical violence in marital relationships, are defined in relation to his pleasures. Significantly, Rachel also indicates that one would feel pleasure watching the dainty way in which Mildmay "twist[s] a woman round his fingers . . . and break[s] all her heartstrings" (I 142). When Rachel defines Mildmay in this way, she frequently speaks in generalities as well, marking not only one man but what any woman marries, a husband.[11] She equates Mildmay with "death" and a "bitter process" of evolving through trauma. She declares that she has "died twice," explaining that "this is [her] third life" and that she knew Colonel Mildmay only "in the other world" (I 146). Only her location in a different world offers her reprieve (but as we will see below, this quarantine has its costs). These scenes of violence are also marginalized, described even by Rachel as melodrama, a remark indicating that her experience is not comprehensible in the realm of realism. It is not long, however, before this melodrama bleeds over into even that which has been marked as real by the narrative, Arthur Vincent.

### The Disintegration of Safety

Arthur's link to Mildmay is first indicated metonymically: when he asks Rachel about Mildmay, she "start[s] as if she had received a blow" (I 141). Mildmay's violence, conjured through Arthur's words, produces the same result as a physical gesture. Further, when Arthur offers to see Rachel "safely" home, she refuses his assistance. His presence avails her of no additional security; rather, she calls upon her fractured identity as her protection, recalling Arthur's first encounter with her. She describes herself as an "equivocal female" (I 139), one with contradictory meanings. The qualities are not only registered in her speech but on her body. Her "face would explain matters better than a volume" (I 140), but her individual safety does not repress the threat that she represents. Immediately after remarking, "Thank you. I am perfectly safe—nobody can possibly be safer than such a woman as I am, in poverty and a middle age. . . . It is an immunity that women don't often prize, Mr Vincent, but it is very valuable in its way" (I 139), her talk turns to "evil creatures pondering in the dark vile schemes against the innocent" (I 143–44). Like the tale of her identity that she refuses to tell when Arthur first visits her and then spends the rest of the novel laying out, Rachel's very presence speaks the danger that she has already experienced and must remain unspoken, betraying rifts in the rhetoric of safety and, increasingly, in Arthur's identity as well. As Rachel cryptically predicts his sister's abduction, she remarks that she often thinks of "dreadful messengers of evil approaching unconscious houses, and looking in at peaceful windows upon the comfort they are about to destroy" (I 143). Her comments evoke the tensions that will destroy not only Arthur's domestic comfort (in Susan's kidnapping), but also the dreadful messenger that these tensions become in the novel overall, threatening the ideology of the serenity of the domestic space. Finally, despite the fact that Arthur knows she did not go to his lecture, she remarks of his talk, "I should not wonder if it made a revolution in Carlingford" (I 141), a prophetic reference to an ideological revolution that the novel begins to address at the site of Arthur's supposed middle-class decorum, a revolution sensation-influenced realist fiction such as *Salem Chapel* takes up. Rachel's expatriation to the working class, then, does not expel the violence from middle- and upper-class homes as it might seem to do. The text betrays its own articulated class boundaries, the violence seeping through the chinks in the barriers the domestic ideology fashions. Rachel's abjection can neither prevent Mildmay or Arthur from threatening her life, nor can it prevent the shattering of the "peaceful windows" in the elite homes of Grange Lane.

The narrative creates a space in which even the domesticity of the middle class becomes aligned with violence, not harmony, and danger, not peace. Oliphant's portrayal of the Mildmays' violence bleeds into her portrayal of the Vincents, the sensational bleeds into the real, the fantastic (no longer so unreal) bleeds into the domestic. This becomes more apparent in a series of formulaic coincidences that strengthens the connection between the two families and grants Mildmay access both to his and Rachel's daughter, Alice, and to Susan. Rachel begs Arthur to allow her

to send Alice to his mother and Susan. Mildmay knows Alice has been
sequestered in one of the country's many towns named Lonsdale, and he
has already investigated the one in which Mrs. Vincent lives. During
these investigations, in fact, he has made the acquaintance of Susan and
Mrs. Vincent and courted Susan under the assumed name "Herbert
Fordham." Arthur, unaware of Mildmay's double identity but discerning
the gravity of Rachel's request, sends Alice to his mother. At the same
time, Mrs. Vincent receives a disturbing note that her daughter's suitor is
not who he seems and visits Arthur for advice. In the past, Rachel has
offered continual warnings about Susan's lover, knowing that Mildmay
has been in Lonsdale: "Your sister is pretty, I suppose? and does your
mother take great care of her and keep her out of harm's way? Lambs
have a silly faculty of running directly in the wolf's road" (I 143). She
urges Arthur to guard against "dangerous strangers" (I 93), and each time
she makes reference to it, Arthur becomes alarmed. Their distress is well
founded; before long they learn that Mildmay has engaged himself to
Susan. Upon this discovery, Rachel recognizes the danger to Susan and
cries to Mrs. Vincent, "We have both thrust our children into the lion's
mouth. . . . Go, poor woman, and save your child if you can, and so will
I—we are companions in misfortune" (I 252).

The doubling of Rachel and Mrs. Vincent as good mothers made
victims to a predatory aspect of their culture with the threat of dangerous
marriages for their daughters, and of Rachel and Susan (as the bride and
bride-to-be of Mildmay/"Fordham"), binds all the women under the
threat of treacherous matrimony, a site at which a woman was expected
to be most safe. There is also a parallel doubling that becomes increasingly
apparent as the novel progresses, that of Arthur and Mildmay. Not only
have they both courted each other's sisters (Mildmay pursuing Susan and
Arthur wooing Lady Western), but they both become increasingly violent and engage in behaviors that Rachel describes as "the inexorable"
manner of men.

### Coming to the Inexorable: The Brotherhood of Man

In what at first seems to be an ironic gesture, Oliphant introduces
Colonel Mildmay in the novel as Arthur's "brother" (I 77). The first
mention of Mildmay comes in a letter from Mrs. Vincent informing

Arthur of Susan and Mildmay's engagement. This gesture binds Mildmay to all the women in the novel with whom Arthur is associated. Not only is Mildmay the intended son-in-law of Arthur's mother and the husband of his sister, but he is also the husband of the parishioner with whom Arthur interacts the most (Rachel) and the half-brother of the woman Arthur loves, Lady Western. Oliphant's pairing of Arthur and Mildmay as "brothers" refigures the characterization of the seemingly mild-mannered minister.

From the first, Arthur—like Mildmay—concerns himself with his own needs, not the women whom he claims to protect. Even after discovering that Mildmay has courted his sister under an assumed name, kidnapped her in an attempt to marry her illegally, and endangered her reputation and, in fact, her very life, Arthur bristles at the threat Susan's difficulties pose to his own reputation. He identifies Mildmay as "Ruin, misery, and horror at the least—death to Susan—not much less to me" (I 258). His thoughts turn from Susan to Lady Western, the woman with whose beauty he has fallen in love. He ponders "the honour and peace of his *own* humble house" (I 258; emphasis added), not the degradation and pain Susan suffers. He fears most of all that snatching Susan from Mildmay's grasp, despite the fact that it could save her life, might offend Lady Western and end her "tantalising intercourse [with him]. . . . He thought of this, and not of Susan" (I 259). The same menacing selfishness and disregard for women that characterizes Mildmay's behavior characterizes Arthur's actions at this time. Throughout Susan's alarming disappearance and uncertain convalescence, Arthur's jealously focuses on Lady Western's former lover, the true Herbert Fordham, and his infatuation for Lady Western. In his pursuit of Mildmay after he has kidnapped Susan, Arthur bemoans, "Oh, hideous fate! it was *her* brother whom he was bound to pursue to the end of the world. . . . Susan floated away like a mist from that burning personal horizon" (I 337). Despite his efforts "to imagine that it was [Susan] who occupied his mind," Arthur "knew in his own mind how often another shadow stood between him and his lost sister," the shadow of Lady Western (I 344–45). Even after his sister has been returned to his home, Arthur cannot for a moment turn his attention to her best interests: "It was not for Susan's sake that her brother's heart closed and his countenance clouded against the man whose name had wrought her so much sorrow. Vincent had arrived at such a climax of personal existence that Susan had but a dim and secondary place in his thoughts. He was absorbed in his own troubles and plans and miseries" (II 296).

Neglect, however, becomes only one in a host of symptoms in Arthur's characterization as a Mildmayan man. When his mother's servant begs him to run for a doctor as Mrs. Vincent swoons, he "thr[ows] the frightened creature off with a savage carelessness of which he [is] quite unconscious" (I 292). He remains inattentive to his violence, repeating it throughout the novel with women who stand in his path. Arthur enlists the genuine Herbert Fordham in his search for Mildmay and Susan after her abduction, and together they decide to visit Herbert's ancestral home in hopes that they will locate there the man who has taken Herbert's name. When they arrive, Arthur "grasp[s] [an elderly servant] by the arm . . . [holds] the terrified woman fast, and thrust[s] her before him, he could not tell where" (I 352). Her screams induce the interference of Herbert, but Arthur remains indifferent to the effects of his attacks.

The most notable parallel between Arthur's and Mildmay's behaviors, however, becomes evident in their treatment of Rachel, and it is ultimately she who offers the most damning argument that the boundaries between Arthur's middle-class propriety and Mildmay's violence have collapsed. Susan escapes Mildmay when Rachel shoots him, and Arthur hopes to imprison Rachel for the crime after Susan's return to Carlingford. Arthur searches her out and takes her captive, mimicking the patterns of Mildmay, who had held and threatened the lives of Rachel, his own daughter, and Susan: "Vincent put out his hand to seize upon the strange woman. . . . He took the door from her hand, closed it, placed himself against it. 'You are my prisoner,' said Vincent. He could not say any more, but gazed at her with blank eyes of determination. He was no longer accessible to reason, pity, any sentiment but one. He had secured her. . . . She was his prisoner—that one fact was all he cared to know" (II 123). His inexorability frames a gendered system of control and domination, basing men's authority on the threat of violence regardless of class and moral codes. It also serves to mark Rachel (or another woman— Susan is also suspected in Mildmay's attempted murder while Mildmay remains free from accountability for kidnapping or assault) culpable for all crimes that occur within the domestic space. Despite the fact that Arthur's role as a minister urges him toward the salvation of life, he threatens

Rachel's execution. He frames her as simply a body to be physically controlled by marking her language and behavior as meaningless, something
she reads as an inevitable characteristic of men's treatment of women:
"'[N]othing you can do or say will help you now.' 'Ah!' said Mrs Hilyard,
with a startled panting breath. 'You have come to the inexorable . . . most
men do, one time or another. You decline meeting us on our ground,
and take to your own'" (II 125). Arthur's ground, as Mildmay's, is the
power of physical suppression and violence, a power that denies the voices
of women. He seizes, silences, and threatens her.

Arthur's acts expose elements of the domestic economy that must
be obscured by the identification of Rachel as the villain and by the erasure of violence against her: if she is bodiless and voiceless, she cannot be
the victim of physical abuse. Despite the fact that she continues to speak,
Arthur is deaf to her: "Yes, you are a man! . . . You are deaf, blind! You
have turned your back on reason. That is what it always comes to"
(II 126). Significantly, Rachel identifies this move with a failure of reason,
though Arthur will later, and with more threatening efficacy, remark on
her loss of reason. Again, the boundaries the novel lays out are retracted
and redefined. Neither reason nor realism can contain what appears in
the depiction of Arthur's behavior, and in spite of the fact that Rachel
names Arthur and his violence as the cause of this break ("You have
turned your back on reason"), she is punished and "imprisoned," her
speech becoming unreal and nonsensical. Ultimately, the middle-class
minister and model of decorum becomes Mildmay himself, bespeaking
the permeability of the domestic boundaries the novel seems on the surface to defend with Arthur's heroics.

Arthur's behavior finally culminates in a rash, vindictive exercise of
authority over Rachel. When he considers the loss of Lady Western to
Herbert, he becomes enraged and wants to lash out at the closest, most
accessible victim. Rachel, who lies at the center of his domestic dream's
destruction, becomes the target: "At that moment the idea of being cruel,
tyrannical to somebody—using his power harshly, balancing the pain in
his own heart by inflicting pain on another—was not disagreeable to the
minister's excited mind. He could have steeled himself just then to bring
down upon her all the horrible penalties of the law" (II 297). Cruelty, the
Victorian legal and social term for physical violence,[12] along with Arthur's
desire to balance heartache with, simply, "pain," suggests a physical form

of retribution for his unfulfilled will. Finally, the narrator describes this ability as his power, Arthur's power, the law and a man's power over a woman to punish or execute. Rachel becomes terrified of Arthur, aware of the authority he holds over her. She has been returned into Arthur's custody by Herbert Fordham, and she becomes an object of barter between the two men. However, she recognizes that Arthur's violence does not directly concern her, but rather centers on the domestic propriety that Lady Western embodies. "She knew very well it was not of her that either of the two was thinking; yet it was her fate, perhaps her very life, which hung in the trembling balance. . . . She was silenced for the first time in her life" (II 302). Her voice becomes inoperable; the discourse of Arthur and Herbert, the discourse that reinforces this domestic ideology, erases her interpretation of the events, making it insignificant madness. The narrative does not, however, point up the tensions in her unspoken evaluation. The emptying out of her speech, her self, leaves only a material body to be acted upon, but also leaves a rich textual body for analysis, rife with Rachel's resistance. The narrative exposes the ways in which she is acted upon, becoming nothing but flesh, a body to take on the violence of men, to screen this violence, and to cure the ills of the domestic space. The materiality of her punishment is made clear in the following passage:

> *She had escaped her crime, but all its* material consequences, *shame and punishment, still hung over her head. After God himself had freed her from the guilt of blood—after the injured man himself had forgiven her—when all was clear for her escape into* another life—*was this an indignant angel, with flaming sword and averted face, that barred the way of the fugitive? Beyond him, virtue and goodness and all the fruits of repentance, shone before the eyes which had up to this time seen but little attraction in them. . . . Just as she had recovered herself—as she had escaped—as remorse and misery had driven her to yearn after a* better life, *to be cast down again into this abyss of guilt and punishment. (II 302–3; emphasis added)*

Rachel, whose violence becomes the explicit reason for Arthur's cruelty, is physically punished—a punishment that serves to obscure Mildmay and Arthur's transgressions. Arthur stands in the way of virtue and goodness, rather than providing an avenue to it. Neither Mildmay nor Arthur are held accountable for their crimes: cruel neglect, kidnapping, threatened (?) rape, and deadly abuse. Rachel remains "waiting [Arthur's] pleasure," a term that evokes Mildmay's cruel pleasures that tortured her in marriage. She identifies Arthur in the same way she defines Mildmay, as "a man and cruel" (II 307). Arthur had already delivered her to the same fate that had awaited her and Susan at the hands of Mildmay, holding over them the threat of an abuse so profound that it amounted to a death threat. Yet Rachel is not powerless and dumb throughout the text, a salient feature of the sensational influence on the novel. The untenable position in which Oliphant places the character—an upper-class woman as the victim of violence—exposes the cultural tensions surrounding marital abuse and, in the strain to maintain the domestic ideal, fragments Rachel's identity and provides landmarks by which to examine these tensions. One manifestation of this splintering, her speech, marks the contradictions that proliferate around marital violence.

## A Woman's Word, a Woman's Parole

### A Woman's Word

Rachel's (in)ability to speak becomes a central issue in the novel's negotiation of gender identity, marital relations, violence, and realism. The domestic violence and sensationalism she comes to represent banishes her speech to the margins of recognizability. Though her speech is marked as incomprehensible and Arthur insists he cannot understand her language and behavior, as well as the abuse that provokes them, they are lucid to other characters and are ultimately manifested in even Arthur's domestic domain. Rachel's expulsion to the margins of the system of linguistic communication is an unsuccessful attempt to deny her presence (though the threat of her extermination is real) and ultimately cannot erase the text she speaks; her "mad" gesticulations burst from the novel's sensational scenes, contaminating the novel's realism.

When Rachel threatens Mildmay—"[I]f I had a knife, I could find it in my heart to put an end to your horrid career; and, look you, I will—Coward! I will! I will kill you before you shall lay your vile hands on my child" (I 166)—she articulates not only her threat but his inadequacies and ultimately those of the system that generated him, shattering ideological assumptions along with Mildmay's body when she fires her fatal shot. Anticipated in *Aurora Floyd,* the dangerous woman of *Salem Chapel* directly assaults the source of the violence, not just his representative, unequivocally placing the threat of marital violence and the unsuppressed rage of the abused women in the homes of the well-to-do. Although Mildmay miraculously survives, the exposed sutures in his head, like the visible sutures in the narrative, fail to conceal the revelatory threat posed by Rachel or the fragility of the fabric her characterization deconstructs, undoing the Mildmay (and the Arthur) that was.

Rachel's ability to rend this social fabric terrifies Arthur. In fact, when Arthur recognizes the potentially disruptive effect of her words and behavior, he pursues her with more fervor than he pursues even Mildmay, a character who nearly destroys his sister's reputation and life, who soils his family name, and who indirectly occasions the loss of his career. As a woman with deadly intentions in pursuit of a man, Rachel shocks Arthur's sensibilities—in essence, launches a more profound assault on domesticity than a forger, a kidnapper, a potential bigamist, rapist, and murderer. Arthur's horror becomes clear when he sees Mildmay and Rachel on the same train.

> *That sight quenched the curses on his own lips, paled the fire in his heart. To see her dogging his steps, with her dreadful relentless promise in her eyes, overwhelmed Vincent, who a moment before had thrilled with all the rage of a man upon whom this villain had brought the direst shame and calamity. He could have dashed him under those wheels, plunged him into any mad destruction, in the first passionate whirl of his thoughts on seeing him again; but to see Her behind following af-ter—pale with her horrible composure, a conscious Death tracking his very steps—drove Vincent back with a sudden paralysing touch. (I 359)*

The text of this passage grants Rachel an almost deific mastery. The capitalization in the last sentence of "Her" mimics a pronoun form reserved for God. The "Death" she threatens also takes on mythic proportions. It is not simply her desire to commit murder that repels Arthur, but the tensions that this, in concert with her gender, implies. Rachel brings her sensational threat into what the novel marks as the normative middle-class realism of Arthur's life. Rachel's behavior enfeebles Arthur, creates an unnatural scene he cannot assimilate. He "sat down on the nearest seat he could find, like a man who had been stunned by some unexpected blow. . . . It was a relief to wait, to recover his breath, to realize his own position once more. That dreadful sight, diabolical and out of nature, had driven the very life-blood out of his heart" (I 359).

Indeed, the kind of tension that Rachel creates in the framework of this culture denaturalizes and thus exposes not only the way gender was constructed, but the way the domestic space was articulated and violence was screened solely by a woman's flaws. Arthur, at this moment, abandons his pursuit of Mildmay and literally identifies with him by experiencing Rachel's pursuit from Mildmay's point of view. Rachel's attack becomes more than an assault on Mildmay; it threatens Arthur and the ideology that kept middle- and upper-class men safe from accusations of marital violence. Arthur reckons this a more terrifying threat than the sacrifice of his own sister to a clearly dangerous man. As A. James Hammerton notes, "Wives who chose to resist their husbands, whether physically or passively, effectively challenged authority which enjoyed the backing of a confident and powerful ideological support system. A legal system which encouraged husbands to equates wives' resistance with provocation and forgiveness with condonation of acts of cruelty could produce knotty legal complications" (123). If Arthur murdered Mildmay, the act would have been a socially authorized act of retribution that would have cleansed Arthur's behavior of implications of violence. He would have been offering his sister protection, salvaging his family honor, and validating Susan's role as a passive creature under his care and control, as well as his authority as a lawgiver—maintaining the social and moral codes already in place. Rachel's behavior in this scene not only usurps his authority, but throws into chaos the system that authorizes male violence. The murder Arthur was ready to commit only moments before suddenly becomes a perversion. Rachel does not have the social authorization to enact murder; rather, she seizes the license to perform it based on the lack of limitations to bound her fluid identity, just as sensationalism speaks to questions that are unthinkable in the realm of realism. Rachel's shifting social position produces a sensational performance that offers up a powerful threat to the ideology from which it derives, a threat that alters both Mildmay's and Arthur's behavior, metaphorically bespeaking the power of this literature to alter cultural notions, revisions that would prove their impact on the law.

Arthur attempts early on to silence Rachel, to repress that of which she speaks. When she tries to communicate to him her predicament, he calls her mad, and she responds, "I speak madly, to be sure, but you don't understand me" (I 304). The use of the conjunction "but" implies that others might understand her, a possibility Arthur cannot allow but that the narrative clearly does. He refuses to let her leave to act on her intentions to kill. Rachel attempts to placate him by saying, "We [women] do have meanings now and then, we poor creatures, but they seldom come to much" (I 304). At this point, Arthur acknowledges that he cannot move her with "reason or argument" (I 304).[13] Her sensational, unreal speech leaves him instead "clutch[ing] her hand," hoping to master her physically, foreshadowing his later violence. She pleads for her release, begging "[d]on't disappoint me now. If I see ghosts behind you, what then? Most people that have lived long enough, come to see ghosts before they die" (I 305). These ghosts are the contradictions that haunt their ideology; they threaten Rachel, who dares to betray their presence, and she challenges Arthur, who embodies them, stands in their stead, and delivers their law.[14] Significantly, Arthur's mother responds to Rachel's pleas. Despite the "strange jumble" of Rachel's speech, the thread seems traceable to her. "I am an older woman than you. . . . You have something on your mind. My son is frightened you will do something—I cannot tell what. . . . Come with me" (I 305–6). Arthur responds to his mother's speech and her attempts to engage with Rachel by labeling her discourse as incomprehensible as well: "Mother, mother! what are you saying?" His mother's communication with Rachel, even if broken and unclear, marks Mrs. Vincent's engagement of the threat Rachel poses, and this again terrifies Arthur. He attempts to interrupt his mother's "extraordinary speech" (I 306), silencing the discourse in which she engages with Rachel. He wishes to terminate any exchange of information to reduce the potential taint of madness, the taint of Rachel's characterization on his domestic circle.

After Rachel shoots Mildmay, Arthur endeavors first to silence her, then to reframe her by engaging her word to perform in socially appropriate behavior. He searches Rachel out, calls for the police, and plans to turn her over to the law that has the authority forcibly to reshape her physical body. He ignores the flood of language that she pours out upon him, including her assurances that Mildmay had already vindicated Susan.

Arthur stands firm in his resolution to see her arrested "without taking any notice of what she said. . . . Her words fell upon his ears without any meaning" (I 124). Rachel simply cannot and does not signify to Arthur as long as she refuses to articulate herself within the cultural boundaries with which he wishes her to comply. Though she begs him to "understand what [she has] to say" in her own terms, he emphasizes the irrelevancy of her speech: "It does not matter. . . . What you say can make no difference" (I 126). Clearly, it does make a difference, to Arthur and in the novel as a whole. Rachel's often successful resistance of what Arthur considers socially appropriate suggests that these definitions are crumbling, perhaps simply because of her presence.

Arthur's persistent refusals to acknowledge Rachel leave her in a "speechless suspense and terror, which no words can describe" (II 128). Her terror and silence derive not from the act of attempted murder she has performed, but from the possibility that she will be marked as far outside the realm of comprehensibility, that she will be utterly effaced through execution, imprisonment, or confinement to the madhouse. Arthur's effacement of her lodges Rachel in a site of prostration; it has none of the power gained by the imperfect engagement with the real. Her successful exposure of male violence and translation of the mythology of female violence and retribution into realism threaten to collapse the firm framework Arthur believes holds his culture together. Arthur attempts to compel her back into a proper silence by materializing the ghosts she has seen and fears: "[H]ere arose before her close and real the spectre which she had defied . . . the inexorable man who had it in his power to deliver her over to law and justice" (II 129).

The ghost Rachel faces is Victorian realism, fraught with the contradictions she has exploited and exposed. Arthur, as a representative of this ideology, attempts to force her into submission, offering the threat of punishment that she experienced at Mildmay's hands. He relents and releases Rachel into Lady Western's custody only when that model of submissive and correct womanliness appears. Lady Western's presence makes Rachel "sacred" by merging her identity with that of a woman who clearly falls within the standards of suitable behavior. Arthur readily responds to Lady Western's entreaties; she poses no threat to Arthur or his ideology. Rachel, under the aegis of Lady Western, again attempts to communicate with Arthur. "I daresay he will understand me when I say that I never could have allowed things to go further" (I 136). Rachel agrees to become a tenant of Grange Lane in the home of Lady Western, moving out of the poverty and horror of her Back Grove Street home. She throws off her working-class habiliments, abandoning her life as a "disguised princess." Once she does so, Rachel takes up a distinguishable, articulable, and controlled position. At this point, Arthur finally concedes to carry on a "secret communication" with Rachel that stays only at the level of eye contact, silencing Rachel and allowing her appearances by Lady Western's side to bring her into proper social focus again. Arthur then refers to them both as "Ladies" and urges, " '[I]t is better you should leave this place at once. . . . Don't say anything; either way, talking will do little good. You are her shield and defence,' he said looking at Lady Western, with an excitement which he could not quite keep under. 'When she touches you, she becomes sacred. You will keep her safe— safe? you will not let her go?' " (II 138).

He demands Rachel's silence to ensure her rearticulation within a socially acceptable space. Lady Western's presence lends Rachel's fluid identity shape and allows for her (temporary) absorption into what Arthur conceives of as a safe social space. The only thing Arthur requests of Lady Western is that she maintain Rachel in this state (literally, by providing her with boundaries), continue to formulate her identity, and "not let her go." Absence from Lady Western's side might dissipate Rachel again—threatening to release her unbounded power, unbounded by law and realism, threatening sensational acts that might eradicate Arthur's control.

### A Woman's Parole

By confining Rachel to Lady Western's home, Arthur attempts to confine her to a socially articulated role. When she leaves Lady Western's, however, she moves outside the boundaries of the domestic propriety to which Arthur had restricted her, and she becomes a threat again. Arthur discovers Rachel outside the confines of Lady Western's home and chastises her, arguing that she has broken her word. She responds, "My word! I did not give you my word . . . No. I—I never said—. . . . [T]he laws of honour don't extend to women. We are weak, and we are allowed to lie" (II 188). It is Rachel's weak boundaries, her precarious position, that make her "lie" possible, even inevitable. Her lie, any speech that lies outside the reality Arthur represents, defines her altered boundaries of perception, behavior, and identity and moves her into the realm of sensation. Her pregnant pause, refusing even to speak the promise that might limit her, also betrays her reluctance to make herself Arthur's victim again. However, in his comment, "You are speaking wildly" (II 188), Rachel recognizes that her identity remains beyond the realism in which he attempts to imprison her: inertia in the domestic space. With her daughter's fate still uncertain, Rachel attempts to negotiate a discourse that will offer Arthur the gesture he desires without drawing her back into his stifling realism and back into submission: "'My word! but women are not bound by their honour; our honour means—not our word,' cried Mrs Hilyard, wildly; 'my parole, he means; soldiers and heroes, and men of honour give their parole; you don't exact it from women. Words are not kept to us, Mr Vincent; do you expect us to keep them?'" (II 191).

Rachel cannot grant Arthur the word he calls for. A woman's honor, her chastity, is bound up in her body, not her speech. Rather, she suggests to him her marginalization in the signifying system. What impact could her dangerous speech have, for it circulates only on the edges of the discursive economy that affects him? According to Rachel, women are always already marginalized in this system: "Words are not kept to us . . . do you expect us to keep them?" This marginalization denies her the right to engage actively in the construction of this system, and the parole she offers, like the temporary reprieve of the captured soldier or prison inmate, is her promise to return "home" when her ends are gained.

Although Arthur fears Rachel's permanent escape, she understands what he does not: escape from this framework is ultimately impossible. Although she may temporarily defy it through the repositioning of cultural terms her identity demands, and although her marginalization allows her to behave in unorthodox ways, she is all the while in mortal danger because there is no way to entirely escape the effects of the cultural economy or its punishments, except through madness or death: "Escape! from what? That is the worst—one cannot escape . . . especially if one keeps quiet in one place and has nothing to do" (II 188). Thus Rachel chooses an effective marginalization, a sensational reality. Her identity and language have granted her a slipperiness that opens "unreal" possibilities. If she keeps quiet and does nothing, however, she becomes the im-

potent lady again. Recognizing the difficulty of her conflicted situation—
a choice between passivity and danger—"she repeat[s] with a miserable
cry[:] 'Who can escape? I do not understand what it means. . . . If I should
go mad it will not matter'" (II 191–92). Rachel's subversive identity and
speech acts redefine the possibilities for behavior; she commits the literally unspeakable acts of sensationalism. "Words," as the narrator reminds
us, "[are] the symbols of life" (I 77). The shape of Rachel's life derives
from the tenuous balance of realism and sensationalism she speaks.

She offers, "I promise—upon my honour. I will not go away—
escape, as you call it. . . . You have taken a woman's parole, Mr Vincent . . . it will be curious to note if she can keep it" (II 192). Despite the
fact that she has indicated she cannot be held to her word, Arthur must
accept her "lie" as a lady or admit that the system he tries so desperately
to defend is crumbling. Unsurprisingly, Rachel does not keep her word
and continues to search for her daughter. She approaches Mrs. Vincent
in hopes of discovering Alice's whereabouts and begs the minister's
mother to "Let [her] speak" (II 249), but Mrs. Vincent understands that
Rachel's speech might endanger her own daughter. Indeed, Mrs. Vincent
wishes to believe that the danger Rachel represents caused the loss of
Susan in the first place, rather than recognizing Rachel as the lens through
which she views that danger. Further, Mrs. Vincent recognizes that if
Arthur's connection to Rachel remains intimate, it may be a "danger
more dismal than the one he had just escaped" when he almost lost his
post (II 254). Were Rachel to persist, the domestic space Mrs. Vincent
treasures, with all its illusions intact, might be lost to her again. Rachel
insists that "[i]t was not God who gave [Susan] back to you . . . it was I—
remember it was I" (II 256). Rachel replaces the morality that Mrs. Vincent trained her son to trust with herself, her sensational identity and
methods. This is, however, a futile attempt to draw Mrs. Vincent out
of the system that defends domesticity and into one that splinters it.
Mrs. Vincent no longer identifies (with) Rachel as she had when her domestic circle was shattered and she was searching for Susan. Despite her
previous contact with Rachel she cannot afford to "remember much
about this woman, who [is] strangely unlike other people in Salem"
(II 249) and who recalls the collapse of the domestic space.

That collapse, though it frees her from Mildmay, also denies Rachel
her daughter. Even after her desperate act to save Alice, the girl has "not

a word for [her]. . . . [N]o word, no look, no recognition" (II 252). Once
Rachel has skirted the bounds of cultural discourse, she becomes unfa-
miliar to her own daughter. Mrs. Vincent struggles with the same non-
recognition and becomes more and more distant as Rachel speaks, holding herself aloof from the woman who represents this drama. Rachel's
marginalization seems to make the mentally incapacitated Alice incapable
of knowing her mother: "she could not know me! and I am not beautiful,
like Lady Western, to please a child's eye" (II 189). Lady Western, dis-
cernable to the simple girl because she is easily framed within the cultural
definition of woman/mother, becomes a substitute for Rachel. Mrs. Vincent can only respond with "Who are—you?" Rachel finally recognizes
that Mrs. Vincent could never "understand; how could she? . . . You
never could be like me" (II 256).

Only in the last pages of the novel, after Alice's safe recovery, does
Rachel returns to the space of protracted silence in an attempt to reposition herself as a lady. Because she has agreed to maintain a submissive
silence, Herbert Fordham petitions for her life with Arthur. Despite the
fact that Herbert is a poor arbiter—the two men have both competed for
the heart of Lady Western and bitterly resent one another—Rachel's fate
lies in their hands. She may not appeal to Arthur on her own behalf:
"They think in Grange Lane that it is only a man who can speak to a
man. . . . [H]ere is somebody come to answer for me" (II 297). Herbert,
if Arthur's enemy, is centrally figured in the cultural discourse, and even
though his wedding to Lady Western, on the day he comes to appeal for
Rachel's life, displaces the minister, it also fortifies the system to which
Arthur subscribes, a gesture toward recuperating idealized marriage and
an effect to which Arthur is responsive. Rachel must also submit. She
indicates that she has "come back to life again, [and] must not manage
[her] own affairs. [She is] going back to society and the world" (II 297).
Once she has surrendered again to the system she abandoned, she must
yield to the inaction that binds a lady. However, her reentry into this
framework is dangerous. She must capitulate to the power of men, for
"only a man . . . can speak to a man," and her betrayal of this system
leaves her vulnerable to its punishments because she has "lost her power
over [Arthur]" (II 297), lost her voice and her ability to act.

Thus, when Arthur responds, he "[speaks] to her, but he [looks] at
Fordham" (II 297). His verbalizations reframe Rachel in silence, insisting

on her identification as a lady. Further, when Herbert explains that Mild-may has agreed to keep his attacker secret, Herbert uses a masculine pro-noun in place of Rachel's name. This shift in the identity of the assassin to a masculine figure, something consonant with cultural standards, re-stores order and lifts the responsibility and burden of the crime from Ra-chel, allowing her to be again made realistic, her venom neutralized and denied.[15] She is made a lady. Herbert reports on Mildmay's remarks con-cerning his attacker: "He is conscious of having wronged—him—and will take no steps against—him. This culprit, it appears, must be permit-ted to escape—you think so?—worse evils might be involved if we were to demand—his—punishment. Mr Vincent, I beg you to take this into consideration. It could be no advantage to you; the innocent shall not suffer—but—the criminal—must be permitted to escape" (II 299–300). These "worse evils" are clearly the cultural confusion (perhaps even cul-tural change) attendant upon Mildmay's violence, Rachel's response, and what they imply about the presence of violence in the middle-class do-mestic space. Rachel rushes to correct Herbert's suggestion of freedom, explaining to Arthur the impossibility of complete alienation from the system: "[T]here is no escape—not in this world. . . . The criminal—Mr Vincent—you know—will not escape" (II 300). Significantly, in this portion of the text, Rachel becomes identified as "Mrs. Mildmay" once again. Taking on her position as the worthy wife, she loses the pseudo-nym that protected her from her husband. She reappropriates the identity of wealth and social status that she abandoned when she left her husband and hid under the name of Hilyard; she regains the status of the name Mildmay "in society and the world" (II 297). Herbert offers to "be an-swerable for her appearance" (II 302). Rachel would be placed under the authority of another man who offers to speak for her, to answer for her speech, and to answer for her physical appearance. However, it is not Herbert's speech but Arthur's lack of it that ultimately saves Rachel.

When Mrs. Vincent appears, Rachel requests a mediator because Arthur is "a man and cruel" (II 307). Although Rachel believes it "might be hard to hear the story of her own sin—[it] was harder to be under the stifling sway of one who knew it, and who had it in his power to de-nounce her" (II 308). Arthur, however, will not allow her to speak the narrative of her cultural betrayal. Nor will he speak it himself; to do so would only compound the dilemma in which he sees himself by sanctioning with his authority the dangers she has performed. In addition, Arthur's audience grows. Tozer enters the room and, impatient to attend to the needs of the "flock," demands as well that Rachel must either state a legitimate reason for imposing upon the minister's time or leave: "[I]t's a swindling of [Arthur's] time to come in upon him of a morning if there ain't a good reason" (II 309). Rachel's reasons are outside of reason, precisely that which Arthur prefers to keep silent. She demands again that he narrate her tale: "[W]ould you judge me unworthy of relief because I once came to see him in a morning? That is hard laws; but the minister will speak for me. The minister knows me" (II 311). Arthur remains silent, faced with the challenge of repeating Rachel's sensation within "good reason," within reason itself, a task that would rend the fabric of the boundaries he hopes to defend. He recognizes that she will be less threatening if he quietly returns her to the system from whence she came. Finally, Rachel "got up wearily, leaning on the table, as indeed she needed to lean, and looked into Mrs Vincent's face: 'May I see my child?'" (II 312). Her request for access to Alice assures Arthur that she will maintain her proper position in order to ensure her contact with her daughter. This act also defines her as nonthreatening and socially manageable. She becomes a needy and disempowered mother—a level of effacement that comforts Arthur. Mrs. Vincent then envelops Rachel as Lady Western had before her. "In [Mrs. Vincent's] tender presence there was protection and shelter even for the passionate spirit beside her. Thus the two went away together" (II 312). Once Rachel is reencompassed in the proper womanly identity, Arthur is divested of the "office of an avenger" (II 312). No longer must he bear the threat of Rachel's speech. With relief he recognizes that she is "out of his hands" (II 312).

## Abductions and Violent Love-making

Arthur's difficulties do not end with Rachel, however; the revolutionary aspect of her behavior is her effect on the narrative overall. Her appearance exposes the contradictions in the domestic ideology of his own middle-class family. His sister, Susan, the pure English girl, becomes the marker of the contamination that Rachel represents. Significantly, the taint is no longer confined to the woman in the precarious social position. A middle-class icon has been adulterated—not by Rachel's presence (they meet only in the wake of Susan's troubles) but by the rifts that Rachel exposes in the ideology of the domestic space. Rachel's husband, Colonel Mildmay, under a pseudonym, courts and finally kidnaps Susan in hopes of making her his bigamous bride. Although she returns in a near frozen, statuelike state of emotional horror, Arthur attempts to deny the sexual violence evidenced all around him. Despite the early tokens of violence in the novel—he has heard a man threaten to kill Rachel; the identity of Susan's fiancé has been called into question, implying sexual misconduct and danger; and his own research has only increased the causes for concern—Arthur defiantly resists the material evidence of danger: "He consoled himself with the thought that these were not the days of abductions or violent love-making. To think of an innocent English girl in her mother's house as threatened with mysterious danger, such as might have surrounded a heroine of the last century, was impossible" (I 150). This self-conscious representation of violence as fictive, an assertion the narrative itself rends at the seams, brings the question of sensationalism to bear fully upon the Victorian notion of reality. The novel displays as fictive the thin veneer between the sensational representation of marital violence and the material experiences of women.

Even Arthur admits the danger in this ghostly rift that is scarcely articulable in his reality. He describes this place as a "dark unknown existence that throbbed and echoed all around," pointing to "those dark streets and houses which hid so many lives and hearts and tragic histories" (I 160). These tragic histories, however, remain silent or marked as unreal sensation, protecting the culture from an awareness of the fissures and contradictions in this ideology, particularly the material dangers affecting women. When Arthur spins his tale of the dark unknown, his homely Salem Chapel audience responds with breathless interest. They are "startled, frightened and enchanted. If they had been witnessing a melodrama, they scarcely could have been more excited" (I 162). The encapsulation of this narrative as a melodrama matches Arthur's attempts to make sexual violence a fantasy, a creation of the fiction writer's mind. The novel ultimately challenges the mythic Victorian (and contemporary) sense of reality that denies the presence of that which his culture defines as fearful and horrific. The presentation of these horrors as sensational realities blurs the boundaries between sensation and the real.

Oliphant's own attempts to recreate reality in fiction suggest that the real may be presented in fictional form, melding "Art" and "Nature" ("Sensation Novels" 567), a comparison that in itself threatens the boundaries between them. By collapsing these boundaries in *Salem Chapel,* the novel calls into question "realistic" Victorian notions of gendered violence in the domestic space and blurs the distinction between the sensation Oliphant rejected and the realism she embraced. Thus when Arthur remarks for the second time, after he has been warned about the identity of Susan's suitor, "Nobody could carry [Susan] off, or do any act of violence; and as for taking advantage of her solitude, Susan, a straightforward, simple-minded English girl, [is] safe in her own pure sense of right" (I 209), the irony in his comments sounds profoundly against his recognition of the dangers in his culture. Further, Susan's Englishness and femininity not only fail to protect her, but because the myths of these discourses suggest that they should protect her, Arthur ignores the possibility of a kidnapping, and she falls into increasing danger. Neither can Mrs. Vincent articulate the possibility of sexual violence. When she mentions the threat Colonel Mildmay poses to Susan, she cannot conclude her statements and only calls out Arthur's name, as if hoping to reinforce the ideology he represents: " 'As for Susan going astray—or being carried off—or falling into wickedness—Arthur!' said his mother, putting back her veil from her pale face" (I 308). By replacing the evils that might follow with "Arthur," she not only makes their effacement by this ideology clear, but aligns Arthur with them. Her comments draw aside the veil, exposing the material danger despite the cultural mythology that urges her daughter's safety.

Arthur also attempts to derive comfort, once Susan returns home an accused murderer and a fallen woman, by claiming Susan's experience and remarking the story. He converts it into his narrative (something the narrative does not do by leaving his retelling out of the novel; in this way the text again demythologizes Susan's story and defies Arthur's attempt to diffuse its horror). This conversion makes the possibility of battery, rape, and kidnapping appear more like discourses over which he has control, banishing them into the realm of the sensation that Arthur refuses to acknowledge as real. He normalizes Susan's experience, editing out tensions in the events, making the only "sensation" in them one of his own comfort. Arthur visits a lawyer and perceives "with a sensation of comfort at his heart, that his story interested the acute attorney, accustomed to the tricks and expedients of crime. . . . The minister himself grew steadier as he entered into his narrative. . . . Under his touch, Susan's dreadful position became one not unprecedented, to be dealt with like any other condition of actual life" (II 95). The question of whose touch leaves Susan's story changed is an interesting one. Certainly, the lawyer's steadiness as Arthur tells his tale implies that the lawyer's calm impacts Arthur's perception of the narrative. The indeterminate referent of "*his* narrative" offers us another interpretation, however. Arthur himself gains control of the tale by reproducing it under his own terms to an authority figure who reframes portions of it in the context of the "tricks and expedients of crime." By placing the difficulties under the rubric of tricks and expedients, Arthur endeavors to erase that which he has expelled to the sensational, drawing the rest into "actual life." Actual life, by this definition, is life in the absence of the dark unknown of sexual violence, the ruptures of the domestic fabric, that Arthur so desperately attempts to marginalize again and again. Certainly, Susan's experience could not be bound by the notions of actual life upon which this discourse builds understanding. For Arthur, such events simply cannot happen to a "straightforward, simple-minded [middle-class] English girl . . . safe in her own pure sense of right" (I 209).

### Sensational Cruelty

The representation of these events, regardless of the fictive or nonfictive character, created culturewide distress. *Salem Chapel* crested the wave of increasing concerns over such representations. In 1859, when considering the difficulties of the Divorce Act, the House of Lords returned continually to the threat of women fictively representing cruelty in divorce cases. These representations were considered serious abuses (rather than violence itself being considered the serious abuse). The mere association of divorce with cruelty might create discursive dilemmas: Was not cruelty a man's right in a relationship of ownership? Was cruelty legal grounds for divorce? Might a woman actually speak of and critique her husband's cruelty?

> *[Lord Campbell] opposed [the] provision [of cruelty in the Divorce Act], because he believed it would be attended with great social danger;*

*he now found that it was the practice in every case where a woman sued*
*for separation on the ground of adultery that she invariably added cru-*
*elty, and sought for the dissolution of the marriage. That, he thought,*
*was a most disastrous consequence, and he called for the earnest consid-*
*eration of their Lordships. Another point requiring careful attention was*
*whether the Court should not have power to sit* foribus clausis, *so that*
*the details of cases of a certain character should not be made public.*[16]

This great social danger was the mere representation of violence in the
sanctified middle- and upper-class domestic scene. This danger was so
pressing and so severe that Lord Campbell felt Parliament should suppress
the publication of this information, preventing the questioning of the
terms of realism and violence, preventing the spread of this potential contaminant, and denying public access to any images of women responding
to cruelty or brutality with demands of protection or a willful desire to
escape. Three years later, only a year before the publication of *Salem
Chapel,* the fear that the publication of these cases would impact public
perception and behavior was realized. In the second reading of the Divorce Court Bill, the Earl of Derby urged that the Divorce Act had only
compounded the sensationalism of earlier cases of parliamentary acts for
divorce. Despite hopes that making divorce a legal hearing as opposed to
a costly parliamentary act would reduce its notoriety, "the Bill had failed
to fulfil all the objects which its promoters had in view. Its effect certainly
had not been greatly to diminish the scandal arising from the publication
of very many indelicate and some indecent cases. Indeed for one such
case previous to the passing of the Act there were now at least twenty
which were just as freely published in the newspapers."[17] The explosion
of this discourse made it increasingly difficult to deny that proper middle-
and upper-class British homes could bear traces of inappropriate, legally
condemnable violence, and that this violence betrayed the boundary of
the working-class limitations Parliament had articulated. Even what Parliament dubbed the "fictional" presentation of an abusive home threatened to rend not only the well-established silences, deafness, and denial,
but the notions of what was fictional. If fictional accounts could appear
in real divorces, might not real accounts appear in sensational/fictional
representations? The publication of novels such as *Salem Chapel,* in concert with the rapidly shifting legal debates and cultural notions of physical

abuse, began to expose the rifts in the ideology, threatening a shift in the authority of the husband in the home, as well as the notion of a wife's province of behavior. They betrayed the boundaries of class and respectability, marking Arthur as a participant in the same kind of violence a working-class "rough" might enact. Most centrally, they disrupted the understanding of what was realistic and what was sensational. Susan's response to these dilemmas becomes a telling rift in itself, one that perhaps offers an alternative approach to marital violence that, unlike Rachel's, does not threaten the disintegration of a woman's identity or body.

### The Marble Woman

Throughout *Salem Chapel,* Mildmay and Arthur endanger Rachel with increasing virulence. She risks violent reclamation to propriety every time she betrays cultural standards in her speech and behavior. Utter silence, which would have eradicated her ability to act on her own behalf or her daughter's, nonetheless becomes the position for which she must finally settle to ensure her safety after her most threatening transgressions. Arthur's sister, Susan, who is marked by the rifts Rachel materializes, represents another formula of self-preservation, not one of fluid, solvent boundaries but of impermeable ones as "the marble woman." A more passive form of defiance, it has as its central manifestation a maintenance of Susan's identity as a gentlewoman, yet it threatens to expose the contradictions Rachel embodies if she is endangered. When Arthur, the police, and Susan's attending physician seek to draw her into compliance, she exposes the rifts they hope to suture, terrifying them and resisting their attempts at control. There are costs to her resistance. Her course of action is limited and she remains in danger, but it is ultimately through this position that Susan attains authority to govern her own behavior (within certain, perhaps wider, boundaries) at the novel's close.

After Rachel shoots Mildmay, Susan escapes and wends her way back to her family. She arrives an altered person and a murder suspect: "Ghastly white, with fixed dilated eyes—with a figure dilated and grandiose—like a statue stricken into marble, raised to grandeur" (II 50). The narrative articulates her as a marble creature over and over again. Her marmoreal state, like a step in the process of her evolution, the hardened chrysalis, prevents others from interacting with her or harming her and alleviates the necessity of response or responsibility on her part. Bound firmly into a single position, Susan does not have to take the risks of dangerous speech that Rachel did. No language passes in to her, and none passes out. In this state, she may not be taken into custody by the police, further insulted, or assaulted.

Although making her inaccessible to physical assault, her marble-ization and silence become a screen for Mildmay's violence, her fall, and even murder. Even in her lifeless state, her unresponsiveness, her unwillingness to reaffirm the absence of violence and the domestic ideology, makes her dangerous, larger than life: "She was a grand form as she lay there upon that bed—might have loved to desperation—fallen—killed" (II 58). Although she lies on the verge of death herself, the text never reads that Susan might have "*been* loved to desperation—been raped—been killed." Rather, as the dangerous woman, she still threatens—a pattern repeated throughout the sensation novel—and she bears the brunt of the punishment for Mildmay's offenses, but she is framed differently than Rachel, firmly bounded in the middle class. Despite the fact that the police know of Mildmay's misrepresentations and the kidnapping, and believe Susan was raped, she alone is the subject of the police's investigation. A woman simply has no just cause for an attempt on a man's life.

Susan's socially characterized evolution, the beliefs others hold about the circumstances that remain unknown to them, subscribes to the role of the woman torturer in the masochistic fantasy. According to Gilles Deleuze, women in this fantasy must pass through a stage of marbleization, just as Susan does, in order to be fitted for the role they will play as the oral mother, who "nurtures and brings death" (55). They evolve a "marble body, [they are] women of stone" (53). Ironically, this form of expression in Masoch's work was not, like Sade's, reviled and condemned, but rather was "fêted and honored. . . . Even the blatantly masochistic elements in his work gained acceptance" (26). Further, many of Masoch's novels were published from mid to late century in the Victorian period, following on the heels of the sensation phenomenon. Not surprisingly, however, Deleuze's analysis of the woman torturer in the masochistic fantasy reveals that she is not a sadist, but rather an element of the masochist's fantasy. Although "the masochistic hero appears to be educated and fashioned by the authoritarian woman . . . basically it is he who forms her, dresses her for the part and prompts the harsh words she addresses to him. It is the victim who speaks through the mouth of his torturer" (22). He attempts in this way to expunge the power of the Oedipal father by destroying it within himself. Susan becomes positioned as an active danger ("[she] loved to desperation—[fell]—killed") despite the fact that she alone has been acted upon and endangered.

Susan's identification as active and dangerous prevents the necessity of marking out Mildmay's abusive behavior as unacceptable, illegal, or inappropriate. Even though Susan is innocent of murder and has not been raped, she must bear the burden of this taint. In order for the law to press this responsibility upon her, however, she must be brought into the social and legal discourse that defines these functions, an attempt that fails. Just as her resistant silence around her sensational story was safely articulated by Arthur when he reframed the narrative for the lawyer, Susan's doctor vies to assert his authority, to force her to take responsibility for her "acts."

Dr. Rider cuts Susan's marbleized arm to release the discourse she has withheld, to force her across the boundary of this silence that protects her and back into the social community. This attempt, however, yields some unexpected and troubling results. When the doctor cuts her vein with a lancet,

> [t]he touch acted like magic. In another moment she had struggled up out of her mother's grasp, and thrown out the arm, from which the blood flowed, up above her head: the crimson stream caught her wild eye as she raised her arm in the air. A convulsive shudder shook her frame. She threw herself over on her face with a cry of horror, far more than a match, in her strength of youth and passion, for the agitated arms that held her. "Mother, mother, mother! it is his blood! it is his life!" cried that despairing voice. . . . [Dr. Rider] shuddered at the touch of that white woman's hand as he bound up the wounded arm. He withdrew his eyes from the pallid grandeur of the stricken face. In spite of himself, horror mingled with his pity. (II 61)

His touch results in an explosion of boundaries only rivaled by Rachel's. Further it employs the same metaphor as Rachel's boundarilessness, doubling in Susan's bleeding arm, Rachel's bleeding fingers. Susan's gushing blood catalyzes her gushing speech, emphasizing again the link between the material and the verbal. However, Dr. Rider does not attain the compliant speech for which he had hoped. Instead it threatens—in the same way Rachel's had—by warning of the murder of an abuser. Just as Rachel's identity had defied social boundaries, so too does Susan's. Just as Rachel had posed a threat to the hegemonic structure of her culture in this posture, Susan does as well. Immediately, Dr. Rider binds up the wound in an attempt to bind her speech, experiencing the same emotions Arthur did when Rachel spoke threateningly: horror and pity. However, the assault of Dr. Rider's lancet's piercing Susan's skin, like a rape, like a beating, has released an unrelenting flood of speech. Susan's response to Dr. Rider is a cry of horror, an attempt to defy the outrage. Her threatening language terrifies Rider, and as her body flies up, asserting itself forcefully, her speech flies up, pouring an "incoherent stream" of language on him as well. Despite its incoherence, however, her speech and posture, like Rachel's, remain dangerous to the man that attends her, and at this point he identifies her as "no longer a girl or innocent" (II 62). He perceives the language she spews as "a heavier stain upon her than those crimson traces on her pearly skin" (II 61). Further, her speech cannot be contained by the boundaries that Arthur and Mrs. Vincent attempt to impose on it after it escapes. Susan's voice, along with her threat, insistently penetrates the "door which hid [her], but did not keep in her cries" (II 88).

Nothing staves off this explosion of language. It forms a striking contrast to the speech that Arthur idealizes, that of Lady Western. Her polite speech, the chattering of an "ignoramus," "kind words" indiscriminately "distributed . . . everywhere" (I 111–13), offers no challenge to Arthur. Arthur, however, repeatedly describes Susan's language as outcries of protest and objection. As long as the police and her own brother and mother see her as the cause of their sorrows, not Mildmay, Susan continues her protest. Arthur must frame her not as a "soft girl, the sudden victim of a bad man," but as a "woman who could avenge herself" (II 90) in order to avoid implicating the system in which he operates. In this frame, Arthur asserts that she had "escaped one horror [rape?] to fall into another yet more horrible" (II 109). Surely, however, escaping an assault with self-defense is not more horrible for Susan but for Arthur, who must be identified with a fallen woman and observe the threat she poses to the domestic ideology that grants only him the power to articulate its frame, and further, conceals any ugly aspects of this ideology, like male violence. Thus, this shift in her articulation, the cries of protest, her "horrible" identity as a woman who would dare to protect herself, produces in Arthur not just "[p]ity and awe; but yet another feeling mingled in the wonder with which he gazed upon her. A thrill of terror came over him" (II 90). She represents the same threat that Rachel does by existing in this state. As long as she "rav[es] with a wild madness which betray[s] in every wandering exclamation the horror upon her soul" (II 62), Dr. Rider and Arthur perceive it as their own horror, something they must fear—she becomes a dangerous woman. Her murderous prose threatens not their bodies directly, for she lies prostrate and immobile, but their authority. It is clear, as the "fictional" reports of abuse disrupting Parliament and the sensation novel disrupting the culture demonstrate, that the public exposure of this discourse lends enough materiality to threaten cultural change. Indeed, when both Arthur and Dr. Rider remark that Susan would be better off dead, it is clear for whom would it be better.

Finally, Arthur physically restrains Susan with the same force he uses with Rachel. When Susan begins to speak her threats explicitly, she releases what even Mrs. Vincent had only held "upon her soul like a frightful, inarticulate shadow" (II 89). Susan calls out in her delirium, reliving the past: "I must, *must* marry [Mildmay] though he has told me lies. I must, whatever he does. Even if I could get through the window and escape; for they will call me wicked. Oh, mamma! and Arthur a minister, and to bring disgrace on *him!* But I am not disgraced. Oh no, no; never, never!—I will die first—I will kill him first. Open the door; oh, open the door! Let me go!" (II 105). At this moment, when she speaks out, threatening to go through the door and cross those boundaries, Arthur "rush[es] forward to control her" (II 105). However, he cannot reign in her speech. As long as Susan is wronged by the threat of punishment, she cries out.

Susan finally becomes silenced again, transformed into a puppet in "dumb apathy" (II 225), when Mildmay's deposition clears her of any wrong and the papers report her absolute innocence. Immediately after Arthur learns of Susan's deliverance, he goes to his sister's room and finds her "lying in an utter quietness which went straight to his heart;—silent, no longer uttering the wild fancies of a distorted brain" (II 173). Her silence relieves him, abates his fears, but the wild fancies have so forcefully invaded his reality that they continue to haunt the narrative.

The silence of women pervades the overt critical resolution of these conflicts. The narrator describes Susan as a "solemn speechless creature" (II 268); Mrs. Vincent has simply "exhausted her language" (II 260), and Rachel becomes "silenced" for the first time in her life (II 302). Susan finally begins to speak again when her speech merges with that of Alice, Rachel and Mildmay's daughter, who on her own speaks only in "strange half-articulate cries" (II 269). Alice, named after Lady Western, parodies her aunt's language, producing literally mindless chatter. Their language mingles, drawing Susan out of her silence, providing an alternative form of operation. Even in this consolidated language, however, Susan marks the ideological rift that cannot be silenced even after they speak no more. In her comment, "Hush! . . . Here are women—women! nobody will harm us" (II 272), Susan implies the danger that derives from men, even in this space of domestic bliss. The operative difference between Rachel and Susan is their position. Rachel, with her working-class garb and rough needlework, is debased, marginalized. Susan, with her firm boundaries, insistently positions herself within the middle-class domestic space and breaks out with sensational danger when facing a threat herself. As the incorporation of sensation within a realistic frame protects the novel from dismissal, yet launches a powerful critique of realism, Susan's internalization both makes her untouchable and exposes the dangers in her brother's home.

### The Dangerous Woman Revisited

Susan speaks again in the conclusion of the novel, and although Rachel temporarily disappears, offering the care, upbringing, and socialization of her child to Susan and Mrs. Vincent, the dangerous rifts she and Susan reveal are not limited to brief outbursts within the narrative; rather, they alter the very nature of the narrative itself. Both Susan and Rachel return, if not triumphantly then steadily, retaining some of the authority they had earlier demonstrated. When Arthur sees Susan again for the first time, he notes that she is a "grand figure, large and calm and noble like a Roman woman" (II 349). The Romanlike marble statuesqueness keeps her firmly within ideological boundaries but evokes the threat that lurks beneath the surface. Further, her voice, like the blood that flows from her and Rachel, exposing the ideological rifts, becomes "liquid" and "fuller than the common tones of women" (II 351). She and Alice learn to communicate "in a kind of dual, harmonious movement of sound" (II 352). Neither of them is silent; neither of them is like a "beautiful mist" to be dispersed by the burning light of day. Susan notes their mutual empowerment: "Somehow most people mind me now, because I am so big, I suppose; and Alice, instead of being foolish, is a little wise woman" (II 351). Susan's authority remains present in such a way that Arthur senses, but does not feel obliged to (or able to?) suppress, it. He feels "glad to escape from Susan's eyes, which somehow looked as if they were a bit of the sky, a deep serene blue" (II 351). Although his fear has transformed into something manageable, he cannot simply put her aside and instead becomes "fascinated" (II 350), perhaps by her power to walk this ideological line.

Ultimately, Rachel's influence on the Vincent family amounts to much more than a taint. The relationship between the Vincents and Mildmays demonstrates that middle-class propriety is no safe haven from sexual violence, nor are the values inculcated in this realm protection against the evolution of a dangerous woman in its midst. It reveals that sensationalism lies at the heart of the proper middle-class home and at the center of a new form of realism. Rachel's involvement, in fact, reveals and makes possible a transformation of the next generation, the Vincents' daughter and her own, revising prescriptions of what women may do to protect themselves from harm by exposing the flaws in a system that assures their safety. Unlike Aurora Floyd, who has committed no crime, or Lady Audley, who is "buried alive," Rachel becomes an assassin, but still maintains her position in polite society, a new mode for the novel and a reflection of cultural changes, as well as a demand for more. That demand, embodied by Susan, offers a renegotiation of this dangerous speech and retains for Susan a significant portion of the power that she gained during her battle of wills with Mildmay and her brother. Finally, despite the fact that Rachel's acts of retribution are never represented within the frame of the narrative, their powerful effects are. Mildmay refuses to speak her name as the criminal, and she remains free to live the life she has chosen, the better life for which she longs. Significantly, we also learn in the last moments of the narrative that Rachel will be the guardian of her daughter again.

Oliphant's representation of Rachel's story does more than entangle her in the incongruities that draw sensation into realism, but in effect makes sensationalism more real. Furthermore, abused women who are wealthy and decorous like Rachel, "born to the name of Rachel Russell, the model English wife" (I 307), and Susan, who spring from the starched propriety of a middle-class minister's family, fail to rescue the ideology when they return to the domestic space with their gentlewomanly identities intact. In fact, the sensation that so clearly lies beneath the surface of Susan's marbled exterior, the grandness that fascinates Arthur, infuses her supposedly realist characterization. By the close of the novel, by blurring the lines between fiction, fictional representation, and realism, between sensationalism and Nature, the female characters do have a response to the inexorability of men, a response that keeps them within the bounds of propriety.

*Salem Chapel,* an amalgamation of cultural tensions and the social efforts to contain those tensions, appeared in the immediate wake of the sensation rage. In an attempt to provide an alternative to sensation, Oliphant exposed how fragile the boundaries she critiqued were. Further, she demonstrated how sensational dissent and confusion could evolve out of a picture of life. Perhaps her choice to entitle the novel after the Dissenting chapel itself marks her recognition of some of these tensions, and the predicaments the novel lays bare. Ultimately, these topics moved out of the confinements of sensation, finding their way into the law and into fiction earmarked, by both contemporary and period critics, as the quintessence of realism. In the years following the sensation fiction of the 1860s, other writers such as George Eliot began to delve into these issues as well. In the next chapter, I examine Eliot's *Daniel Deronda* to view the way in which realist fiction in the wake of the era of sensation approached the subject of sexual violence.

# V

## Gwendolen's Madness: Sensational Performance and Reasonable Fear in *Daniel Deronda*

*Behind the slim girl Bertha, whose words I watched for, whose touch was bliss, there stood continually that Bertha . . . with the barren selfish soul laid bare; no longer a fascinating secret, but a measured fact, urging itself perpetually on my unwilling sight. Are you unable to give me your sympathy—you who read this? Are you unable to imagine this double consciousness at work within me, flowing on like two parallel streams which never mingle their waters and blend into a common hue?*

—George Eliot, *The Lifted Veil*

### Sensation and Realist Fiction: The Novels of George Eliot

Sensation novels introduced into the discourse of Victorian Britain a language of sexual violence in the middle and upper classes and a reconceptualization of realism that shaped and was shaped by the social and political debates over women's autonomy, authority, and political rights. However, these novels were simultaneously marginalized by their identification as sensation. In part because of the distance these novels seemed to maintain from mainstream ideology, writers in this genre were granted a great deal of discretionary freedom in working through questions that were beyond the pale—and they used it. The sensation genre directly discussed and depicted marital violence, both emotional and physical, as well as its consequences and the constellation of screens that surrounded it in polite society. Decried as a less significant genre during the Victorian period, despite its popularity, the sensation novel generated and was generated by "unseemly" political concerns that lay outside the realm of the so-called serious artist. After the advent of sensation, however, the tone of realist fiction shifted, and within the bounds of the respectable, high-culture, realist novel, sexual violence appeared in new terms.

George Eliot's thoroughly canonized novel *Daniel Deronda* allows us to examine the ways in which sensation novels altered the discourse of realist fiction[1] and the social ideology of the period, in part because Eliot provides a remarkably apt deconstruction of the terms that marginalized sensation, denying both its influence and significance in Victorian literature. Eliot's novella *The Lifted Veil* charges the reader to imagine the horror of a life in which one man can see, without reserve, beyond social proprieties and into the minds of his peers. It suggests Eliot's early interest in uncovering the ordinarily unseen, that which was obscured by polite conventions. Written just after *Adam Bede*, *The Lifted Veil* was not published for five years because of the discomfort the lead character's supernatural vision caused Eliot's publishers, yet she repeatedly stressed that the ideas and concerns in the novel were of great importance to her, and it was ultimately published with *Silas Marner* and *Brother Jacob*. This early work is no aberration, as many critics have suggested (Gray 70); Eliot's concerns with lifting the veil of sociability run throughout her fiction. Primarily considered a realist author,[2] Eliot incorporates the tensions of the sensation novel surrounding violence, gender, and class identity, along with those between sensation and realism, to give us the uncanny sight of *The Lifted Veil* in her final novel, *Daniel Deronda*. Published in 1876 (following the explosion of sensation fiction in the '60s and early '70s) and set in the midst of the sensation years, *Daniel Deronda* presents the life of Gwendolen Harleth and her husband's mysterious and sensational death alongside a seemingly distinct plot line of a young man's search for religion and truth.[3] Eliot's letters demonstrate that she was aware of the sensation novel and had "looked into three or four novels to see what the world was reading" in her research for *Daniel Deronda*.[4] Significantly, she also noted of her own work that she "melt[ed] off the outlines of things" (*George Eliot Letters* 5 : 367, qtd. in Rowe, 10), blurring the boundaries and blending these plot lines and the terms they encompass,[5] sensation and the real. In this way, *Daniel Deronda* provides a critique of the legal and social separation of sensation and realism.

### The Screens of Violence

Gwendolen Harleth, the "spoiled child," performs the part of a great actress and, in fact, becomes the star of her own sensational story within the novel. Gwendolen is a clever manipulator of circumstance and language, and her social success derives not so much from her beauty as from her wit and precocity. Courted by a seemingly cold and dispassionate man, Henleigh Grandcourt, who is the presumptive heir to titles and fortune, Gwendolen rejects his suit and flees when she discovers that he has a lover and four children. Suddenly stricken with poverty as a result of a failed financial investment, she searches for alternatives to provide herself and her family with a sufficient income. When she is unable to secure a satisfying position and is discouraged from pursuing a professional career in acting, Gwendolen marries Henleigh and embarks on a life in which she sacrifices her customary imperial authority and bends to the subtle and severe commands of her husband.[6] Finally, wishing him dead for cruelties she cannot articulate—particularly to Daniel Deronda, who has become her confidant—she believes herself to have murdered Henleigh by supernaturally making her "wish appear outside of [her]" (761). Although the novel culminates in what many critics have described as a sensational plot line, Eliot calls this easy appellation into question by exposing the screens in Henleigh's cruel behavior, making the things that Gwendolen and her society seem unwilling to articulate in polite language flood into that discourse by the novel's close.

### *The Perfect Gentleman*

Henleigh never does anything for which one might call into question his title as a gentleman. Although he has fathered children with a married woman and fails to legitimize them when granted the opportunity, even the punctilious rector of Pennicote and Gwendolen's uncle, Reverend Gascoigne, can find no fault in Henleigh's behavior: "Whatever Grandcourt had done, he had not ruined himself; and it is well known that . . .

a man who has the strength of mind to leave off when he has only ruined others, is a reformed character" (125). Eliot emphasizes Henleigh's remarkable self-management and lack of passion, the narrator commenting that "the English fondness for reserve will account for much negation; and Grandcourt's manners with an extra veil of reserve over them might be expected to present the extreme type of national taste" (467). These characteristics would seem to suggest that Henleigh is incapable of violence as Parliament and much of the culture imagined it.[7] Indeed, Eliot emphasizes Henleigh's hatred of the appearance of violence. When he engages in a frustrating discussion with his abandoned lover, Lydia Glasher, the narrator notes that "there was nothing [Henleigh] hated more than to be forced into anything like violence even in words: his will must impose itself without trouble" (396). His refusal to elevate his voice, his insistence on behaving within the bounds of decency by providing liberally for his former lover and their children, and his generosity in granting Gwendolen all a woman of her debased stature "could expect" seem to mark his propriety in all arenas. However, the narrative exposes Henleigh's cruelty and violence through the critique of his rational and calm behavior and the reason and realism that advocate and screen it.

### Exposure: The Contradiction of Terror

Through Gwendolen's tortured articulations, the narrative dismantles reason and composure as blinds for violence, drawing to the surface the contradictions Gwendolen experiences between reason and her sensations by pairing her expressions of terror in and about her marriage with oppositional terms of self-assertion or power. From the beginning of her relationship with Henleigh, Gwendolen's behavior changes. For the first time in her life, and well before she learns of Henleigh's lover, she is overcome with indecision. She experiences difficulty in "fulfil[ling] her deliberate intention[s]" with regard to Henleigh; suddenly her "favourite key of life—doing as she liked—seemed to fail her" (174). The strong-willed Gwendolen cannot express her will, nor can she discern the reason why.

These signs become increasingly apparent as the relationship progresses. When their small community discerns that Henleigh means to propose to Gwendolen, Gwendolen's contradictory impulses rise to the surface. Henleigh suggests a walk away from a group gathering, securing the opportunity to speak to her alone, and Gwendolen feels "rather pleased, and yet afraid" at his invitation (170). In a gesture that indicates her discomfort with Henleigh rather than pleasure at their intimacy, Gwendolen snatches up her whip "automatically" as they leave and "giv[es] a harder grasp to the handle." One of the only scenes that furnishes a description of Gwendolen's carrying a whip in Henleigh's presence, it features Gwendolen's awkward manipulation of the implement, an indication of her crumbling preeminence.[8] As Henleigh steers toward a marriage proposal, Gwendolen notes that, like plants, "women must stay where we grow, or where the gardeners like to transplant us. . . . [T]hat is the reason why some of them have got poisonous" (171). Suggesting the ability of even a passive plant to cause injury, Gwendolen "lightly whip[s] the rhododendron bush in front of her" (171), evoking her fear of the threat men pose to the stationary womanly plant and simultaneously playing out the possibility of male threat and (her own) female response. Sensing that the seemingly passive Henleigh may have a whip of his own, she repeats the gesture when he suggests that she must care about him, and then in a startlingly direct deconstruction of the terms, Eliot offers up this translation of the following events:

> *"You do care, then" said Grandcourt. . . . "Ha! my whip!" said Gwendolen in a little scream of distress. She had let it go—what could be more natural in a slight agitation?—and—but this seemed less natural in a gold-handled whip which had been left altogether to itself—it had gone with some force over the immediate shrubs. . . . She could run down now, laughing prettily, and Grandcourt was obliged to follow; but she was beforehand with him in rescuing the whip, and continued on her way to the level ground, when she paused and looked at Grandcourt with an exasperating brightness in her glance, and a heightened colour, as if she had carried a triumph. (172)*

The strange conjunction of conjunctions—"what could be more natural in a slight agitation?—*and*—*but* this seemed less natural"—emphasizes the tensions in what is natural in this moment. Gwendolen's unusual inability to manage a socially appropriate motion to abate her discomfort leaves her awkwardly escaping Henleigh. Gwendolen simply has no natural formula to which to resort in order to dissipate her fear nor a reasonable explanation to justify it. The novel offers this paradoxical distress marked by unconventional imagery of violence while reinforcing Henleigh's adherence to social convention. Henleigh behaves with the utmost propriety, and Gwendolen whips the feminine foliage. Further, Gwendolen must sacrifice her gold-handled whip to escape, and it is only with some effort that she can rescue it—one last time—from Henleigh's hands. She must, in fact, sacrifice naturalness in order to regain it momentarily. Socially contradictory terms, violence and propriety may not appear together in the same structure, particularly not when the proposal of an advantageous marriage is imminent. However, here they meet and produce feelings of terror for which Gwendolen has difficulty accounting.

Later, when Gwendolen receives a note indicating that Henleigh is coming to propose marriage, she wonders whether it is "triumph she [feels] most or terror" (337). This pattern of conflicted terms appears again when Henleigh arrives: "Whatever was accepted as consistent with being a lady she had no scruple about; but from that dim region of what was called disgraceful, wrong, guilty, she shrank with mingled pride and terror" (342). The boundaries of a lady's behavior offer her a frame through which she can comprehend and understand the world around her. However, when behavior, language, or thought falls outside of those bounds, into that dim region that remains virtually inarticulable, Gwendolen begins to feel terror—not horror, disgust, or confusion, but terror.

The narrator reinforces Henleigh's connection to Gwendolen's paradoxical experiences by providing another instance of this complex feeling following the couple's marriage. As Daniel Deronda ponders Henleigh's power over Gwendolen and the contradictory nature of her response to him, the narrator describes Henleigh as follows: "Grandcourt had a delusive mode of observing whatever had an interest for him, which could be surpassed by no sleepy-eyed animal on the watch for prey. . . . If Grandcourt cared to keep any one under his power he saw them out of the corners of his long narrow eyes, and if they went behind him, he had a constructive process by which he knew what they were doing there. He knew perfectly well where his wife was, and how she was behaving" (465). Gwendolen, however, responds to Henleigh's attempts at complete control with a combination of "perilously-poised terror with defiance" (467). The reappearance of terror in this formulation highlights Henleigh's predatorlike observance and control of Gwendolen. A trope in sensation novels that emphasizes a fear of abuse within the domestic space and a woman's potentially dangerous response, terror invokes the tensions at the heart of *Daniel Deronda*. Gwendolen is "frightened at everything" in her new life with Henleigh, but she is equally frightened at herself. She explains, "When my blood is fired I can do daring things—take any leap; but that makes me frightened at myself" (508). Her fear is the same terror that her counterparts in sensation fiction feel and inspire: she fears that her terror of her husband will drive her to murder him.[9] The mingling of these seeming contradictions—terror and defiance, terror and triumph, and terror and pride—collapses the distinction between them. This collapse forms one avenue through which the novel critiques the frail social boundaries that safely frame sexual violence well outside of propriety. Language serves as another avenue through which Eliot launches this critique.

### The Unspoken Threat

Gwendolen's fear of Henleigh derives in part from what Eliot describes as his "two remarkably different voices." One is a "superficial interrupted drawl suggestive chiefly of languor and *ennui*"; the other, suggesting the "sleepy-eyed animal on watch for prey," is one of "subdued, inward, yet distinct tones,[10] which [his intimates would] recognise as the expression of a peremptory will" (162). It is, in fact, Henleigh's public voice of ennui that first attracts Gwendolen. The only characteristics she points out to her mother to define her acceptance of his advances revolve around his speech. "He is quiet and distingué," she remarks gravely (175). Henleigh's public reticence and silence, however, operate much differently than the simple absence of commanding speech. Even before they marry, Gwendolen begins to lose the mastery and animation characteristic of her own speech as she becomes silenced in Henleigh's presence. Her mother notices an unusual lack of satire in her discussions of Henleigh; in fact, she remains in "total silence about his characteristics" (167). Further, Gwendolen herself notices that he "caused her unusual constraint [and] that she was less daring and playful in her talk with him than any other admirer she had known" (173). During his proposal to her, Gwendolen finds difficulty in expressing herself; in fact, at the moment of his offer she "remained quite pale . . . and with her hands folded before her stood in silence" (347). She realizes that Henleigh has left her no room for any other answer but yes, and "wait as long as she would, how could she contradict herself? What had she detained him for? He had shut out any explanation. 'Yes' came as gravely from Gwendolen's lips as if she had been answering to her name in a court of justice" (348). Henleigh's request seems entirely reasonable; she would not only contradict herself, but her culture, indeed, the entire system of reason around which her culture operates. Not only is Henleigh forcing her to say yes, but for a rational, reasoning person within this frame, there simply is no other answer.

As Gwendolen becomes increasingly silenced and her answers to Henleigh's questions formulate his desired responses, his private voice becomes increasingly apparent to her. Eliot defines Henleigh's private voice as his peremptory voice. "Peremptory" derives etymologically from the Latin terms "destructive" and "deadly" and is also a legal term that indicates a bar to further action. Henleigh's absolute and dictatorial commands bar Gwendolen's behavior, becoming deadly threats to which she must remain passive and mute. However, his speech remains subdued, inward, not conspicuously harsh, not triggering the well-articulated social cues of violence. Rather, Henleigh's speech itself becomes a threat to Gwendolen: "His words had the power of thumbscrews and the cold touch of the rack" (745).

We see the first evidence of this dangerous speech after the couple is married. Henleigh wishes Gwendolen to wear the family diamonds that his former lover, Lydia, has sent her. Lydia has secretly enclosed an acidic critique of Gwendolen and of the marriage she had promised Lydia she would not make. Overcome with horror and guilt, Gwendolen protests to Henleigh that she does not want to wear the jewels.

> *"What you think has nothing to do with it," said Grandcourt, his* sotto voce *imperiousness seeming to have an evening quietude and finish, like his toilet. "I wish you to wear the diamonds."*
>
> *"Pray excuse me; I like these emeralds," said Gwendolen, frightened in spite of her preparation. That white hand of his which was touching his whiskers was capable, she fancied, of clinging around her neck and threatening to throttle her; for her fear of him . . . had reached a superstitious point. (481)*

Henleigh's language has the polish and icy composure of his appearance, betraying nothing within the frame of their cultural mores, yet infusing Gwendolen with not simply a vague fear, but an emotion that, although impossible to justify with his literal comments, fills her with a dread of losing her life. The absence/presence of Henleigh's violence points up the difficulties of its representation within the frame of realism. Gwendolen's fear becomes one of superstition because she cannot contain it within the linguistic frame she understands as reality. Gwendolen knows well that "she had neither devices at her command to determine his will, nor any rational means of escaping it" (480). Reason, rationality, reality can provide her with no way of skirting his fusion of gentility and violence.[11]

Gwendolen's inability to express Henleigh's danger does not prevent its insistent presence in her life. When Henleigh breaks a promise to her by inviting to their home a man whom she finds repugnant, she wishes to oppose Henleigh but fears it. "Gwendolen's heart began to beat violently. . . . She was as frightened at a quarrel as if she had foreseen that it would end with throttling fingers on her neck." Despite her desire to respond as "one wants to return a blow," she answers in a "tone rather of defeat than resentment" (626). She feels the force of this "blow," and remains powerless to respond, defeated as if she had been in a physical battle. When Gwendolen later offends Henleigh, she has the "expectation that she [is] going to be punished." And indeed his punishment comes in the form of a "silence which was formidable with omniscience" (674).[12] He wishes her to match his strict silence and keep her "unrealistic" fears to herself. Her struggle with these desires and the conflicts she experiences give him "intense satisfaction in leading his wife captive," and her "private protest . . . (kept strictly private) [only] add[ed] to the piquancy of the despotism" (736). The only way in which Gwendolen can comprehend Henleigh's threat of violence is through his muted voice and her silence.

His silence, Gwendolen knows, is not merely a blank, but rather the presence of something she has difficulty expressing. Her understanding of his abuse and her fear seems unspeakable within the bounds of reason: "The sort of truth that made any excuse for her anger could not be uttered" (743). Further, although Gwendolen grows to recognize more and more clearly that Henleigh has her on the "rack" (745), Eliot emphasizes that her dumbness does not result from lack of feeling, but an inability to articulate the horrors she feels. The epigraph to chapter 54, in which Gwendolen and Henleigh embark on an excursion together, serves to highlight Gwendolen's frustrated silence:

> *The unwilling brain*
> *Feigns often what it would not; and we trust*
> *Imagination with such phantasies*                    —Shelley
> *As the tongue dares not fashion into words;*
> *Which have no words, their horror makes them dim*
> *to the mind's eye.*

The horrors, which are unspoken, remain dim. They become inaccessible and silent, but embodied in fantasies, in feelings and sensation. If there are any doubts as to what these horrors might be, the narrator follows with an account of Madonna Pia, "whose husband, feeling himself injured by her, took her to his castle amid the swampy flats of the Maremma and got rid of her there." This woman, she tells us, "makes a pathetic figure in Dante's Purgatory," and she encourages us to "infer with some confidence that the husband had never been a very delightful companion." The narrator introduces Gwendolen into this chronicle by suggesting the reader should feel more sympathy for her because she remains undelivered from her tormentor's presence and suffers "inward torture" (731–32). Gwendolen feels the sway of Henleigh's authority as she recognizes that "she had sold herself . . . had sold her truthfulness and sense of justice, so that [Henleigh] held them throttled into silence, collared and dragged behind him to witness what he would, without remonstrance" (733). Gwendolen's truthfulness and sense of justice have been sacrificed not to Henleigh, but to the contradictions she cannot identify in his behavior. Gwendolen only understands that she hates him, a hatred, the narrator informs us, of the most intense variety, a hatred "rooted in fear" (737).

Thus Gwendolen does not speak about her experience, nor would Henleigh permit her remonstrance; he countenances no response but utter compliance: "[C]lashing was intolerable to him: his habitual want was to put collision out of the question by the quiet massive pressure of his rule" (656). Although he is quiet, his dictates provide a slow, steady, and painful pressure on Gwendolen, a pressure that she cannot define because of the contradictions it offers to her worldview. Peter Brooks argues that in George Eliot's narrative style, "[t]he language of the body at moments of crisis exceeds articulated speech and resists conceptual translation" (246). The excess and resistance of which Brooks speaks are not absolute. If we read the tensions that exceed and resist the normative narrative structure of the novel (its realism) through sensation, elements that otherwise would not appear become lucid.

### Dogs and a Long Whip

*Daniel Deronda* as a whole emphasizes and collapses the dichotomies that leave Gwendolen unable to respond, underscoring cultural tensions that make violence unspeakable and sensational by metaphorically representing Henleigh's ability to enact violence through a medium that recurs throughout the sensation genre: the pet dog.[13] On the couple's wedding day, a young woman remarks that gentlemen could never "behave badly" to their brides. Her mother responds, "Oh, child, men's men: gentle or simple, they're much of a muchness. I've heard my mother say Squire Pelton used to take his dogs and a long whip into his wife's room, and flog 'em there to frighten her" (400–401). Using the cultural certainty that working-class men could be physically violent with their wives[14] as an avenue into the discussion—gentlemen behave the same as simple men—the mother provides an instance of a dog serving as a substitute for a wife in the privacy of the home and visible only to servants, as a proof that gentry could behave badly, threaten their wives with beatings, or beat them just as working-class men did. The women also note the relationship between a man's speech and his ability to execute physical abuse by marking the distinction between one who attacks with his tongue and one who attacks with a weapon. Proceeding with the metaphor of the whip and dog, one notes, "Mr Grandcourt has wonderful little tongue. Everything must be done dummy-like without his ordering," to which her companion responds, "Then he's the more whip, I doubt" (401). Henleigh's silence not only represents authority, it also indicates to these women, for whom the discourse of domestic violence is readily accessible, that Henleigh uses the whip behind closed doors to accomplish his desires. His sedate demeanor, Eliot notes, "without raising his voice or looking," indicates that "he counted on attention to the smallest sign" (161). The key the narrative provides to this cultural cryptography furnishes the reader with ample evidence of the authority that lies behind Henleigh's gentle voice.

Henleigh's dog Fetch becomes a representation of his proficiency at imperturbable cruelty. He intentionally teases his spaniel by drawing its attention to another dog in his lap and caressing it.[15] Fetch, the "poor thing, whimpered interruptedly, as if trying to repress that sign of discontent, and at last rested her head beside the appealing paw, looking up with piteous beseeching." Henleigh, however, ignores the dog's protests, deriving pleasure from its discomfort: "But when the amusing anguish burst forth in a howling bark, Grandcourt pushed Fetch down without speaking . . . [experiencing] some annoyance against Fetch as the cause" of a trivial irritation, and immediately orders his companion to "[t]urn out that brute" (161). As soon as Fetch voices her discontent, Henleigh has her "dispos[ed] of," identifying her as a "brute" to cloak his unkind behavior. Interestingly, Eliot defines Fetch in this scene as a bitch: "she gently put her large silky paw on her master's leg," but in a scene less than ten pages later, Fetch becomes "he." This gendered shift emphasizes the significance of the dog's femaleness in the earlier scene, drawing a more striking contrast to Squire Pelton and to the animals Henleigh toys with as he does the women, Lydia and Gwendolen.

Other comments on Henleigh's relationship with his dogs provide insight into his behavior: "Grandcourt kept so many dogs that he was reputed to love them; at any rate, his impulse to act just in this way [his cruelty with Fetch] started from such an interpretation" (161). Similarly, although Henleigh seems to have great love for Gwendolen, rescuing her from the grip of poverty, he manipulates and terrifies her. He understands, however, the significance of the appearance of love, and he therefore does not choose to "kick any animal, because the act of kicking is a compromising attitude, and a gentlemen's dogs should be kicked for him. He only said things which might have exposed himself to be kicked" (164). In the public arena, Henleigh will never risk compromising himself; like his speech, his behavior has both a public and private persona, one that is, however, dismantled by this novel, along with the boundaries between public and private issues, sensation and realism. Henleigh clearly indicates to Gwendolen, without triggering the explicit social cues, that the implicit threat of a kick for her or any of his dogs lies beneath his calm demeanor. Further, although always careful to seem a gentle caretaker of his pets in public, if he suspects any insurgency and is "out of temper," he will "at once [thrash] his horse or [kick] his dog in consequence" (741). Gwendolen perceives this possibility early on and remarks, "He delights in making the dogs and horses quail: that is half his pleasure in calling them his" (482). Finally, even Daniel notes of Henleigh, "although he generally observes the forms," he "can bite" (487).

### The Spectral Law

As Anne Cvetkovich notes in *Mixed Feelings,* sensation pivots on affect, on the private and personalized. However, *Daniel Deronda* and the sensation narratives that preceded it use sensation to draw the private into public discourse, exposing the conventions that maintain the camouflage of intrafamilial violence. Once visible, sensation provides a rhetoric for introducing these issues into convention, offering a framework for the material experience of women who could not describe their fears otherwise. Even characters such as Daniel (and his friend Hans Meyrick) who remain distant from Gwendolen and Henleigh comprehend that in the privacy of the Grandcourts' connubial relations Henleigh "can bite."

The narrative delineates these contradictions metaphorically as ghosts. Images that terrify, ghosts remain outside of reason but surround the women in this novel.[16] As Nina Auerbach notes in *Private Theatricals,* the Victorian image of ghosts "manifests truer, if trickier 'own selves' than the authorized cycle of life accommodates" (18). By employing ghosts as a metaphor, Eliot exposes the marginalization of the material selves that were not visible in contemporary social and legal discourse.[17] Sensation becomes its own vehicle, briefly materializing the mystical, the scandalous, into reality. This metaphor also betokens the ephemeral articulability and the diaphanous quality of marital violence in Gwendolen's polite social world. These spirits, contradictions of realism and confirmation of Gwendolen's terror, buttress Henleigh's attempts to control Gwendolen. She cannot avoid "the nightmare of fear" he imposes; she can neither rebel nor speak, even outside of his presence, for "[h]er husband had a ghostly army at his back, that could close round her wherever she might turn" (503). The specter of sexual violence haunts the novel, and the laws and social conventions that ensured its secrecy provide a ghostly army to sustain Henleigh's position and keep Gwendolen in a state of terrified submission.

Despite her desire to flee Henleigh or act according to her own will,

Gwendolen cannot defy these ghosts, bowing to the rational considerations that imperceptibly require her to stay in this dangerous situation.[18] These spirits rise up whenever Gwendolen experiences the threat of Henleigh's violent behavior or the structure that maintains its privacy. When Mr. Lush comes to inform her of Henleigh's intention of providing handsomely for Lydia and their children in his will, her "words were no better than chips" and she could only perceive "Lush [as] getting merged in a crowd of other feelings, dim and alarming as a crowd of ghosts" (662). Their dimness does not, however, diminish their threat or authority, and Gwendolen feels their danger as much as she does Henleigh's. Henleigh's Will/will still becomes the law, entrenched in a misogyny that, like parliamentary law, callously determines her future.

When Sir Hugo, Henleigh's uncle and Daniel's guardian, remarks that the ghosts of the past generations lie in their homes, Gwendolen replies, "It is very nice to come after ancestors and monks, but they should know their places and keep underground. I should be rather frightened to go about this house all alone. I suppose the old generations must be angry with us because we have altered things so much" (461). This heritage of legal and religious sanction lies at the foundation of Henleigh's behavior, keeping Gwendolen terrified. Further, these ghosts are threatened by any change, any shift in the ministrations of their authority. As long as Henleigh remains within the bounds of propriety, Gwendolen's resistance to his abuse would draw this ghostly army down upon her from all its quarters: religious, social, and legal.

Henleigh himself becomes a ghostly vision to Gwendolen. Her desire to leave him leaves her with images that "instead of freedom, [offer up a] palsy of a new terror—a white dead face from which she was for ever trying to flee and for ever held back" (738). His absence will not erase her fear of the sway he holds over her, because the power of such predominance does not lie in Henleigh alone, but in the battalion that stands all around her and at his side. Like Rachel in *Salem Chapel,* who acknowledges the impossibility of escape, Gwendolen recognizes that even if she were alone, she would remain within the same frame, "for ever held back" in this world of confusion, with ghostly boundaries and blurred signifiers. Even after Henleigh dies, Gwendolen remarks that she "will never get away from [his dead face]." Daniel, the unhappy attendant to this lament, wonders if Gwendolen makes these comments because she is experiencing reality "through an exaggerating medium of excitement and horror . . . in a state of delirium" (753). Gwendolen's sense that Henleigh and his power remain with her seems absurd to Daniel, but Gwendolen's remarks sum up the irony: "Sometimes I thought he would kill *me* if I resisted his will. But now—his dead face is there and I cannot bear it" (758). She must live in terror for the rest of her life; Henleigh's absence does not erase his authority, just as his silence did not indicate a lack of signification.

The culminating moments of the novel are not the only points at which Gwendolen's fears are defined as superstitious and outside the realm of rationality. From the beginning, Eliot marks Gwendolen's dread of these ghosts, despite her inability to define the dread. Behind a locked panel, Gwendolen's family discovers a "picture of an upturned dead face, from which an obscure figure seemed to be fleeing with outstretched arms" (56). More than simply a foreshadowing of Gwendolen's flight from Henleigh's dead, upturned face, this image demonstrates her dread of the ghostly faces that hover around her before she meets Henleigh. Gwendolen angrily asks her sister, "How dare you open things [the panel] which were meant to be shut up?" A woman who initially asserts her will against the men in her life, Gwendolen understands that she must protect herself from these ghosts. Later, during a performance of a tableau from *The Winter's Tale* that Gwendolen has orchestrated, the panel flies open, terrifying her: "[T]he [eventual] touch of her mother's arm had the effect of an electric charge; Gwendolen fell on her knees and put her hands before her face. She was still trembling, but mute, and it seemed that she had self-consciousness enough to aim at controlling her signs of terror" (92). The terror, which appears here as it does in her relationship with Henleigh, seems to the audience to derive from spirits and mystery. The narrator's rational explanation of the exposure of the ghosts at a peak in sensation—Gwendolen's performance of the performance of Hermione [19]—doesn't dissipate the mystery and terror surrounding the ghostly face. Indeed, Hermione's situation in *The Winter's Tale* foreshadows Gwendolen's dilemma in which seeming "justice prove[s] violence" (II.i.128–29). Just as Leontes's cruelty is legalized, but revealed through the mystically pure vision of Paulina, Henleigh's aggression must be viewed with a special lens. As Leontes unwittingly predicts early in the play, the magical and real must become "coactive arts" (I.ii.141) for the good to be achieved. This blurring of the magical and the real vexes everyone in *Daniel Deronda*. Even after learning of her sibling's tampering with the panel, the event still "seemed [to Gwendolen] like a brief re-membered madness" (94).

### A Madwoman in a Play

Forced to face viewing life through the window of Henleigh's oppres-sion, "like a piece of yellow and wavy glass that distorts form and makes colour an affliction" (736), Gwendolen rejects the frame that Henleigh provides and, along with it, the discourse of reason he embodies. Like Gwendolen, whose confusion between the bounds of reason and sensa-tion leaves her in the realms of performance and madness, all the women in the novel (with the possible exception of Mirah[20]) find reprieve from the distortion of their lives that results from abuse by engaging in a min-gling of sensation and reality, performance and truth (which may be de-fined as that which they understand as their culture's manner of framing itself). For Gwendolen and Lydia, a radical recontextualization of reality, a shattering of the yellow window—even to the point of performing madness, inserting the sensational into the real[21]—grants them a modi-cum of control over their relationship with Henleigh. I want to distin-guish the performance of madness that results from the host of contradic-tions in which these characters find themselves from madness as "the opposite of rebellion . . . the impasse confronting those whom cultural condition has deprived of the very means of protest or self-affirmation" (Shoshana Felman in Showalter, *Female Malady,* 5). Though, as Judith Butler has persuasively argued, performance may not be easily distin-guished from the real, I am interested here in the multiplication of that frame as a means to draw attention to the framework itself, by exploiting rifts and contradictions. These tensions leave some characters recourse only to the sociopolitical blurring of terms found in sensation and in a Butlerian performance of madness. This performance, which Butler de-scribes as a "perpetual displacement constitut[ing] a fluidity of identities that suggests an openness to resignification and recontextualization; pa-rodic proliferation depriv[ing] hegemonic culture and its critics of the claim to naturalized" identities (*Gender Trouble* 138), might become a subversive act, which not only reframes female identity but also rescripts the "natural" absence of sexual violence in the domestic space.

Though clearly not an unequivocally beneficial construction of female identity,[22] these characters' excursions into performance alter the boundaries of their behavior. As long as their performance skirts the dangers of institutionalization,[23] they may be able to shift the ground of social understanding to make possible a new vision of the real. An indeterminate line separating performance and madness not only makes performed madness possible, but also refigures madness. A trope of sensation, the fictional madwoman became a central figure in the genre's subversive protest against the limitations in women's lives. Similarly, sensation figures in the realist narrative of *Daniel Deronda,* altering its generic shape and theme.[24] For many Victorian physicians, "violations of conventions of feminine speech" characterized madness (Showalter, *Female Malady* 81), so this disruption of text, like the disruption of sensation, provided access to language that would otherwise be denied—from specific forms of language, such as cursing, to topics considered indelicate for a woman, such as marital violence.[25] Language outside the script of normative womanhood redefined the terms of representation. Elaine Showalter has argued for the connection between sensation fiction and the undoing of constructions of female madness (*Female Malady* 71, 48), and Sandra M. Gilbert and Susan Gubar's landmark study of madness and gendered identity, *The Madwoman in the Attic,* provides the groundwork for many of the assertions I make here. My contention is that madness as a trope disrupts and refigures reality, rather than rejecting it entirely. A performance, then, such as those in *Daniel Deronda,* reveals "a fluidity of character that decomposes the uniform integrity of self" (Auerbach, *Private Theatricals* 4). Eliot, however, does not repudiate this phenomenon, as Auerbach and other critics suggest, but rather offers up in *Daniel Deronda* a recasting of traditional theater and performance, which Auerbach argues "shared— and eventually, self-consciously aped—the paradoxes of Victorian culture as a whole" (16). By staging the novel as an examination of performance (it was even cast into a play by Eliot herself [Auerbach 13]) and paradoxes, the novel interrogates the ways in which performance offers women a potentially subversive, if risky, alternative to silence.

### Gwendolen: Act I

Performance in *Daniel Deronda* amounts to a blending of the real and the sensational that results from an inability to integrate experience and "reality." In the early scene in which Gwendolen plays Hermione in a tableau in her home and the portrait of the dead face so insistently associated with Henleigh is exposed, Eliot is not only, as Auerbach suggests, marking "the realization of a pervasive Victorian fear of soullessness within the portrait of the lady" ("Alluring Vacancies" 47), but also drawing the connection between visible but unspoken terror of death and a woman's performance. As Gwendolen performs a performing woman, she employs a method associated with that performance that offers resistance to the suppressed terror of her culture. When Gwendolen speaks of this performance with her mother prior to its staging, she invokes many of the themes discussed here:

> *"Do I look as well as Rachel, mamma?"* . . . .
>
> *"You have better arms than Rachel," said Mrs Davilow; "your arms would do for anything, Gwen. But your voice is not so tragic as hers: it is not so deep."*
>
> *"I can make it deeper, if I like," said Gwendolen, provisionally; then she added, with decision, "I think a higher voice is more tragic: it is more feminine; and the more feminine a woman is, the more tragic it seems when she does desperate actions."*
>
> *"There may be something in that. . . . But I don't know what good there is in making one's blood creep. And if there is anything horrible to be done, I should like it to be left to the men."*
>
> *"Oh mamma, you are so dreadfully prosaic! As if all the great poetic criminals were not women! . . ."*
>
> *"Well, dear, and you—who are afraid to be alone in the night— I don't think you would be very bold in crime, thank God."*
>
> *"I am not talking about reality, mamma," said Gwendolen, impatiently." (84–85)*

In this passage, Gwendolen aligns herself with the (in)famous Victorian actress Rachel, an identification she is later urged to abandon when she hopes to escape marriage to Henleigh and that, for a time, Daniel's mother, Leonora, employs successfully to escape her father and husband. As John Stokes notes, the historical figure Rachel invoked both the betrayal of the created self in performance and the dangerous identity of the

performing woman, a combination of the "Racinian actress who inten-
sified tragic convention and a Shakespearean actress who naturalized
tragic experience" (784). Tampering with notions of female identity gave
Rachel not only an independence and autonomy that few women of the
period enjoyed, but also guarded her character (here, clearly a loaded
term) (783) in what Auerbach describes as an increasingly respectable
profession. Stokes further argues that the tableau Eliot chooses, the climax of *The Winter's Tale,* was a piece known for its "theatrical ambiguity"
(786), emphasizing the difficulty of discerning the real from the performance. Stokes, however, calls this Gwendolen's "fail[ure]" (788), and I
read it as a narrative triumph, as a means of expressing what might otherwise be inexpressible through the blending of realism and performance.
Gwendolen finds performance in the blurred boundaries between sensation and reality. In the final moments of the novel, she voices a consistently unspoken crime and tragedy like the one she alludes to above,
maintaining still her feminine tone.[26] She becomes one of the great poetic
criminals, not so much for the "murder" of her husband as for her willingness to draw this sensational scene into Daniel's jealously guarded reality.[27] Gwendolen's fear/performance at the exposed painting when the
tableau is acted seems to her like a "brief remembered madness" (94), the
form that these performances most often take in the novel.

### Brief Madness

The first explicit performance of madness that gives a woman mastery
over Henleigh occurs when he approaches Lydia to inform her that he
has decided to marry another woman and to recover the family diamonds
of which she has been in possession. Lydia initially responds with anger
and bitterness, and when she lashes out with a venomous critique, Henleigh remarks severely, "I advise you not to say that sort of thing again,"
and a second time warns her "not to say things that [she] will repent of"
(394). Her ordinary speech is conscripted, managed by the strictures he
applies when she speaks the same language she has always spoken. As long
as they remain within the realm of ordinary social discourse, Lydia must
maintain the same silence that stifles Gwendolen. Despite the fact that
Henleigh's treatment of Lydia is like the torture of "the thumb-screw

and the iron-boot," she fears to respond. She "knew her helplessness and shrank from testing it by any appeal—shrank from crying in a dead ear. . . . She did not weep nor speak" (392). As his assault continues, like a "surgical operation" (394), "[s]he dare[s] not answer" (393).

As Butler's revision of her thesis indicates in *Bodies That Matter,* the performances that rend the social fabric, that alter the social codes—and certainly this alteration occurs and we must account for its processes— are not produced by the will of the actor. I would argue that they are a product of the tensions present in the conflicting structures I have described above. Placed in this painful impasse, Lydia bends to the contradictory impulses that pervade *Daniel Deronda* (as Margaret Oliphant did in writing *Salem Chapel*) and finds herself embodying what the novel locates in these sites, "the one suicidal form of threat within her power" (397). She was "suffering the horrible conflict of self-reproach and tenacity" and the horrible conflict between what she experiences as abuse and the way reason defines Henleigh's behavior. When she begins to speak from this space, a space that wildly cites both sensation and reality,[28] Henleigh quickly responds, attempting to overpower this posture that threatens to dissemble the ideology on which his authority is based: "Of course, if you like, you can play the mad woman." Lydia's execution of what Henleigh himself defines as performed madness turns the tables, in one of the only instances in which Henleigh does not gain his will. Lydia refuses to give up the diamonds and "madly" offers to deliver them herself, so she might exact her revenge against Gwendolen. Henleigh "remain[s] silent without turning his eyes upon her" (397); the tables turn, and he realizes that he cannot move her when she does not stand on familiar ground. He abandons his brutal speech and simply remarks, "What's the use of talking to mad people?" Lydia's behavior after this comment ensures the fulfillment of her desires.

> *"Yes, I am foolish—loneliness has made me foolish—indulge me."*
> *Sobs rose as she spoke. "If you will indulge me in this one folly, I will be very meek—I will never trouble you." She burst into hysterical crying, and said again almost with a scream—"I will be very meek after that."*
>
> *There was a strange mixture of acting and reality in this passion. . . . Even Grandcourt was wrought upon by surprise: this*

*capricious wish, this childish violence, was as unlike Lydia's bearing as*
*it was incongruous with her person. (398)*

Lydia's foray into performed madness, into the paradoxical behavior that
results from her situation, leaves Henleigh without access to his formidable arsenal of torturous language. Her language, her hysteria, her
screaming protestations shift her from the realm of rationality and reason
that has granted Henleigh so much authority. She informs Henleigh that
she means "to keep her [own] word" and not to do as he tells her. She
immediately recognizes the potentially "suicidal" danger involved in
speaking against Henleigh, yet the novel makes clear the power of this
language to reshape the context, to reshape the lives of the characters. In
spite of the hazard, the narrator proclaims of Lydia's language: "the word
had been spoken" (396)—a remark of biblical gravity. The significance
of her speech is not lost on Henleigh. With an agitated sensation of fear,
he orders her to "[b]e quiet, and hear what I tell you" (398). Almost
pleading, he asserts his authority by calling for a return to a normative
structure. Though the shift is brief and Henleigh is granted verbal command of the conversation, which very well could have saved Lydia from
the asylum, she gains her point and Henleigh grants her the right to deliver the diamonds to Gwendolen as she chooses. Henleigh departs with
the "baffling sense that he had to deal with something like madness [in
which] he could only govern by giving way." Lydia's performance im-
presses Henleigh with "a sense of imperfect mastery" (399). Momentarily, the corpus of the real has been punctured—a wound that even if
healed will alter the surface of the skin, change its very shape. We gain a
key to understanding both that which is incomprehensible in Gwendolen's terror and the method by which Gwendolen herself ultimately begins to challenge Henleigh's successful formula of control, by examining
the way in which realism is rewritten in the novel.

### Gwendolen: Act II

Gwendolen initially becomes infected with this madness when Lydia
communicates it to her in the letter she encloses with the diamonds she
delivers to Gwendolen on her wedding day. The note contains a bitter
curse, the effect of which is surprisingly mixed. Initially, the jewels seem

to carry only negativity, in spite of the fact that they announce a rise in Gwendolen's position out of the poverty for which she had been destined: "[t]ruly here were poisoned gems, and the poison had entered into this poor young creature." This poison, like madness, leaves Gwendolen "scream[ing] again and again with hysterical violence" at the sight of her new husband, a scene that clearly unnerves Henleigh.[29] In fact, he believes that it must either be madness or "the Furies [who] had crossed his threshold"[30] (407). This eruption of madness foreshadows the incorporation of Gwendolen's threat, not as *Salem Chapel* or *Aurora Floyd* had conceived of it—in an act of responsive physical violence—but more profoundly, in an explicit reconceptualization of the very terms by which these situations are framed. A pattern that threatens to reconfigure and challenge Henleigh's authority, Gwendolen's more intentional management will produce what Henleigh will only be able to call madness. Even in this early scene, Henleigh describes Gwendolen's new behavior as the seeds of that "oddity, [which in the 'old time'] end[ed] in that mild form of lunatic asylum, a nunnery." These seeds, Gwendolen's "threatening moods," require him "peremptorily to check" her, exercising his authority with the "quiet massive pressure of his rule" (656). Still, the seeds may grow, and he cannot predict what fruit they will bear.

Gwendolen employs this performative madness, just as Lydia had, to achieve ascendancy over Henleigh only when she understands that he "would do just what he will" and that she has "neither devices at her command to determine his will, nor any rational means of escaping it" (480). It is precisely this engagement with rationality that Gwendolen must lose to gain any safety or autonomy in her relationship with Henleigh (as she earlier loses her whip to gain safety when caught in the contradictions between sensation and realism). Her fear of him, her sense that "his eyes showed a delight in torturing her" (481), leaves her with the alternative that the narrative fashions here—to take means other than rational ones to escape. Performed madness is this absence of rationality that Gwendolen uses when her social script leaves her no alternative within reality, within reason, to gain her desires.[31]

Gwendolen, thus, embodies this madness at the crises in her relationship with Henleigh, and again, it plays out in relation to Gwendolen's jewels. Many of the elements of this scene evoke the earlier one in which Gwendolen collapsed hysterically after reading Lydia's clandestine note, enclosed with the necklace that marked Gwendolen's new position as Henleigh's wife. Gwendolen, like Lydia, uses her jewels to communicate furtively, and like Lydia, speaks through them her resistance to the position in which she has been placed by Henleigh—a resistance that Henleigh again perceives as performative madness. When Gwendolen desires to communicate with Daniel against Henleigh's wishes, she wears a necklace that she had lost gambling and that Daniel had redeemed for her, rather than the dazzling family diamonds that might be expected in her first public appearance as Henleigh's wife. Despite the fact that she "[d]ared not to offend her husband, . . . [she was] determined to wear the memorial necklace somehow" (495), and her determination both communicates her will and resists Henleigh's—an end she achieves by moving outside the realm of reasonable behavior. A bauble unbefitting her new rank and station, Gwendolen's unpretentious trinket not only adorns her at the grand dinner party and ball, which would have been strange in itself, but she winds it around her wrist in a clumsy fashion that is "necessarily conspicuous" (499). Finally, when she and her husband return to their room, "Grandcourt threw himself into a chair and said, with undertoned peremptoriness, 'Sit down.' She, already in the expectation of something unpleasant, had thrown off her burnous with nervous unconsciousness, and immediately obeyed. . . . 'Oblige me in future by not showing whims like a mad woman in a play'" (502). Gwendolen has achieved a successful performance of madness that, although it leaves her chastised, permits her to behave as she desires. She communicates with Daniel by visually performing her message for him, converses in spite of the fact that Henleigh demands her silence. Henleigh informs her that like Lydia, she must "not make a spectacle of [herself]." If her performance of madness must occur, she must take care to regulate its structure, to step back into realism and legitimate the power of these sensational outbursts. A performance too spectacular, too sustained, might carry grave consequences: "You are my wife. And you will either fill your place properly—to the world and to me—or you will go to the devil" (503).[32] Gwendolen must continue to fill her role, secretly suffering its tensions, or suffer the wrath that Henleigh has in store for her, whether lunatic asylum or emotional and perhaps physical torture.[33]

Not only does this mode provide Gwendolen with a fleeting autonomy, but it also grants her the means of comprehending her situation.

This "madness" is a blurring of the boundaries between the rational and the irrational, the real and the sensational, that had been signaled in *Salem Chapel*'s Rachel. If Gwendolen can fracture the barriers that separate these two worlds, she can conceive of Henleigh's violence. Within sensation, understanding Henleigh's behavior as violence—despite his class, wealth, and composure—becomes possible. Only when Gwendolen remains confined to traditionary frames does she have difficulty identifying Henleigh's behavior as cruel and comprehending his private voice, his "long whip," his private rod. For example, Gwendolen's secret wish to be separated from Henleigh seems unreasonable to her in the realm of the rational: "Search as she would in her consciousness, she found no plea to justify a plaint" (659). In the conscious, a world Jacques Lacan would argue is ordered by the Law, Gwendolen finds no relief. Only when consciousness is distorted, reconsidered, rewritten can she gesture toward an understanding of Henleigh's cruelties. If she remains within the bounds of realism, "[s]he had absolutely nothing that she could allege against him in judicious or judicial ears" (665). Being unable to name his cruelties in realistic speech, acknowledging the impossibility of addressing them within the historical framework she has been given, Gwendolen retreats to the only other means available: a play of madness—what generically is marked as sensation.

Ultimately, this madness aids in freeing her from Henleigh. On their first and last voyage together, they are forced to dock in Genoa, where unbeknownst to them, Daniel is staying to visit his mother. Once they learn of Daniel's presence, Henleigh refuses to allow Gwendolen any solitude or freedom, taking her out on a small sailboat with him to prevent her from seeing Daniel. Gwendolen's hatred of Henleigh, along with her fear that "her life was a sailing and sailing away" (760), initiates the novel's most dramatic melding of sensation and reality. As Athena Vrettos notes, Eliot frames this final scene as a performance: "the scene was as good as a theatrical representation for all beholders" (*Daniel Deronda* 745). It culminates in Gwendolen's "dread" of Henleigh (761) and a wish that he were dead. At this crisis, and in isolation, she is again trapped in a place that strains the terms of her understanding, and she says "wildly," "I think we shall go on always like the Flying Dutchman" (746). When she later relates the narrative to Daniel, she affirms that she "did not want to die" herself: "I was afraid of being drowned together. I knew no way of killing him there, but I did, I did kill him in my thoughts" (760). Gwendolen believes that Henleigh, knocked overboard by the sail and drowned, was a victim of a sensationally magic wish for his death: "the evil longings, the evil prayers came again and blotted everything else dim, till, in the midst of them—I don't know how it was—he was turning the sail—there was a gust—he was struck—I know nothing—I only know that I saw my wish outside me. . . . [T]here he was again—his face above the water—and he cried again—and I held my hand, and my heart said, 'Die!'—and he sank" (761). As she describes the moment to Daniel, Gwendolen becomes increasingly silent, "submerged by the weight of memory which no [rational] words could represent" (760). Even the following day, she remains in fear, "hindering" her talk and only offering facial expressions that "did not issue in speech" (763). Gwendolen cannot speak about the madness that made it possible for her to "imagine Henleigh to death," nor can she return to her normal "well[ness] and calm" as Daniel orders (766). The narrative voice alternately sensationalizes and naturalizes this event, consistently blurring sensation and realism and enabling Gwendolen to perform the most radical act she can against her husband: murder. By wishing for another world and manifesting that wish "outside [her]," Gwendolen's thoughts do, in their revision of her worldview, kill what Henleigh represents.

### The Novel of "Real Life"

The narrative of *Daniel Deronda* provides us with the metaphors of drama and fiction through which to read the permeation of the real with sensation, to decode the blurring of boundaries it manufactures in order to communicate the screened violence of Victorian culture. The representation of lives and experience collapses the framework that separates performance and reality and, novelistically, sensation and realism. Gwendolen's "yeasty mingling of dimly understood facts with vague but deep impressions, and with images half real, half fantastic" (402) furnishes the reader with a clue to the space in which this language must be rendered and understood. It is within the half-real and half-fantastic that we must direct our inquiry in order to comprehend the novel, the violence of characters such as Henleigh, and the response of those such as Gwendolen.

Eliot points up the necessity of analyzing the text in these terms by noting that Henleigh's life is "so little suggestive of drama" that Gwendolen has difficulty imagining that any sensational or dangerous situations might occur behind the facade of his polite discourse. However, the reader can discern that which lies behind the barriers of decorum by examining the tensions in the novel. Without this lens, Henleigh's behavior and public language remain beyond reproach. The narrator tells us that although his conduct does not "seem black in mere statement," something in Henleigh's motives circulates outside the language in which he communicates, something that might reveal the blackness now concealed. The reader, in fact, must map Henleigh's cruelty by indicators that lie outside of his explicit, normative persona. We learn that Gwendolen's "inward torture is disproportionate to what is discernible as outward cause" (732), and thus we must not confine our examination only to that which is outwardly discernible in ordinary terms if we wish to learn the cause of Gwendolen's anguish.

We must risk the intrusion of the sensational into our comprehension of reality in the same way that the novel incorporates sensational moments into realism, refiguring realism itself. Gwendolen's novelistic life can only be figured if it becomes understood as a novel within a novel, a parody of the novel's own realism. "Real life," the narrator remarks of Gwendolen's marriage, "was as interesting as 'Sir Charles Grandison'" (354). Unsurprisingly, Clementina, often described as the most complex and interesting character in *Sir Charles Grandison,* goes mad over her potential marriage then recovers to rebuke her suitor, the same method by which Gwendolen and Lydia eventually negotiate their relationships with Henleigh. This coincidence of the novel (*Sir Charles Grandison*) within the real (Gwendolen's life) that is the novel (*Daniel Deronda*) serves to emphasize the point that realism must be understood through a larger fiction (or what seems such) to read the realistic well. Only when we examine the real through the more fictional fictions can we begin to perceive those things that culture screens for the sake of propriety. Further, those novels that were considered representations of reality are not adequate tools. The discourse they employ, that of polite society, cannot provide the critical edge that sensation can. Even Gwendolen's "uncontrolled reading, though consisting chiefly in what are called pictures of life, had somehow not prepared her for this encounter with reality" (193), a reality that requires a dose of sensational realism, like *Lady Audley's Secret*. Gwendolen's attempt to read the great masters she assumes Daniel must have read leaves her as unprepared as the realist novels.

There is, however, tremendous resistance to the possibility of blurring these lines—a resistance *Daniel Deronda* outlines and critiques. Framing manners with a strict division between the real and the performance of sensation provides a culture with some security. Sensation, often horror, can then be contained by these boundaries and described as existing only outside of the domestic space. Transgression of the boundaries would indeed be alarming and threatening, as the narrator explains: "It is to be believed that attendance at the *opéra bouffe* in the present day would not leave men's minds entirely without shock, if the manners observed there with some applause were suddenly to start up in their own families" (193). A situational subplot demonstrates the same social nod to, even a passion for, sensation within the novel, but an extreme repugnance for the appearance of it within the real. When Mrs. Arrowpoint learns of her daughter Catherine's intention to marry her music master—a drama that Mrs. Arrowpoint's own writings glorify—she furiously chastises her daughter for refusing to agree to the social conventions of reality that those around her have accepted. Eliot draws out the friction between Mrs. Arrowpoint's enjoyment in producing drama and sensation within a novel and her indignant rejection of it in her own life: "It is hard for us to live up to our own eloquence, and keep pace with our winged words, while we are treading the solid earth and are liable to heavy dining. Besides, it has long been understood that the proprieties of literature are not those of practical life" (288). Mrs. Arrowpoint immediately assumes, as Henleigh does of Lydia and Gwendolen, that Catherine must be mad to engage in such a performance. Catherine, however, wins her point by allowing these lines to blur and eventually retains the fortune her parents threatened to refuse her.

Not surprisingly in this context, Gwendolen attempts to secure a position as a performer when her family loses its fortune. Hoping to avoid marriage to Henleigh, Gwendolen consults the renowned musician Klesmer about her chances of success. He informs her that her notions of real performance "have no more resemblance to reality than a pantomime. Ladies and gentlemen think that when they have made their toilet and drawn on their gloves they are as presentable on the stage as in a

drawing-room" (301). Middle- and upper-class notions of performance
do not suffice to encompass all that it must entail. The reality of performance, Klesmer explains, is one of hardship and little reward. The real
and the horrible bleed together in performance, requiring a diligent mastery of both. Further, he informs Gwendolen that reality encompasses
"indignities . . . such as [he] will not speak of" (304). He cannot speak of
these dangers, yet Klesmer reveals the connection between performance
and a response to danger, implied in the "dead face" evocative of Henleigh and revealed during Gwendolen's performance. Though Gwendolen screams with real terror and falls to her knees, Klesmer teaches her
the value of performance over paralyzing fear: "A magnificent bit of *plas-
tik* that!" (92). The only foreshadowing of the terror she experiences in
her relationship with Henleigh, the performance embedded in this scene
at so many levels (including the performance that Klesmer models when
he pretends to believe Gwendolen's fear is performative and she pretends
agreement) introduces these themes in this crucial and richly symbolic
moment. Klesmer perceives Gwendolen's unpreparedness for a career on
the stage, for her life to this point has been only a "narrow theater which
life offers to a girl of twenty, who cannot conceive herself as anything else
than a lady, or as in any position which would lack the tribute of respect.
She had no permanent consciousness of other fetters" (94). She must
conceive of herself differently and become conscious of fetters to perform
effectively.

Klesmer urges Gwendolen to marry, which he believes will entail
less hardship for her. The weight of public and private opinion heavily
favors Klesmer's urgings, and Gwendolen feels obliged to take on the role
of wife, which she believes will not require the sort of arduous performance Klesmer had mentioned. She does not remain long in this role,
however, without negotiating her life as it hangs in the balance of her
ability to perform. She must enact the role of "Mrs. Grandcourt" to the
satisfaction of her husband and the cast around him, and she must engage
in much riskier performances than Klesmer's to forge any reality in her
contradictory life. Mirah, who watches her within the bounds of her
marriage, notes that Gwendolen is "a grand lady . . . coming out of some
unknown drama in which parts perhaps got more tragic as they went on"
(621). Significantly, however, Gwendolen must not only execute the
tragedy of her marriage, but she must also perform adequately for Daniel

Deronda, who serves as another kind of threatening critic and yet another ghost in the gallery of judges who haunt Gwendolen but remain outside the range of polite articulation.

### Making the Law Real and the Making of Real Law

Daniel Deronda searches, throughout the novel, for something that will lend his life meaning and purpose; he eventually finds this calling when the mother who has been unknown to him reveals that he is Jewish. Judaism gives Daniel a spiritual mission as well as a bride in the form of a beautiful young Jewish woman he has rescued from despondency and suicide, and his search seems to be advocated by the narrative. Although the tale lauds Daniel's choice to acknowledge his Jewish heritage and his wisdom in uncovering this fact, it does not depict his regeneration as a step to heal the tensions that revolve around marital violence. For Daniel, Judaism satisfies the need for an overarching law that can guide his life, a "vocation" (792) that lends itself to his desire: to "urge him into a definite line of action, and compress his wandering energy" (413). Daniel desires a measure with which to mark out his life, an authority to "justify partiality" and enable him to engage in absolute and assured moral judgment and action. Though the Judaism he discovers supplies different codes, the differences are not of a sort to address Gwendolen's concerns. Daniel's search for moral authority (often translated into a legal lexicon, concerning judging, defending, and prosecuting) participates in the commentary on the moral and legal codes that much sensation fiction calls into question, codes that authorize and screen violence.[34] Although many critics have read Daniel as an unblemished hero, I find a richer texture in his character that suggests not only a longing for moral authority and purpose in the novel, but a discomfort with the available solutions. Gwendolen's agonizing afterlife in the face of Daniel's abandonment points to that dissatisfaction.

Daniel's obsession with framing life inside an appropriate moral law, along with his rejection of drama, becomes another source of Gwendolen's fear. Just as her husband embodies the cultural authority of matrimonial and social law compelling her to remain with him despite her desires, so does Daniel reaffirm the command for her to remain within this system. Unlike Gwendolen, Lydia, and his mother, Leonora, who long to find an alternative to the legal and social barriers that limit their range of action, Daniel seeks the security of their solidity, hoping to contain the unmoored identity that leaves him adrift in the patrilineal system.[35] Asserting the authority of this law with Gwendolen assures his place within a system that threatens to exclude him as a bastard.

The novel opens with an assertion of Daniel's domination of Gwendolen. Fittingly, Gwendolen, attempting to escape Henleigh's authority after learning of Lydia, makes her appearance while engaging in another kind of play[36] at the gaming tables. These scenes circulate around Daniel's morally imperious correction of Gwendolen's attempt to assert her will and evade Henleigh's. Daniel's critical observance of her sends her away from her formerly successful pageantry in frustration. His gaze acts as an "evil eye" that dethrones her from the "supremacy" she had gained at the gaming table (38), "arresting" her, policing her behavior, and jarring her out of her alternative universe of performance that she governs. Rather than nurturing the growth of a new Gwendolen (even if we read Daniel's behavior as "tough love"), "[t]he basis of her thinking [receives] a disagreeable concussion" from him (40). Rather than offering salvation or liberating her, his attention acts like a blow, a pattern that continues throughout their relationship. Daniel later admits that her presence at the tables troubled him because she is a woman (382), a woman engaged in a performance that seemed to "coerce" him (35). Daniel feels obliged (as a man and insecure purveyor of the law) to squelch Gwendolen's unorthodox behavior. Conformity secures the order of things for Daniel, secures his authority.

Thus, just as Henleigh's rule of Gwendolen becomes a painful and terrifying pressure, attempting to drive her into submission, Daniel's observance of her is "like a pressure which begins to be torturing" (39). His glance frames and shapes her as uncomfortably as Henleigh's. Daniel's conclusion, that Gwendolen must be more evil than good because she engages in the play at the tables (35), authorizes him to chastise her behavior not only with a critical observation, but also with an invasion into her private play. Despite the fact that they are strangers, Daniel redeems a necklace Gwendolen pawns for gambling money and sends it to her with a message: "A stranger who has found Miss Harleth's necklace returns it to her with the hope that she will not again risk the loss of it." Gwendolen's performance must be morally "redeemed" by Daniel, and she recognizes immediately that his action places her in a position of obligation and moral inferiority: "[H]e knew very well that he was entangling her in helpless humiliation: it was another way of smiling at her ironically, and taking the air of a supercilious mentor" (49).

Daniel's authority over Gwendolen expands as her situation worsens, as she becomes increasingly threatened with marriage to Henleigh, and she searches for an alternative law to Henleigh's, hoping to regain her self-respect and the "confidence" she has lost in her "destiny." Her "hidden helplessness gave fresh force to the hold Deronda had from the first taken on her mind, as one who had an unknown standard by which he judged her. Had he some way of looking at things which might be a new footing for her?" (484). Gwendolen hopes his authority will provide her with a liberating alternative to Henleigh's pressure and mistreatment, particularly since he seems an atypical figure. In his difference, she seeks another vision, one that might have the perception and authority to release her from her situation. However, the hold he takes on her serves not to liberate her from the cycle of abuse and self-repression; rather, it reinforces those patterns, submitting her to a standard of behavior that not only remains as obscured by proprieties as Henleigh's, but ultimately matches Henleigh's in the tenor of its commands.

Daniel's standard remains enigmatic to Gwendolen because the social and moral law to which he subscribes mirrors Henleigh's in unexpected ways. The English moral and legal codes in which he has been raised are unmitigated by anything more than his desire to be unlike Sir Hugo, the man he suspects is his father. In response to what he believes has been a moral lapse in his birth, Daniel vows to subscribe to the ethical and social codes even more rigidly. This belief system causes him to reject and even despise the possibility of drama, performance, or sensation in real life—a possibility that haunts Gwendolen's experience with her husband. Daniel defines performance as existing outside the province of English gentlemanliness (208); as a child he vehemently rejected the notion of becoming a performer himself. As he grows older, he learns to despise the manifestation of performance in anyone else. He admires Mirah's repulsion for acting and feels disgust at Gwendolen's facades, even though they serve as her only refuge from Henleigh. When Daniel "perceive[s] in her an intensifying of her superficial hardness and resolute display [it makes] her abrupt betrayals of agitation the more marked and disturbing to him" (656). The contrast between propriety and the sensationalism that lies beneath her performance leaves Daniel distressed. Each of her performances provides evidence that the law cannot absolutely frame the reality of her experience, a notion to which he clings, urging upon Gwendolen dictates that he hopes will draw her back into the moral and legal scheme he finds comforting.

In the midst of the contradictions between social propriety and the material reality of her terror, Gwendolen defers to the moral loftiness Daniel broadcasts and other characters esteem, hoping to achieve security in what Daniel seems to promise are alternative boundaries to Henleigh's. Yet Daniel's nebulous standard continues to "measure [Gwendolen] into littleness," regardless of her attempts to reform. She begs him to "tell [her] what to think and what to do" (501) over and again. If she could make Daniel's moral dictums concur with her experience, she might be able to find a rational cause for her fear and a rational means of escape, a choice outside of the performance to which Daniel objects. However, Daniel's objections to her do not dissipate, and Gwendolen feels compelled to absorb his wishes so completely that she becomes less and less likely to leave Henleigh, even as she falls prey to Henleigh's increasing abuse. She continues to follow Daniel's injunctions despite her own desires because he is "not her admirer but her superior: in some mysterious way he was becoming a part of her conscience" (468). Daniel serves as Gwendolen's internalized authority, an authority for which Henleigh provides the external threat. As many critics have pointed out, Daniel becomes the Foucauldian monitor, a most effective means of suppressing dissent and contradiction. However, the element that this formulaic assignment of internal authority neglects is the implicit threat contained in Daniel's presence, the violence at the heart of his monitoring. Just as Henleigh traps Gwendolen with the jewels he confers upon her, the necklace Daniel redeems for Gwendolen creates an "ungainly form of bondage" for her, a mastery through which he can compel her to submit (Rosenman 251).

Ultimately, Gwendolen feels the same sensations at Daniel's hands that she experiences with Henleigh: subordination, constraint, and fear. Daniel sheds the angelic image that his surface characterization seems to suggest, and his admonitions produce more than results; they produce dread. Gwendolen admits to Sir Hugo, Daniel's guardian, "You don't know how much I am afraid of Mr Deronda . . . [b]ecause when he came to look on at the roulette-table, I began to lose. He cast an evil eye on my play. He didn't approve it. He has told me so. And now what-ever I do before him, I am afraid he will cast an evil eye upon it" (461–62). Indeed, she considers herself increasingly "evil" in Daniel's eyes, "[a]lways uneasily dubious about his opinion of her . . . lest he might think of her with contempt" (468). She becomes so afraid of his judg-ment, and the consequences that it might bring, that she dreads his au-thority as another boundary she must not cross. When Henleigh offers that Daniel behaves like other men and that in her naïveté she "takes Deronda for a saint," Gwendolen replies, "Oh dear no! . . . Only a little less of a monster" (649). Yet, her fear that she might have laid her last hope on a man who is no different than Henleigh leaves her in horror: "Even in the moments after reading the poisonous letter [she had re-ceived from Lydia on her wedding day] she had hardly had more cruel sensations than now; for emotion was at the acute point, where it is not distinguishable from sensation. Deronda, unlike what she had believed him to be, was an image which affected her as a hideous apparition would have done. . . . It had taken hold of her as pain before she could consider whether it were fiction or truth" (650). At this moment, Daniel becomes an apparition, one of the army of ghosts that authorizes Henleigh's law, and Gwendolen becomes lost in "sensation," in the belief that blurs the line between fiction and realism—hoping for relief from the pain, cru-elty, and suppression that men may heap on her. By abandoning the con-sideration of the line between fiction and truth upon which Daniel and Henleigh insist so forcefully, she might simply trust her sensations, sen-sational as they might be.

Daniel's desire to prevent Gwendolen from shaping an alternative law by reframing realism becomes the sole thrust of his conversations with her. He feels just as threatened by Gwendolen's performance, which might render the law imaginary and eradicate his sense of purpose, as does Henleigh. Regardless of the fact that Daniel intrudes his will upon Gwen-dolen and not vice versa (Gwendolen argues: "[Y]ou found *me* and wanted to make me better" [755; emphasis added]), he retreats farther and farther from her as she fails to comply. Moreover, Mirah appears increasingly attractive to Daniel because her constantly reiterated ability to submit, even under the most harsh rule, buttresses his authority to institute the law. Thus, even as he distances himself from Gwendolen, he constantly casts her back into the structure against which she struggles.

When Gwendolen turns to Daniel in desperation, hoping that her "intolerable fear [about his judgment of her was] an infection from her husband's way of thinking" (671), the only response that he offers her, despite her "helpless misery," is a dictate that plays directly on the terror Gwendolen feels for Henleigh: "Confess everything to your husband; leave nothing concealed" (673). A bizarre, even cruelly absurd demand in the face of his own negative opinion of Henleigh, it simply serves to reinforce the notion that Daniel's seemingly alternative ethic falls in line with the one he appears on the surface to reject. At the height of Gwendolen's repression at Henleigh's hands, she is haunted by Daniel's injunctions in her dreams. She "felt herself escaping over the Mount Cenis, and wondering to find it warmer even in the moonlight on the snow, till suddenly she met Deronda, who told her to go back" (740)—back to Henleigh and his abuse, back to her enforced submission, back within the law. Although Gwendolen perceives safety and warmth over Mount Cenis, away from Henleigh—in spite the apparent freeze and darkness of social prohibition—she always sees the threat of Daniel's critique over the horizon of safety.

Despite Daniel's understanding that Gwendolen is despondent, along with his recognition that Henleigh's private deportment lies at the heart of her unhappiness, Daniel urges Gwendolen back into her husband's authority. When Gwendolen turns to him because she desires to "make herself different," yet "can alter nothing" with the methods he has offered her, Daniel's language collapses. He remains entrenched in the law he reveres, able only to observe the "horrible" sensations he refuses to express. His "[w]ords seemed to have no more rescue in them than if he had been beholding a vessel in peril of wreck" (672–73). Acknowledging Gwendolen's horror and the power it might have to topple the strict boundaries he has negotiated between the real and the sensational—the strict boundaries of the law—terrifies him, and he becomes "afraid of his own voice." Left unable to affirm Gwendolen's fears, Daniel "[feels] himself holding a crowd of words imprisoned within his lips, as if letting them escape would be a violation of awe before the mysteries of our human lot" (673). His reverence of the structure that maintains these mysteries, the horrors behind the veils he cannot recognize, leaves him with only the alternative of returning Gwendolen to the hands of Henleigh, releasing himself from the responsibility of comprehending her fears.

This cruel abandonment becomes increasingly clear as the novel progresses. Gwendolen reaches out to Daniel, rushing to meet him alone in the drawing room before a large group of guests appears. However, when he spies her, "[h]e turn[s] aside and walk[s] out of the room. This was behaving quite badly. Mere politeness would have made him stay to exchange some words before leaving her alone" (469). When she relates to him the narrative of Henleigh's death, she begs him not to "turn away from [her] and forsake [her]" (755), yet Daniel again feels "impelled to turn his back towards her and walk to a distance" (759). Finally, these metaphoric forms of abandonment become concretized in spite of his promise that he "will not forsake [her]" (755). In the novel's denouement, Daniel becomes engaged to Mirah and plans to travel to the East, yet does not inform Gwendolen of these momentous changes in his life. Their emotional intimacy continues, with Gwendolen confiding her feelings in him, and the social community in which they circulate suspects a marriage between them at any time. Despite this fact, when a friend of Daniel's proposes that Gwendolen might remarry, Daniel remarks, "Is it absolutely necessary that Mrs Grandcourt should marry again?" His friend retorts, "You monster! . . . do you want her to wear weeds for *you* all her life—burn in perpetual suttee while you are alive and merry?" (871). The language reveals tensions on several levels: one burns in suttee only for a husband and only for one who is dead. Daniel has become a husband like Henleigh, mastering Gwendolen, requiring her submission, but dead to her agony while he remains alive and merry. Like the dead face of Henleigh, he would become another departed partner, another threatening ghost, absent but lurking in the shadow of her failure to comply with the moral standards he offered. Indeed, the task of informing her of his plans becomes one of "utmost cruelty"; her plea that " 'he must remain near her—must not forsake her'—continually recurred to him with the clearness and importunity of imagined sounds" (684). These imagined sounds, like the invasion of sensation in his law-bound world, are sounds that Daniel has chosen to deny. Therefore, even while he makes his pronouncements, he turns his back on Gwendolen again, "prop[ping] himself up against the corner of the mantelpiece, at a different angle from her face" (874). When his plan to leave her becomes apparent, Gwendolen "stretche[s] out her arms straight, and crie[s] with a smothered voice—'I said I should be forsaken. I have been a cruel woman. And I am forsaken.'" She becomes the "victim of [Daniel's] happiness," and he admits, "I am cruel too, I am cruel" (877).

Gwendolen's desire to communicate the horrors of her life to Daniel fails her when she remains within the bounds of reality that he demands. She understands this restriction and fancifully "wish[es] he could know everything about [her] without [her] telling him" (485). Her fears that speaking her experiences would alienate him are borne out in the narrative. As soon as she has communicated the spectrum of her sensational anxieties after Henleigh's death, Daniel does indeed abandon her. And as he steps away from her, it appears that they have a "difference of native language" (873). We may begin to imagine the things Gwendolen would say were she permitted to perform for Daniel by examining the language of a woman who does not hesitate to perform for him. The Princess Leonora Halm-Eperstein boldly speaks of the terrors that remain suppressed in Gwendolen's breast.

## A Woman's Frame

Aligned through the descriptions Eliot provides of them and the ways in which they begin to define their experience, Leonora and Gwendolen share many characteristics. Both rebel against customary gender roles; both resist religious definition; both perform. Leonora, however, serves as a mouthpiece for the things Gwendolen cannot or dare not say in her dangerous situation. Leonora, Daniel's mother, had felt the bit of an oppressive man just as Gwendolen did. Leonora negotiated a different path of action, however, because the man was her father, not her husband, and when she grew older she married a man who would bend to her wishes. Leonora represents the preeminent model of performance. A superb actress and vocalist, she achieves that which Gwendolen and Lydia—who have no stage and ultimately must remain within the margins of reality— cannot: the authority to act and speak on her own by virtue of her ability to perform an identity that extends beyond the boundaries set in place for her. Leonora's profession as an actress, her position on the stage, the cruelties of her father, and the early death of her first husband make her life a metaphoric embodiment of the transfigured sensational performance of

Lydia, Gwendolen, and herself, as well as leaving her with a wide field in which to perform and few fetters to prevent performance in her own chaotic (mis)understanding of the boundaries between the stage and her life. Catherine Gallagher argues that, for Eliot, women's performance in *Daniel Deronda* is a form of prostitution, an "'unnatural' reproduction of mere signs" as opposed to the "natural" female reproduction of children (41). Although Gallagher believes Eliot disdained the reproduction of signs (something she aligns with sensation/popular novels) as a nonlabor void of "origination of substance" (55), I would argue that Eliot, like Oliphant, recognized the impossibility of escape from the linguistic system and saw the manipulation of signs as a powerfully subversive—if dangerous—tool. Leonora deploys this tool, her voice resounding with the transgression of the borders between stage and reality, speaking those things that belong to sensation as if they were veritable.

> *The varied transitions of tone with which [her] speech was delivered were as perfect as the most accomplished actress could have made them. The speech was in fact a piece of what may be called sincere acting: this woman's nature was one in which all feeling—and all the more when it was tragic as well as real—immediately became a matter of conscious representation: experience immediately passed into drama, and she acted her own emotions. In a minor degree this is nothing uncommon, but in the Princess [Leonora] the acting had a rare perfection of physiognomy, voice and gesture. (691)*

In Leonora, sensation and feeling are as much real as they are performed. Her expertise provides her with the ability to move beyond the structures that limit Gwendolen and Lydia. Daniel notices immediately when he meets her that "her eyes were so piercing and her face so mobile that the next moment she might look like a different person." She masters an alternative speech with her performance, offering a "play of the brow and nostril which made a tacit language" (687). This language loosens the constraints of ordinary social discourse through performance, leaving Leonora with a dialect of her own and a new frame through which to present herself. This language even powerfully alters patriarchal authority, granting her the ability to name and transform names. When Daniel learns that his father and grandfather bore another surname, he questions Leonora about the veracity of his own: "'Oh, [it's] as real as another' said his mother indifferently" (701). To her, naming remains unbounded by the desires of the father and the Law.[37] Daniel, however, dislikes the elasticity of her language that denies his forefathers the right (and by virtue of his birthright, his prerogative as well) to create meaning and identity. Leonora's fluidity of identity and language empowers her to abandon the reason that would deny alternative autonomous action. In fact, she removes herself so far from these restraints that Daniel perceives her as "not quite a human mother, but a Melusina, who had ties with some world which is independent of ours" (688). Leonora creates another world and, like Mélusine, moves fluidly from one to the other.[38] At both levels, acting serves as the tool that allows her a "chance of escaping from the bondage" (694) formed of realism, social and religious law. Leonora could combat the force of her father's domination and have her own will "by seeming to obey." She notes that "[w]hen a woman's will is strong as the man's who wants to govern her, half her strength must be concealment" (695). This concealment does not simply veil what is present; it produces a new means of understanding, a new epistemological mode, as Leonora's distance from the norms indicates. Leonora lauds the voice she gains through this performance, and Daniel demonizes it.

Leonora thus speaks freely of the bonds that limit women's freedom of motion and thought, describing her father's rigidity and domination with an anger and hatred that remains predominately suppressed in the novel's other characters. She describes her youth as a "slavery" to her father, who like other men "[threw] all the weight of [his] will on the necks and souls of women" (694). She felt herself less bound by his will, however, as she became an increasingly adept actress. His commandments became "thunder without meaning" (693) as she moved away from the standards that guide women's lives and, more generally, the culture in which he lives. Still, he attempted to rein her into this social and religious frame, into his notion of womanhood: "[He] never thought of his daughter except as an instrument. Because I had wants outside his purpose, I was to be put in a frame and tortured" (726). Yet she rejected the "frame that got tighter and tighter as [she] grew," creating another through play (693).

Leonora plainly articulates the difficulties women experience in fighting the violence, the torture, that binds them to certain proprietous behaviors and words. When Daniel attempts to convey his empathy with the "hardship of an enforced renunciation" of choice, Leonora rejects his efforts and genders the issue more clearly: "No, . . . You are not a woman. You may try—but you can never imagine what it is to have a man's force of genius in you, and yet to suffer the slavery of being a girl. . . . [A] woman's heart must be of such a size and no larger, else it must be pressed small like Chinese feet" (694). Evoking widespread and accepted forms of cultural torture, Leonora's metaphors of slavery and foot-binding bespeak a kind of ingrained value system that depends upon repression, often in the guise of morality. Daniel's experience of her pronouncements calls up the relationship of morality to these issues; observing her seems to him like a "strange rite of religion which gave a sacredness to crime" (689). As Joanne Long Demaria notes, Daniel perceives Leonora's behavior as criminal because she subverts the laws of motherhood and wifehood. Despite this "sacredness," Daniel finds a shrine that no longer contains any "symbols of sacredness"; Leonora's alteration of these values alters the essential womanhood he had imagined to find in her before their meeting (723).

Leonora seems to Daniel the half-serpent, half-woman Mélusine, who conceals her identity through trickery and performance. Like Gwendolen, described with snakelike imagery throughout the first chapter, Leonora's reptilian fluidity grants her the ability to play with the identity that repulses and threatens Daniel. As his grandfather before him, Daniel wants Leonora to stop acting and to comply with his notions of reality. In the wake of a recognition that his language may become cruel to counter her remarks, Daniel says, "I see no other way to get any clearness than by being truthful. . . . The effects prepared by generations are likely to triumph over a contrivance which would bend them all to the satisfaction of self" (726–27). He desires her to abandon performance and return to reality and truthfulness, succumbing to the will of generations, which cannot be reshaped by her alone. However, in Daniel's assertion that Leonora's shift alone cannot alter larger systems, the novel suggests the possibility of change in the communal acceptance of these terms. If Gwendolen, Lydia, and Leonora all resist, what then becomes of the "effects prepared by generations"?[39]

Daniel's efforts to return Leonora to a state of submission are unnecessary, for her "father [has gotten] his way now" (696). For the same reason that Gwendolen complies, the "army of ghosts" surrounds

Leonora as well. Her father's companion encounters and recognizes Daniel and seeks out the dying princess to curse her. He threatens Leonora with precisely that which keeps Gwendolen under his rule when Henleigh's dictates alone do not suffice, the "shadows . . . rising round [her]" (691), who terrify her more than one man alone could. Her father's death does not leave Leonora free from restraint; another man ultimately discovers her transformation of terms (in Daniel's name and her identity) and punishes her. Her father's and his comrade's threats make her feel subject to "evil enchantments . . . apparitions in the darkness." To these apparitions, she must show subservience, she must fulfill the wishes of the great law that Daniel worships as well: "I don't consent. We only consent to what we love. I obey something tyrannic . . . I have been forced to obey my dead father" (693). Even as she speaks to Daniel, "her large eyes [fix] on something incorporeal," leaving her silenced with her brow knit (692). She admits to him that the hauntings do not confine themselves to the dark of night or to discreet places. Rather, even in moments of comfort and ease, she finds her father and all his progenitors "beginning to make ghosts upon the daylight" (699). Leonora acknowledges that her choice to be independent and autonomous makes her a "monster" in the eyes of her culture, an appellation nearly as dangerous as that of madwoman. She achieves this status precisely because of the difference in her behavior from those within the bounds of the traditional lady's identity: "I am not a monster, but I have not felt exactly what other women feel— or say they feel, for fear of being thought unlike others" (691). Despite this fear, however, the effects of her naming remains; the counterforce to her resistance tells on her, and she ultimately submits, but not until she has shaped herself and her will into something visible—and audible— even to Daniel. Even following her submission, Leonora's voice rings beyond the boundaries of her life on the stage, and her performance continues.

## Real Villains and Sensational Heroines

The tensions of *Daniel Deronda* belie the labeling of a villain or a heroine. Without a doubt, Henleigh Grandcourt embodies the vicious, controlling, and manipulative persona possible within the gentry and aristocracy. Yet Daniel Deronda seems no less a villain when his moral whip-cracking leaves Gwendolen terrified of acting without his sanction, particularly when he abandons her both physically (by leaving the country) and emotionally (through his marriage to Mirah and the spiritual distance he puts between them). However, Eliot does not thrust Gwendolen forward as a role model for Victorian identity either. She begins the novel a selfish child and ends humbled, submissive to the wishes of those she had scorned, insecure and cowed. Leonora's emotional anesthetization to other characters seems as unattractive as the disease that eats her body and leaves her at her father's mercy. Nor does Mirah, a character so one-sided and flat as to be translucent, inspire in the reader much devotion. Readers who pledge their favor to Gwendolen do so perhaps less because she appeals to us as a model of perfection than because the tensions of the culture become so apparent in her struggles between what laws and newspapers recommended as real and what women experienced in the dangerous frames of madness and performance. Gwendolen becomes the visual vanishing point of all the trajectories in the novel. She is the space toward which all of the contradictions between what was represented as violence and what women experienced as material consequences outside the province of violence move. Eliot leaves us with no discernible heroine because this is not a text about victory; rather, she offers us the struggles and the tensions that became increasingly apparent in the law and in fiction as and after sensation novels appeared on the scene. *Daniel Deronda* offers no simple solution to the difficulties represented here. There are risks on all sides, and many of them are literally deadly. Yet, the novel clearly critiques the culture's rigid notions of reality that leave women such as Gwendolen, Lydia, and Leonora sickly and gray in the face of oppression.

However, the possibility exists within the most sensational moments of the novel that women can begin to accomplish what Auerbach describes as the "transform[ation of] private moments into public spectacles" (82), exposing sensation within realism and violence within the domestic scene. As Eliot offers in the epigraph to chapter 1, even science, the standard of reason, must exist with "a make-believe of a beginning," an invented frame—and if this frame has been invented, surely we can invent another.

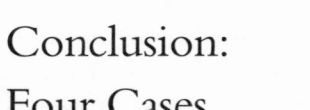

# Conclusion:
# Four Cases
# of Victorian Values

*Why is a woman still not safe when she's in her home?*

—Tracy Chapman, "Why?"

## The Clitheroe Decision

I have attempted to show that the lens of sensation provides a way of seeing patterns that were rendered obscure by nearly two centuries of selective vision. Though the lens is imperfect, marked by the kind of flaws the narrator of *Middlemarch* finds in the pier glass, the scratches fall into concentric circles when illuminated and reveal patterns heretofore unseen. Sensation fiction may be said to have dominated the 1860s, and we may trace one impetus for many literary and legal changes in the ensuing decades to this new fictional mode. Realist literature reflected the impact of sensation, especially in addressing those issues that were most intimately connected to women's bodies and the laws that governed them. Women's bodies were considered a "dark continent" whose impenetrability lent itself to sensational exploration. (Another important issue, imperialism, begs for similar analysis in relation to sensation.) Such complex issues, however, were not resolved by sensation. Instead, the tensions that were embedded in the culture's representation of marital violence became evident in the wake of sensation. One late-century marital rights case, the Clitheroe Decision, which Maeve Doggett claims is of "pivotal significance in the history of law relating to wife-beating" (ix), reveals the impact of sensationalism.

In 1891, Edmund Jackson and two other men forced Edmund's estranged wife, Emily Jackson of Clitheroe, into a waiting carriage as she
and her sister left church. From there they took her to Edmund's house
and she was held within, eventually under guard, while her family gath-
ered outside and attempted to communicate with her. When the details
of this case hit the presses, the response was public outrage—but what
shocked the public the most? That Edmund should employ physical violence to secure Emily and hold her captive against her will, perhaps demanding his legal right to sexual access, while her distraught relations
stood helpless below her window? Or was it that Emily had the audacity
to resist her lawful husband's commands to return home, in direct violation of marriage law and social custom? Was the implication of marital
and sexual violence at the heart of the attention riveted on the case, or
was it the failure of a wife?

Three and a half years earlier, the couple had married against the
wishes of Emily's family. Despite their concerns that Edmund was marrying Emily for her money, the family was unable to prevent the union;
Emily was 42 years old and had an independent income—circumstances
that demanded a kind of independence and freedom of choice. Edmund
left for London the evening of the wedding ceremony and shipped out
to New Zealand days later, intending his wife to follow. He returned after
eight months, but Emily refused to live with him, she and her sister alleg-
ing that the couple had quarreled in their correspondence. Edmund sued
for restitution of conjugal rights (which legally enforced the cohabitation
of a married couple) and used this order to prevent police interference in
her detainment.

Emily's family eventually attempted to procure a writ of habeas corpus to have her released. Initially, the writ was denied, one justice remarking, "[T]hough generally forcible detention of a subject by another
is *prima facie* illegal, yet *where the relation is that of husband and wife the detention is not illegal*" (Shanley 180). The family appealed the decision, and the
court overturned the ruling of the Queen's bench. During the appeal,
with the same assemblage of facts, the Lord Chancellor noted that a husband's right to forcibly hold, imprison, or do violence to his wife did not
exist nor "ever did exist" in British law—remarks that ran directly
counter to those of the Queen's bench. Ironically, in the course of his
statements, the Lord Chancellor himself quoted legal dicta that autho-

rized the violence about which he claimed discussion was absent in Victorian statutes, not to mention the Victorian home (Doggett 3).

The Clitheroe Decision became what both Mary Lyndon Shanley and Maeve Doggett describe as one of the most sensational events in marriage law and provides us, as modern readers, with insight into the tensions still surrounding marital violence at the end of the century. Public attention was riveted to the case and the ruling. Reaction from legal professionals and women's groups was radically mixed. A variety of newspapers and legal journals debated the case. Eliza Lynn Linton saw it as the destruction of the institution of marriage, Elizabeth Wolstenholme-Elmy[1] as the "grandest victory the women's cause has ever yet gained" (Shanley 182). Because of the level of disagreement, these legal decisions and the coincident public furor seem to provide little illumination about the accepted beliefs about marriage and violence. This tension, however, allows us to read the continuing complexity of Victorian attitudes about violence in marriage, attitudes critics have often neglected to study because they were perceived as self-evident. Violence, the story goes, was intolerable, except, perhaps, in the working classes, where it was the subject of much criticism. The Clitheroe case indicates that even late in the century, and after the passage of many legal acts that secured greater rights for women, the question of what was disturbing about marriage and violence (who, for example, was behaving violently?) remained unresolved.

The tensions that emerged so publicly in the Clitheroe case arose from the contradictions in social and legal notions of maritally authorized violence—contradictions that made it possible for one justice to assert its absolute propriety while another casually declared its illegality. The association of sensation with this case suggests that marital violence, disruption, and sensationalism were figured together throughout the period in which the laws governing Caroline Norton in her time of marital distress varied radically from those Emily Jackson faced in the 1890s courtroom. Sensation participated in the evolution of the discourses regarding the domestic space, sexuality, and violence and, by contaminating realism, by revealing the fissures in its logic (like those evident in the Clitheroe case), redefined what was identified as realism, along with Victorian "truths" about marital violence. A. James Hammerton argues that, by late in the century, judges in the divorce courts were experiencing "new-found flexibility" with regard to marital cruelty cases (131). Although he cites the role of education on the job, I contend that the shift toward a new vision of marriage and violence resulted largely from the shifting ideological climate made possible by an education in sensation, a primer increasingly available to a broad group of people throughout the century.

### Sensation in Victorian Britain

Richard D. Altick notes that until the 1860s, "sensation" was a term that was confined to the theater (*Deadly Encounters* 7). It is not surprising, then, that sensation novels took on this term when they began performing scenes in the Victorian family that called into question what had been commonly asserted as a reality. "Wife torture," it was believed, simply did not occur in the middle and upper classes of this civilized nation; moral imperatives prevented it. As the tensions between what was possible and what was unnatural or impossible erupted in the newspapers, in the fiction, and occasionally in the lives of respectable Victorians, notions of what was real became less and less trustworthy. Altick outlines one such case concerning a man named Major Murray, brought before a coroner's jury for murder. Murray claimed to have been lured into a strange man's home in a respectable district, shot in the head twice, and then to have viciously beaten the man (who later died) in self-defense. The press ridiculed Murray's claims as fancy, sensation, and unrealistic prevarication. Murray was identified as a murderous charlatan—until voluminous evidence emerged to support his seemingly wild story. Altick argues that the "strange but (as it proved) true story of Major Murray dispensed them [sensation novelists (and realist novelists?)] from the obligation that normally binds the writer of realist fiction" (151). Significantly, Altick blurs the referent of the pronoun "them," blurring also the generic classification of sensation and realist fiction. Along with this Altick notes that the social conditions of the day, the news media, and the fiction offered up a hypothesis to the middle-class Victorian: "it can happen to you" (154), a message that pervades not only the plot and subject matter of the sensation novel, but the rhetorical style as well. No one is safe from the imposition of sensation upon his or her reality. No one can ensure that his "private rod" will not be exposed to public scrutiny.

The public scrutiny the sensation novel affords in its tenuous negotiation of the real and the not real offers us an opportunity to examine the presence and possibility of marital violence in the domestic scene of Victorian Britain. It also provides us with a means of rereading, through the lens of gender and marital relations, Michel Foucault's notion of the disciplinary regime that evolved over the eighteenth and nineteenth centuries. Clearly, juridical modes of power were in place—not in the prisons, mental institutions, or marketplaces, but in the home. Sensation became the spectacle that Foucault argues was extinguished along with "spectacular manifestations of power" (*Discipline and Punish* 217). I argue that these modes of power were not extinguished, but privatized, internalized, and domesticated—a function the sensation novel reveals. In those revelations, voices increasingly considered reasonable spoke to marital violence. Frances Power Cobbe's campaign against wife torture was in full swing by the late 1870s, and several papers were published that addressed the issue of marital violence. Lydia Becker's *Women's Suffrage Journal* carried several articles on wife abuse, and Serjeant Pulling's "influential paper . . . on crimes of violence at the Liverpool Social Science Congress of 1876" appeared (Hammerton 53). The new voice, which could now, over the shifting ground of realism, be considered authoritative cemented legal and social changes that continued to grant women greater freedoms and more expansive rights. Perhaps the reason that fiction was not so frequently labeled as sensation later in the century is that what made it sensational was being incorporated into the shifting ground of the real.

### Lorena Bobbitt and Other Dangerous Women

The ideological shifts I outline here do not provide unambivalent success for feminists, nor do they offer a clear strategy for shelter within the confines of the family. Indeed, we see the same patterns reiterated in many contemporary arguments about domestic violence. When director Oliver Stone discussed *Natural Born Killers,* a film he called a critique of violence and sensationalism, he listed several serial killers he believed had been sensationalized and glorified by the press. Surprisingly, the first villain on his list was not any of the array of contemporary mass murderers or sexual criminals who have become media stars: Ted Bundy, Son of Sam, Richard Speck, Danny Rolling. Rather, Stone's primary target was Lorena Bobbitt, acquitted of reckless endangerment for severing her husband's penis after what she claimed was a night of terror, assault, and rape. Stone made no mention of John Wayne Bobbitt's long documented history of domestic violence, which reappeared in his relationship with his new fiancée, or of the terror that women experience when they are in a physically, sexually, and/or emotionally abusive relationship. Stone focused instead on the feminist championing of a woman who fought back against her attacker, describing her act as sensational, mercenary, brutal. John Wayne Bobbitt's assaults remain nearly invisible, and Lorena Bobbitt becomes a threat to cultural safety, a dangerous woman, not a hero who fought back against a series of criminal assaults, but a figure to be reviled for her resistance. Her act of violence serves to screen the brutality of her husband and has itself been regarded as a sign of social decay, as sensation fiction was in its day.

In a similar trend, the O. J. Simpson case was consistently described as sensationalized. The coverage of Simpson's arrest (for the murder of his ex-wife, Nicole Brown Simpson, and her friend Ronald Goldman), the jury selection, the omnipresence of the trial, and the announcement of the verdict have all been critiqued for their sensationalism. Although the case clearly involves a wide range of elements besides marital violence, including racial tensions that many writers seemed reluctant to address (until the verdict was read, and then the tensions were distilled to an oversimplified complaint about the race of the jurors),[2] class issues, and questions about the relationship between violent popular sports and heroism, murder lies at the center of this case. *Newsweek* columnist Meg Greenfield, writing on the case in a column entitled "In Defense of Sensationalism," noted that "the air has been full of complaint about all the attention being paid the case—prurient, sick, unworthy, sensationalistic attention. . . . Since the first news of it broke we have been told at least twice a day that we should be thinking about something else and what is the matter with us anyway?" She went on to add that "[it] is ridiculous to assume, as so many of the exasperated do, that [sensational stories] are somehow not serious. . . . [T]he startling crimes and trials, the passions that wreck lives and destroy families and other institutions[,] [don't go] to ancient, even primal human concerns" (72). As I have shown, sensationalism *is* linked with the ancient concerns, concerns that a civilized nation wants to reject as real.

Despite this fact, Lorena Bobbitt's resistance provided another way of imagining domestic violence for many women, just as the dangerous women in sensation novels offered new conceptions of marriage and gender in their day; and the O. J. Simpson case prompted a rash of new reports of domestic violence and, at least temporarily, supported an increase in funding to domestic violence shelters across the country. Lorena Bobbitt and Nicole Simpson join a cast of women—such as Anita Hill, who according to most accounts of social history facilitated an exponentially increased reporting of sexual harassers in the workplace, and Patty Bowman, who fought for a rape conviction of William Kennedy Smith despite his popularity and fame—who threaten cultural values, not necessarily because they defied them themselves, but because they revealed persistent tensions surrounding our value system. (If we think domestic violence is wrong, why is it so difficult to get a convicted batterer any jail time?) Although Bowman lost her case, the challenge dangerous women provide to a notion of domestic, moral, and male realism offers women a chance to appear from behind the blue dot that elides their faces in trials that materialize on our television screens, in our neighborhoods, and in our homes. Sensationalism may often be dismissed as unreal, but the way it shifts the terms of realism often hits home with those who remain oppressed by ideological assumptions of their equality, safety, and security. Sensational cases are still altering our values. Though we may seem Victorian at times, the terms of our value system continue to evolve.

Years of work in shelters handling hotline calls from victims of rape, battery, and incest taught me to regard with suspicion the dismissive categorization of any depiction of sexual violence as sensational or fictional, and to reexamine the categories that make it possible to marginalize and trivialize these representations. Although the public, and often sensational, exposure of these issues has launched what Susan Faludi has dubbed a tremendous backlash, people are talking—just as they were in Victorian Britain. It was in Victorian Britain, amidst and following the sensation of the 1860s and '70s, that the first legislation designed to protect women from brutality in marriage, financially and physically, was passed. Despite the fact that much of the legislation then, and today, reifies notions of domestic privacy and nonenforcement, there has been change—the kind of change that makes it possible for me to offer a study such as this one. If critics continue to examine these issues and the complex associations that make domestic violence an entrenched and widespread cultural ill, interrogating what has been considered real and what fiction, we can help articulate a shifting understanding of our culture—perhaps one of the most important services academics can provide.

# Notes

## Introduction

1. "Fantoccini" referred to either marionettes on strings or the performance of the show itself. The *Oxford English Dictionary* provides literary examples that suggest this performance was one that the elite could attend without fear of besmirching their names, a more fashionable and socially acceptable formulation of puppetry and performance than Punch.

2. In a three-part series titled "Our Novels," *Temple Bar* compares the characters in the "Sensational School" to the puppets as a means of indicating how shallowly constructed the figures are (488). Such a comparison is evocative because of the precise naming of this puppet show in relation to sensational text.

3. I am particularly attentive here to the interrogation Jacques Derrida makes in Stephen Scobie's "Signature Event Context" into the distinction between "serious" and "performative" text and speech, calling for a collapse of the boundary between these terms. I am also interested in the ideological investments embedded in the distinction between feminine romance texts and male, realist, intellectual texts that Elaine Hadley discusses in chapter 4 of *Melodramatic Tactics*.

4. Similarly, Catherine Gallagher argues in *The Industrial Reformation of English Fiction* that Matthew Arnold's efforts to remark and redress the tensions present in industrial fiction during the debates about the Second Reform Bill have left us a canonical legacy—the virtual absence of industrial fiction, which had rendered visible the tensions Arnold hoped to reframe.

5. Certainly, academics are not the only people who reproduce and regenerate the patterns I will lay out in the chapters to come. Popular culture is rife with examples of the same tensions: for example, the cases of O. J. Simpson and Lorena Bobbitt, which I discuss in the conclusion. The connection between pop culture media and the epistemological assumptions of academics is in many ways similar to that between sensation fiction and the law.

6. Žižek indicates that our awareness of this phenomenon is vital in order to prevent a materialist study from "ensnar[ing] us in the historicist relativism that suspends the inherent cognitive value of the term 'ideology' and makes it into an expression of social circumstances" (10), rather than an "elusive network of implicit, quasi-'spontaneous' presuppositions and attitudes that form an irreducible moment of the reproduction of 'non-ideological' (economic, legal, political, sexual . . . ) practices" (15).

7. Many critics extend the frame of sensation fiction, noting the way in which novels much earlier and later employ sensation tropes or techniques. I have chosen novels

that were self-identified and labeled explicitly by contemporary criticism as sensational. The label of sensation itself became significant in the construction of these novels (as Jonathan Loesberg has noted) and in the laws regarding women's rights. This study, however, culminates in a breakdown of these terms, examining the social and political effects of such labeling.

8. Wilkie Collins has commanded the attention of scholars such as Winifred Hughes (*Maniac in the Cellar*) and Jenny Bourne Taylor (*In the Secret Theatre of the Home*). Other authors, such as Dickens, have occasionally been studied for their relation to sensation, but not at length for their generic classification as sensation novelists. Richard Altick, Thomas Boyle, Ann Cvetkovich, and Lyn Pykett provide compelling examinations of the phenomenon of sensation as well as sensation versus realism. However, this pioneering work often remarginalizes sensation as a fictional Other by which the real is defined.

9. Interestingly, the Sadleir Collection at the University of California, Los Angeles provides an official definition of the genre that describes sensation as "those works dependent on a fair smattering of rape, near rapes, suicides, murders and other mysterious happenings" (qtd. in Boyle, 120). Although rape can certainly be a form of marital violence, this definition does not suggest the kind of battery we traditionally define as domestic violence despite its insistent presence in these novels. This omission perhaps betrays a continued reluctance to mark the domestic space as a potential site of violence.

10. I have chosen to employ the phrase "marital violence" to indicate the phenomenon of physical and mental abuse that occurs within the confines of the fictional Victorian, heterosexual, middle-class marriages or common-law or regularized marriages in the working class (like that of Nancy and Bill in *Oliver Twist*). I am focusing particularly on the gendered nature of violence in the home, violence predominantly enacted by men against women, along with the resulting political tensions that are often mapped out along gender lines. I have not used the common Victorian phraseology "wife beating" because this term often would not have been applicable to the texts I study. To imply that the passages I examine would have been defined contemporarily as describing wife beating would be misleading. The difficulties of making such a phrase stick to anything other than certain socially demarcated situations—primarily those involving "working-class alcoholic men" and "irresponsible working-class women"—concealed the violence in middle- and upper-class homes, and I wanted to make visible a phenomenon that often went unnamed. The phrase "marital violence" (one that would not have seemed foreign to the Victorians themselves) also avoids the trap of specifically signifying only the wife, which eliminated the husband from the formula and seemed to make the wife the only factor in the violence, implicitly suggesting that she was responsible for the abuse she suffered. Although I was initially drawn to the phrase "sexual violence," since it clearly indicated the gender dynamic and the threat of sexual power, including rape (which was not a crime in marriage, unless a woman was sodomized), I wanted a term that would avoid the suggestion of only rape or something that was exclusively physical. "Sexual" was so bound to the body, I feared that it would prove too limiting. See A. James Hammerton's *Cruelty and Companionship* for an excellent discussion of sexual assault as well as other forms of violence in marriage as they appeared in the news, the courts, and the law.

11. Eliot's realism has been contested since her novels first appeared, and the sheer volume of work debating this issue indicates the significance of the term in her writing. George Levine says of Eliot's *Daniel Deronda* that "[t]he complexity of reality as George Eliot imagines it makes for a reality unimaginable in traditional realistic forms" (272). He sees in her work a "new science . . . being shaped and 'reality' . . . being transformed" (274). Daniel Cottom argues that "[i]n Eliot's conception, realism transcends romance. However, it does not do so by a simple rejection of the values or inversion of the stylistic characteristics of romance; it transcends romance as the liberal intellectual transcends society in general: by interpreting it, understanding it, and so gaining the power to patronize it" (*Social Figures* 125). Richard Altick notes that "reviewers of . . . George Eliot's novels in particular . . . could scarcely have done their job without ["daguerreotype" and "photograph"] in their inkwells. Eventually [those words] were supplanted by *realism* and *realist*" (*Presence of the Present* 338). Jerome Meckier argues that, in the fiction market, "the goal was to establish one's credentials as a realist, hence a reliable social critic, by taking away someone else's— generally Dickens's. Trollope, Mrs. Gaskell, and especially George Eliot attempted to make room for themselves in the 1850s and '60s by pushing the preeminent Dickens aside" (2). Karen Chase says, "George Eliot's realism has most often been regarded as a commitment to 'ordinary life'—'the faithful representation of commonplace things'(144). Since my study hinges on the attempt, and often failure, to define writers and subject matter as sensational or realist, it is not as important that Eliot be a realist as that she was often defined as such.

12. In "Illegitimacy, Insanity, and Insolvency," Stana Nenadic constructs a lengthy argument concerning the use of novels, particularly sensation novels, for insight into Victorian culture.

13. Frances L. Restuccia concurs with this assertion and critiques Nancy Armstrong and Leonard Tennenhouse's introduction to *The Violence of Representation* as I critique Foucault himself below. Restuccia argues that Armstrong and Tennenhouse generate a totalizing narrative in terms of violence and its reproduction in text; she reads this as a product of their failure to examine the various means of approaching representation and of their insistence upon confounding the differences between a batterer's violence, a woman's responsive violence, and a sympathetic resistant portrayal. Restuccia makes important points about the way in which the complexity of the narratives she studies resist a reading of simple complicity. See my discussion of Cvetkovich in the final section of this chapter.

14. Ground-breaking feminist work has been done by critics such as Nancy Armstrong (*Desire and Domestic Fiction*) and Elizabeth Langland (*Nobody's Angels*) using Foucault's theories to illuminate the role literature, gender, and class play in shaping various Victorian discourses and in turn reshaping those discourses themselves.

15. Foucault notes in *History of Sexuality* that power has often been examined only in those places in which it is most visible, "irreducible to the representation of the law" (89). This narrow research focus been translated to the study of legal statutes as sufficient cultural authority regarding questions of gender, violence, and the home, and fictionally to the study of high realist fiction and the canon. Perhaps one of the most significant contributions Foucault has made to research in the academy is his insight that all ephemera, not simply those that are visible, hold juridical and monarchic power and provide a valuable means of examining culture. He suggests that we must

"cut off the king's head" in order to more adequately examine political systems (*Power/Knowledge* 121). However, his analysis does not venture into the realm of the fictional. William A. Cohen (*Sex Scandal*) and D. A. Miller (*The Novel and the Police*) have remarked upon the ways in which Foucault himself was reserved in his study of literature. Cohen argues that the study of literature attends to "richly ambiguous, subtly coded, prolix and polyvalent" discourses, offering us access to what he calls the "unspeakable."

16. As Susan Faludi argues in *Backlash,* many of the intimidating claims made in recent years that damaged the political efficacy of feminism through fear—for example, about the dilemmas in which women who delayed marriage or childbirth to facilitate their careers found themselves—erroneously represent information and produce a desire for a return to the safety of traditional behaviors. Critics may have failed to see other representations of violence simply because many forms of discourse suggested there were no other representations. In searching for those in sensation fiction, I have encountered an alternative voice to the one typically represented.

17. Though all of the novelists mentioned here had successful writing careers, the best-selling novels of the period were often the sensational works. Mary Elizabeth Braddon, for example, was enthroned as "Queen of the Circulating Libraries." See both *The Presence of the Present* and *Victorian Studies in Scarlet*.

18. There are, of course, notable exceptions, such as Virginia B. Morris's *Double Jeopardy*. Morris is primarily concerned with examining the fictional presence in mid-century literature of "unmarried mothers [who] did kill their infants, abused wives their husbands, and abandoned women their lovers," but she also argues that the authors "seemed to feel justified in ignoring the political implications of their women's deeds" (152–53). The political implications of these fictional representations are impossible to ignore or escape. Many other critics mention domestic violence tangentially without making it a primary concern. (Interestingly, it has only been in recent years that the *MLA Bibliography* has provided an indexical cue for domestic violence, an indication, perhaps, of both the lack of critical matter on the subject and resistance to the issue itself.)

19. The disregard with which many critics have dismissed sensation has recently been called into question. Pamela K. Gilbert says that the "task of cultural power groups [such as literary critics] became . . . [the] organiz[ation] and control [of] these other voices" (45). She argues that sensation was a category articulated to contain; I argue that this project necessarily fails, since discursive purity is impossible (the very act of naming indicates its movement into the mainstream), and that it then becomes a hermeneutic device, a means of reading the previously undecipherable.

20. This is not to suggest that sensation novels were unregulated. Many of them appeared as selections in Mudie's Circulating Library (which, to some extent, explains their remarkable popularity), and Mudie's reputation was established on maintaining a library of literature appropriate for a young lady's consumption. Yet, the scandal of sensation was by no means a subtle aspect of its oeuvre. William A. Cohen's *Sex Scandal* details the complex relations of public exposure and privacy.

21. In Patrick Brantlinger's fascinating discussion of culture and credit in Britain, *Fictions of State,* he notes that realism was a move away from social criticism in novels and toward a discussion of "moral currency" (like that in *Daniel Deronda* through Daniel and Mordecai's proto-Zionist vision). Brantlinger sees this move as paralleling the

"increasing privatization of issues of debt and (monetary) credit" (143). Brantlinger's argument does not touch upon popular fiction such as sensation, though he studies the link between the production of novels and capital (clearly a concern for and a charge against sensation novelists), yet I see a link between his sense of the increasing privatization of credit and the increasing privatization of the domestic space that was fractured by fiction such as sensation—fiction that did not move away from social critique. Wilkie Collins, perhaps the most explicitly critical of all sensation novelists, grappled with the failings of the law, and Mary Elizabeth Braddon and others with the social tensions the law produced.

22. Not all texts that were besmirched by the name of sensation retained this dubious distinction, and some writers, such as Charles Reade, were sometimes held above this category as writers of the real (see Margaret Oliphant's "Sensation Novels").

23. Athena Vrettos notes in her study of somatic fictions that she reads "not merely instances of parallel rhetoric, but interactive patterns of thought that signal points of conceptual blockage, social transformation, or cultural obsession. Somatic fictions are not the unified products of a coherent cultural logic; rather, they are emblematic of the promiscuous interaction and semiotic drift of cultural forms" (178–79).

24. Certainly, part of the dilemma for women who are victims of domestic violence today is that police and the courts still tend to view marital disorder as a matter for private resolution. However, there are laws that specifically address and provide for the intervention of the state into a violent home. Further, the face of the laws has clearly shifted since a century and a half ago. Prior to mid-century legislation concerning cruelty, a man could legally beat his wife, even if it resulted in crippling, maiming, and, occasionally, death, particularly if the courts felt there was provocation. See Francis Power Cobbe's "Wife Torture in England" and Nancy Tomes's "A 'Torrent of Abuse.'"

25. William A. Cohen explains in *Sex Scandal* that sensational narratives of scandal actually reinforced the notion that such matters were private through their articulation of them as scandalous. This is true, but as he notes, these still privatized scandals "provide the opportunity for new types of knowledge about sexuality to circulate publicly" (11). It is this circulation that transforms the social structure by generating particular social effects. Public engagement is the element in which I am most interested.

26. According to Victorian critics, sensation novels were primarily responsible for this inversion. They failed to offer the desirable "quiet picture of common every-day life" ("Recent Novels" 103). Rather, sensation "would have us believe that crime is not an accident, but is the business of life" (Rae, "Sensation Novelists" 104). These crimes were often explicitly related to failed, disrupted, or illegal marriage in reviewers' analysis. Henry Mansel suggests that it is a school of fiction peopled with "highly-coloured portraits of beautiful fiends and fast young ladies burdened with superfluous husbands" who reduce marriage to a "temporary connection" (256–60).

27. Nancy Armstrong also presents a persuasive argument about the domestication of women through a novelistic reification of gendered terms in *Desire and Domestic Fiction.* See my discussion of her argument in chapter 3.

28. Elaine Showalter discusses these questions in her landmark essay "Desperate Remedies," regarding *Lady Audley's Secret,* one of the first and most important sensation novels.

29. Winifred Hughes lays out, with fine precision, the tensions between realism and sen-

sation, arguing ultimately that authors such as Thomas Hardy and Eliot did produce novels with sensational elements. I am interested in understanding not just how sensational elements might have been co-opted in the service of realism, but also how realism was epistemologically reconceived in ways that make sense only if we understand the impact of sensation fiction.

30. Georg Lukacs also speaks to the transforming nature of realistic fiction, which "appears as something in the process of becoming. That is why, from the artistic point, the novel is the most hazardous genre, and why it has been described as only half an art by many who equate *having a problematic with being a problematic*" (73). Though Lukacs uses his terms to distinguish art from its "caricatural twin, . . . the entertainment novel," my argument would deconstruct the dichotomy he sets up here to apply his claim to sensation fiction as well.

31. I would like to address briefly my reasons for excluding some of the novels that might seem obvious choices for a study of marital violence and sensation. I have not included Anne Brontë's *Tenant of Wildfell Hall* or George Eliot's novella "Janet's Repentance" in *Scenes of Clerical Life* because they are significantly complicated by the question of drunkenness, a "moral disease" that was believed to go hand in hand with marital violence, another screen that marked violence as an anomaly. Brontë's novel of regency decadence consigns abuse to the past, the gothic, and the rollicking derelictions of a dissipated aristocracy not yet tamed by middle-class values. Elaine Showalter notes the role of moral renewal as well, suggesting that unhappy marriages such as the one in "Janet's Repentance" are depicted as "spiritual opportunit[ies]" ("Desperate Remedies" 5). I would argue that these opportunities exist primarily for the wife—Janet, not her abusive husband, must be the one to repent of her sins. Both of these novels, however, support my claims about the role of middle-class morality in the formation of an understanding of marital violence not yet refashioned by sensation. *Aurora Floyd* and *Salem Chapel* also conduct a token moral rebirth of their heroines in the last few pages of the novel, yet their heroines must be reformed by (the violence of) their partners—a much more sensational proposition. Rather than simply conforming to the notion of the woman's moral excellence, sensation novels as a genre "shake that mutual confidence by which societies and above all, families, are held together" by questioning the morality and identity of (dangerous) women as an avenue to question the morality of the family and of husbands (*London Quarterly Review,* qtd. in Page, 157). Evolving at the heart of the century, when middle-class morality and the solidity of the family were vital to Victorian notions of order, propriety, and identity, sensation novels portray the crumbling exterior that functioned to conceal marital violence and bolster the sanctity, and privacy, of the family. The novels I have examined here provide a fascinating path through the Victorians' struggles with the reality of marital violence.

## I. A *"Pound"* of Flesh

1. To "ride Skimmington" was another ritual that was reserved to ridicule a man beaten by his wife. It consisted of "a man riding behind a woman with his face to the horse's tail, holding a distaff in his hand, at which he seems to work, the woman all the while beating him with a ladle" (Hazlitt 551). They are accompanied by rough music.

2. In *Desire and Domestic Fiction,* Nancy Armstrong argues that conduct books "at-

tacked . . . traditional notions of the female body in order to suggest that the female had depths far more valuable than her surface. By implying that the essence of the woman lay inside or underneath her surface, the invention of depths in the self entailed making the material body of the woman appear superficial" (76). Armstrong also discusses the role of Richardson's *Pamela* in "deflecting eroticism away from the material body and onto writing" (120). Though in Charlotte Brontë she sees a revision of these notions, the scene of seduction converted to the scene of reading, she does not read Brontë as "offering resistance in the face of political oppression. . . . Like virtually every other novelist who is well known today, she displaces class conflict onto sexual relations and inscribes them within a modern institutional culture. Thus contained, they come to represent two poles within middle-class discourse rather than the hegemonic struggle between that discourse and cultural voices capable of speaking another political truth" (200).

3. It is important to note that criminality encompasses more than pickpocketing and kidnapping in the novel; it also includes housebreaking (a violent disruption of the domestic space), domestic murder, and what was later to be more explicitly criminalized in the Divorce Act, physical abuse.

4. A collection of short and graphic true-crime narratives bearing the name of London's infamous prison, *The Calendar* contained parables of community and family relations fragmented by acts of violence and the standards of the law.

5. In later works, Dickens would revise this pattern in characters such as Little Nell. Matthew Rowlinson, however, identifies Nell as a manifestation of the sublime, which would suggest that her death is merely another form of her own vexed immateriality and materiality.

6. Helena Michie notes in her analysis of this novel in *The Flesh Made Word* that Nancy increasingly cloaks her body as the novel progresses, "focus[ing] far more obsessively on what [she puts] on than on what [she takes] off" (76). This cloaking does not obscure the body, but rather draws attention to it (as Michie indicates elsewhere in her argument). Nancy's physical cloaking is a gesture toward repression that always remains at the level of the material, but it never effects the kind of purity available in the social disembodiment we see in Rose and Oliver. Note, for example, that we are never granted detailed accounts of Rose's garb, even though she is a central character, described in great detail.

7. Elizabeth Langland notes in *Nobody's Angels* that Arthur Munby, the gentleman lover of working-class women, perceived the women in whom he invested his affection as "not 'wom[e]n' within his culture's signifying practices," in part because of their "sinewy" animal-like strength and "grace" (127). Many contemporary social critics, Members of Parliament, and physicians argued that working-class women were more animalistic because they lacked the civilizing influence that culture provided women of greater means. Thus, one minister wrote that "these are living persons, with strong animal instincts . . . [whose] passions are uncontrolled" (qtd. in Barrett-Durocq, 37).

8. A genre of popular fiction known as Newgate novels evolved in the early nineteenth century. Its most famous practitioner was William H. Ainsworth, but the work of other writers, including Edward Bulwer-Lytton, Dickens, and Thackeray, has been classified in this way. In Dickens's case, I will challenge the argument (as Dickens himself did) that he might simply be classified as a Newgate novelist. Hollingsworth argues that *Oliver Twist* qualified for classification as a Newgate novel because of its

representation of criminal characters, some of whom likely corresponded to real people. I point to the way that, though Dickens did employ some of *The Newgate Calendar*'s strategies, he resisted others, revising them significantly.

9. See chapter 2 for a discussion of the Divorce Act and the debates that preceded it.

10. Beth Kalikoff discusses a range of nineteenth-century narratives, from street literature to melodrama to fiction, arguing that women's sexuality was often punished with death, particularly in early nineteenth-century working-class narratives and, later in the century, in sensation fiction. She also indicates that in popular fiction early in the century, the murderer's gallows repentance "mend[ed] the moral fabric murder rips" (15). I find the murderer's repentance to be absent in those cases that deal with lethal marital violence and, thus, important for consideration on those grounds, particularly in terms of the contrast I will offer in the person of the victim.

11. There are several fascinating discussions of Oliver's innate genteel identity. Michael Peled Ginsburg's "Truth and Persuasion" tackles the question of Oliver's polished speech that never bears traces of its working-class history.

12. See Garrett Stewart's *Dear Reader* for an extended discussion of the position of both the reader and the text.

13. Jacques Lacan describes this process as the fundamental engagement with the Other that constitutes the self in the signifying process. Derrida and critics following his argument, such as Julia Kristeva, note that in iteration there always lies the possibility for disruption, which is certainly built into the movement of these signifiers too. Though we can only understand these movements in their iteration, it is in their imperfect mimesis that I find the space for social change.

14. "[A]ll ideology hails or interpellates concrete individuals as concrete subjects, by the functioning of the category of the subject. . . . [I]t 'recruits' subjects among individuals (it recruits them all), or 'transforms' the individuals into subjects (it transforms them all) by that very precise operation which I have called *interpellation* or hailing, and which can be imagined along the lines of the most commonplace everyday police (or other) hailing: 'Hey, you there!' " (130–31).

15. Schön and Stewart are arguing here for this displacement only in silent reading because of the termination of the musculature movement associated with enunciation, like this moment in the Maylies' study. I am suggesting that even in those acts of orality there is a displacement of the material onto the text, not a literal evaporation of the human body but a substitutionary, representational shift.

16. We see this potential for danger again with the degraded Bumbles, who circulate in the criminal world rather than with the middle classes: Mrs. Bumble commands her husband to "say as little as you can, or you'll betray us at once" (335). When he does dare to speak, Mrs. Bumble chastises him by saying, "You are a fool . . . and had better hold your tongue." Monks concurs, and links this to bodily violence, saying, "He had better have cut [his tongue] out, before he came, if he can't speak in a lower tone" (339). The encounter ends with the couple promising their silence. "You may depend upon my not saying a word to you, young man," Mr. Bumble says, "or about you, on no account" (344). Later, Mrs. Bumble again silences Mr. Bumble, as "peaching" sends them out of their life of workhouse mastery and into the workhouse: "Hold your tongue, fool" (460). Indeed, she indicates, since Monks "has been coward enough to confess, as I see he has[,] . . . I have nothing more to say" (461). As

a result of this talk, Mr. and Mrs. Bumble are "reduced to great indigence and misery, and finally became paupers in that very same workhouse in which they had once lorded it over others" (477).

17. Grahame Smith notes that Dickens had a "burning ambition to be a financially independent, professional writer" (71) and that he valued a "public assertion of his profession" (16). I read this as a desire to generate himself in a specific social frame, the same frame in which Oliver is being tutored.

18. Some critics, such as Judith L. Fisher, Mary Saunders, and George J. Worth, have cited particular scenes in Dickens that bear the mark of sensationalism by virtue, for example, of its relationship to melodrama. I argue that those sensational moments gesture to the figures that will come to fruition in the sensation genre. Dickens's work serves as a forerunner to sensation fiction, not simply an incorporation of the modes of the past.

## II. Brutality and Propriety

1. The essay cited in the epigraph to this chapter appeared in *Argosy,* a journal edited by Mrs. Henry Wood, the author of *East Lynne,* considered one of the trinity of novels that gave birth to sensation.

2. Lillian Nayder agrees, arguing that Collins speaks to the evils of coverture while still expressing anxiety about female autonomy (*Wilkie Collins* 85). Nayder's excellent analysis finds different impulses at the core of Collins's resistance than I do, pointing to overarching themes in his oeuvre.

3. Gail Turley Houston discusses the sensation novel *Lady Audley's Secret* in relation to the Divorce Act in her essay "Mary Braddon's Commentaries," arguing that the novel causes its audience to interrogate the soundness of English law. Houston speaks to the role of fiction in demonstrating and playing out the tensions in the law. I am arguing that the tensions present in the social and legal understanding of what was called, globally, the "Woman Question" actually helped generate the genre of sensation fiction and that the genre participated in a discourse that generated legal reform.

4. Though alternative, these representations were not the radical innovations of sensation—rather sensation played out in narrative social tensions already circulating in the culture, undoubtedly aggravating the anxieties further—nor were they necessarily more true than what was considered real, but they did reshape notions of what was possible and real.

5. Hansard Parliamentary Debates, 3d ser., vol. 145 (25 May 1857), col. 801–2. Hereafter cited as 3 Hansard 145 (25 May 1857), 801–2.

6. 3 Hansard 141 (3 March 1856), 800.

7. 3 Hansard 145 (25 May 1857), 797.

8. Jan Lambertz notes that the problem of wife abuse was set "in the broader context of working-class urban manhood, a contextualization aided by mass press accounts of court decisions. These generated a stereotype of the culprit in 'wife-torture' as a 'lower' type of working-class man, an insensitive, drink-crazed brute, a primitive" (27).

9. 3 Hansard 143 (3 July 1856), 240.

10. 3 Hansard 146 (23 June 1857), 215.

11. 3 Hansard 141 (3 March 1856), 1693.

12. 3 Hansard 143 (3 July 1856), 247.

13. 3 Hansard 146 (23 June 1857), 215; 3 Hansard 145 (25 May 1857), 814; 3 Hansard 141 (3 March 1856), 1688.

14. 3 Hansard 145 (25 May 1857), 813.

15. Philip O'Neill also argues for this dual function of propriety "Janiform" in Wilkie Collins's fiction. He sees it as a means "to hide the truth and . . . reveal the truth" (106). He further argues that the gender ambiguity in the novel reveals Collins's insistence that propriety is a thoroughly ideological, rather than natural, formation.

16. The walking stick, cane, or whip appear in all of the novels discussed here and also in other narratives that discuss violence, including Anne Brontë's *Tenant of Wildfell Hall* and George Eliot's "Janet's Repentance."

17. 3 Hansard 145 (25 May 1857), 800.

18. Ibid., 803, 805.

19. *Feme sole* status, literally "woman alone," allowed a woman to act independently on her own behalf and at her own risk and responsibility as single women did: to make contracts, incur debt, and apportion her money and property any way she chose.

20. 3 Hansard 145 (4 June 1857), 1098.

21. 3 Hansard 145 (25 May 1857), 811.

22. The construct of dangerous women is developed at greater length in chapter 3 of this text.

23. See Judith Butler's *Gender Trouble* and *Bodies That Matter,* discussed in more detail in later chapters.

24. 3 Hansard 146 (23 June 1857), 200–201.

25. Domestic animals often serve as indices of tensions in the domestic space, a convention of Victorian fiction that evolves from the animalistic bull's-eye Nancy becomes in *Oliver Twist* to the genteel purebreds in sensation fiction, a theme I develop in chapters 3–5.

26. Fosco's disciplinary surveillance is comprised not just of the internalized (or external) monitoring Michel Foucault describes in *Discipline and Punish.* Rather, Madame Fosco's submission comes as a result of the employment of a private rod as well. This exposure of the privatized violence for public consumption exposes as well the instabilities of Foucault's theories when inflected through gender. In this disciplinary relationship, the juridical exercise of power plays a significant role. Teresa de Lauretis argues in "The Violence of Rhetoric" that gendered material violence is precisely what Foucault's theories neglect: "[O]f the three—the concept [of family violence], the expression [of the same], and the violence—only the first two belong to Foucault's discursive order. The third is somewhere else, like 'bodies and pleasure,' outside the social. Now, for those of us whose bodies and whose pleasures are out there where the violence is (in that we have no language, enunciative position, or power apparatuses to speak them), the risk of saying yes to sex-desire and power is relatively small, and amounts to a choice between the devil and the deep blue sea" (246).

27. Evasion of the law becomes a vexed issue for the Members of Parliament. Collusion and circumvention represent "serious evil[s]" for the community, precisely because they are unpunishable; they fall outside the framework of what is legislatable (3 Hansard 143 [3 July 1856], 248–49).

28. The growing trend to value those goods that are the product of personal labor (a belief that has a historical precedence in Locke's claim that one may own only what

one produces with one's own hands), especially as the middle class worked to establish the validity of earned income over inherited wealth, may be why we see representations such as this one in *The Woman in White* and images in Trollope's novels such as *The Duke's Children* and *He Knew He Was Right,* in which Americans identify themselves as wage earners against what they perceive as an indolent aristocracy. Though the narrator in Trollope's novels assures us that the "middle-class values" expressed by vulgar Americans are mistaken, they are insistent in the texts and certainly had some coincidence with Trollope's own sense of production for income.

29. Certainly, the rule of the middle classes was not complete. Indeed, a profound reverence for the aristocracy continued to exist alongside stringent criticism. Similarly, the middle classes were experiencing economic distress as well as economic development, visible in the anxiety over genteelly "redundant women" and economically disenfranchised sons sent to the colonies to earn their bread. It is in part from this tension that the need to designate the middle classes as morally authoritative derives.

30. Significant studies have laid out various claims about the precise nature of these value systems; see Nancy Armstrong, Jeffrey Weeks, Elizabeth Langland, and Mary Poovey, for example. What concerns me here is, narrowly, the way in which economic motives are structured by class, imperialism, and violence (not individually, but collectively) and translated as moral, not the abstract Victorian sense of those moral imperatives themselves.

31. Daniel Bivona argues that "[m]id-Victorian England saw the rise to political and intellectual power of a middle class strongly influenced by the moralism characteristic of Evangelical and Dissenting Protestantism. Not surprisingly, the growing demand for a 'serious' moral purpose for empire fittingly conformed to this more general 'tone' of moral earnestness" (ix). He discusses ways in which this was resisted with a discourse of play. My argument focuses on the way in which the former discourses were generated and deployed.

32. Patrick Brantlinger notes that imperialism "served as a reservoir of utopian images and alternatives that helped energize reform impulses at home" (*Rule of Darkness* 28). Walter's heroism is evidence of this pattern, as is the kind of attention to legislative reform that I speak to in this chapter. 33. Collins develops this theme at length in *Man and Wife* (1870). Blaming cultural degeneration on the rage for muscular cultivation, Collins calls the youth of England "aborigines" and "primitives."

34. I wish to point to the role of establishing foreignness within the rhetoric of imperialism as a means of laying out the modes of propriety and moral efficacy—as well as justifying violence.

35. Langland discusses how this visibility serves to facilitate the authority of the middle class and gentry, pointing to the ways in which it demands the asexuality of the lady of the house (a "childishness" Langland associates with both madness and innocence). She cites Mark Giroud's *Life of the English Country House* to point to moral authorization of class power, a thread I develop here at greater length to demonstrate how morality figured in gendered domestic relations and sanctioned violence within that space and the larger social deployment of those terms through the discourse of imperialism.

36. The construct of the dangerous woman served to displace the responsibility for intra-marital violence (a maneuver that pointed up the anxiety concerning male violence

within the domestic space) and exposed cultural dread concerning women's desire/ capability to respond retributively to abuse.

## III. The Dangerous Woman

1. As Mary S. Hartman points out in *Victorian Murderesses,* this was not an alien notion to the mid-Victorians: "[I]n England from 1855 to 1874 the annual totals of women tried for murder, which ranged from twelve to forty-two, twice exceeded those for men and normally were at least half as high, whereas women were only a fifth to a quarter of those tried in assize court for felonies" (5). Further, in the decade leading up to the publication of *Aurora Floyd* and in the years following, several women from France and England were accused in widely publicized trials of poisoning their husbands or fiancés with arsenic or tartar emetic.

2. Hannah Cullwick's diaries not only demonstrate the physicality of kitchen labor, but through her relationship with Arthur Munby they indicate the complex association of sexuality and gender identity that accompanied labor and pain. Her journals catalog her unending work and the hazards of her labor: "Got up & come down to the wretched-looking kitchen & I felt so sick & bad from so much dirt & hard work." Injury was commonplace in the midst of strenuous labor: "Felt a little stiff this morning but nothing to speak of. I found one or two bruises on my knees but that was all. I swept & dusted the rooms. Clean'd the glasses. Laid the hearth & got breakfast up. Clean'd 2 pairs of boots. Made the beds & emptied the slops. Clean'd & wash'd the breakfast things. Got our dinner; clean'd away. Got the parlour dinner ready. . . . I wash'd the plate and to bed at 11" (Stanley 171, 107).

3. According to Winifred Hughes, Braddon knew "exactly what she [was] doing; she ha[d] no exalted opinion of her material or her mission; she [was] quite willing and capable of playing around with her chosen conventions and making her own ironic compromises with the ticklish requirements of Victorian taste" (122). Katherine Montweiler takes this claim a step further in her discussion of *Lady Audley's Secret* when she suggests that "Lady Audley [does more than] threaten class boundaries, her creator shows her readers how they can as well" ("Marketing Sensation" 43). Montweiler sees Braddon's novel as a handbook for resistance to social norms.

4. Although Butler refers here to drag performance and the closeting of homosexual identities, her analysis provides an apt model for conceiving of domestic performances and the closeting of marital violence.

5. Still, *Lady Audley's Secret* unveils many of the suggestive tensions that *Aurora Floyd* would develop. Though Lady Audley bears the onus of the failure in the home, her first husband, George Talboys, deserts her, forecasts his own death as likely, and promises to never return unless he makes his fortune. Later, when he arrives on the scene after her second marriage, and Lady Audley supposes that she has killed him by pushing him down a well, we discover that he employed physical violence in the conversation that led to his "death." Lady Audley appears in the drawing room that night with nasty bruises on her delicate wrists. One wonders what other marks of violence are vaguely obscured by the lady's well-practiced social demeanor, and certainly the narrative leads us to speculate about those, though they are not overtly mentioned again. Even this possibility undermines the domestic heroism of George and his champion Robert Audley.

6. 3 Hansard 203 (20 July 1870), 576.

7. Ibid., 1346.

8. It is important to note, however, that even in the absence of explicit signs of engagement such as Braddon's express intention to tackle these issues, the correspondence of these narratives would be analytically important. As Jacques Derrida remarked, "There is a sort of paradoxical historicity in the experience of writing. The writer can be ignorant or naive in relation to the historical tradition which bears him or her, or which s/he transforms, invents, displaces. But I wonder whether, even in the absence of historical awareness or knowledge s/he doesn't 'treat' history in the course of an experience which is more significant, more alive, more *necessary* in a word, than that of some professional 'historians'" (*Acts of Literature* 54–55).

9. Legally, this term frequently referred to physical abuse, which was rarely described in any more explicit way than "cruelty" or "brutality." It seems likely, then, that James's connubial behavior may have included corporeal correction of Aurora.

10. This remark links John's threat of violence to the working class, as violence had been marked in the Divorce Act. It also suggests Aurora's working-class heritage, which I will discuss below.

11. Madness, however, is a notoriously slippery cultural structure that fails to contain feminine danger, as critics such as Elaine Showalter explain. See also chapter 5 for a discussion of madness.

12. The dog as a metonym through which marital violence can easily be enacted becomes a pattern reiterated in this novel and others examined here. The loyalty, docility, and reliability of the domestic pet, a metaphorically stinging portrayal of the idealized middle-class woman, serves as the explicit site on which this violence is dramatized. This displaced representation allows the narrative to continue to identify the Mellishes' marriage as a model domestic scene while danger appears in its midst. Earlier in the novel, when Aurora's first suitor becomes unsettled by his inability to control Aurora's interactions with other men, he beats a dog she is affectionate with on the nose with his cane—a common metaphor for male phallic authority.

13. Although the absence of a direct representation of this violence is what I am analyzing through the responsive female violence, there is a moment in the novel in which John explicitly addresses this in a "jest." He looks forward to a visit from Talbot and Lucy with the interest in "how our little Lucy looks, and whether solemn Talbot beats her in the silence of the matrimonial chamber" (II 95). Michel Foucault notes in *Discipline and Punish* that mechanisms of power are integrated and naturalized by the redistribution of power in the "ordering of human multiplicities" (218). I believe the enactment of violence is managed, and rendered nearly invisible, by the same ordering in the domestic space.

14. This poem (1842), written in the voice of one who "saw [her] snare" and escaped, details Lady Clara's "murder" of one of her suitors. The following contains the lines alluded to in the novel. See Strange (46) for the complete text of the poem.

> *You put strange memories in my head.*
> *Not thrice your branching limes have blown*
> *Since I beheld young Laurence dead.*
> *O, your sweet eyes, your low replies!*
> *A great enchantress you may be;*

*But there was that across his throat*
*Which you had hardly cared to see.*
. . . . . . . . . . . . .

*Lady Clara Vere de Vere,*
*There stands a spectre in your hall;*
*The guilt of blood is at your door;*
*You changed a wholesome heart to gall*
*You held your course without remorse,*
*To make him trust his modest worth,*
*And, last, you fix'd a vacant stare,*
*And slew him with your noble birth.*

The "spectre" in Lady Clara's hallway could indeed represent the specter of domestic violence that haunted the Victorian home. This hypothesis is developed at length in chapter 5.

15. In her lament, Aurora condemns a character named Claude Melnotte from a popular contemporary play, an honest working-class man who marries a wealthy woman. It is his performance that convinces her that a marriage to James is safe. This novel provides a counterperformance in which all marriages are depicted as unsafe for the same reason Aurora and James' was—the husband's brutality.

16. See "'Listeners in the Corners'" below on the connection between the working class and surveillance.

17. In "Nationalisms and Sexualities," Eve Kosofsky Sedgwick points to the ways in which the use of nationalism/colonialism and the Orientalized Other "has become a central tool of liberal analysis; and it is the explanatory aegis of the Other or Othered that has, for the most part, allowed people of variant sexualities, along with non-Christian, non-white, and medically-disadvantaged people, to become visible in liberal narratives about the origins of nationalism. . . . [T]he trope of the Other in relation to nationalism must almost *a priori* fail to do justice to the complex activity, creativity and engagement of those whom *it* figures as simply relegated objects" (238–39). Mindful of this critique, particularly Sedgwick's concern about reductive analyses, I point to the ways in which the metaphor of the Other becomes emplaced in the discourse of gendered violence at the site of "woman" in order to justify its appearance in a cultural construction that it contradicts and to veil the presence of male violence in the domestic space.

18. Susan Meyer speaks to the way in which women novelists of the nineteenth century employed race as a metaphor in order to speak to limiting gender hierarchies, an act that also called race hierarchies into question. I see the same metaphorization of race in *Aurora Floyd,* uncovering in the yoking of racial and gendered terms a critique of the production of both. My argument reads sensation as the form of this critique and considers class, in the person of the prostitute (as the appropriate victim of violence), and the role of violence in the construction of such terminology.

19. In "Three Women's Texts," Gayatri Chakravorty Spivak describes Bertha's function in *Jane Eyre* as a colonialist "render[ing] indeterminate of the boundary between human and animal . . . thereby [weakening] her entitlement under the spirit if not the letter of the Law." She further argues that in Jean Rhys's retelling of *Jane Eyre* in *Wide Sargasso Sea,* it is the "dissimulation" and, indeed, cruelty of male characters "that

prompts [Bertha's] violent *reaction*" (803). The pattern is similar to the one I draw here, but my focus is the male violence that is not just recuperated but screened by this construction of Oriental identity.

20. Edward Said notes in *Culture and Imperialism* that there are five characteristics to the mature British imperialism of the late nineteenth century:

> One is a self-forgetting delight in the use of power—the power to observe, rule, hold, and profit from distant territories of people. . . . Another is an ideological rationale for reducing then reconstituting the native as someone to be ruled and managed. . . . Third is the idea of Western salvation and redemption through its "civilizing mission." . . . Fourth is the security of a situation that permits the conqueror not to look into the truth of the violence he does. . . . Fifth is the process by which, after the natives have been displaced from their historical location on their land, their history is rewritten as a function of the imperial one. This process uses narrative to dispel contradictory memories and occlude violence. (131–32)

These elements are anticipated in *Aurora Floyd* and other novels like it, and serve as metaphors for the relative invisibility of violence in the upper- and middle-class domestic space. The appearance of these themes in the fiction of mid-century demonstrates not only the mutually constitutive nature of fiction and culture, but also, by virtue of the fate of the figures in this novel, an implicit critique of this violence.

21. One often sees the manifestation of desire in the subject's fantasies that the Other desires him. See the Lacanian notion of the subject's desire as the Other's desire of the self in *Four Fundamental Concepts* (103).

22. Elizabeth Langland notes that women were responsible for "signifying wealth and class" in the country home. She indicates that "the [country estate's] owners' coffers were emptied not in developing the lands, which could have produced greater profits, but in augmenting the size and grandeur of the house, which could yield no profit" but which could serve to mark their social power ("Enclosure Acts" 6). I argue here that the lady of the house might be marked as the culpable party in the cost and destruction that might occur in this process. Particularly, I am interested in how this functioned to complexly mark the lord's authorization to enact this same process on his lady, primarily by deploying the rhetoric of imperialism.

23. In her excellent study *Rule Britannia*, Deirdre David points to the intrusion of the colonized into the realm of the colonizer and argues that this is an inevitable result of an act of imperialism.

24. Mary Poovey argues in *Uneven Developments* that the governess, although intended to be a "bulwark against the erosion" of middle-class identity, collapsed those distinctions by imitating a "middle-class mother in the work she performed, but [being] like both a working-class woman and man in the wages she received" (127). The contradictions in her position left her in a site of social, sexual, and class ambiguity.

25. As Foucault argues in *Discipline and Punish*, panopticism functions to "assur[e] the ordering of human multiplicities" (218) by ensuring in all persons "a state of conscious and permanent visibility that assures the automatic functioning of power. . . . [S]urveillance is permanent in its effect, even if it is discontinuous in its action" (201). Aurora becomes more and more painfully aware of a surveillance she aligns only with the servants.

26. Again, Foucault notes in *Discipline and Punish* that "[a] power to punish that ran the

whole length of the social network would act at each of its points, and in the end would no longer be perceived as a power of certain individuals over others, but as an immediate reaction of all in relation to the individual" (130). This process allows for Aurora's (potential) punishment not by the individuals who are most explicitly engaged in the process of scrutinizing her behavior, but by her society as a whole. This attribution of surveillance to the working class alone allows Talbot and John to avoid being implicated in Aurora's surveillance or the violence that follows, relegating violence to the lower classes and outside of the domestic space.

27. See chapter 2 for details about the invisibility of the stick and the significance of its manipulation with ease and nonchalance. See also Foucault, *Discipline and Punish,* on the naturalization of disciplinary power.

28. Jeni Curtis discusses the violence of Lucy and Aurora's pruning, noting how the metaphors of the naturalness and construction of womanhood are vexed, rendering the text indeterminate in terms of its assignment of proper authority and the gendered ideal.

29. Deirdre David argues, and I agree, that women often served as contrapuntal, though not always disparaging, voices in the deployment of imperialism as a metaphor. However, in her discussion of *Dombey and Son* and *The Old Curiosity Shop,* David argues that women bear domestic violence, like the natives, but contrition for violence against women becomes the site at which "cruel colonialist practices are rehabilitated through instructive punishment for domestic violence. The dark servant, however, remains in painful bondage" (72). However, the contrition David mentions does not ensure the termination of domestic violence. The victimized wife remains in a painful situation as well, a phenomenon I interrogate here. Once the arm is raised, the possibility of renewed violence haunts the narrative. David agrees, however, that gender "conjoins with race in subordinating millions of indigenous peoples to Britannic rule and maintaining women in their private sphere" (44).

30. 3 Hansard 201 (24 May 1870), 1332.

31. Ibid., 1265–66.

32. 3 Hansard 203 (20 July 1870), 604.

33. Ibid.

34. 3 Hansard 201 (24 May 1870), 1333.

35. 3 Hansard 203 (20 July 1870), 594.

36. Ibid.

37. Ibid., 597.

38. 3 Hansard 201 (24 May 1870), 1318, 1326.

39. *Westminster Review* in 3 Hansard 201 (24 May 1870), 1308.

40. 3 Hansard 201 (24 May 1870), 1312, 1313–14.

41. Nayder links new marriage law reform and the Indian Mutiny to isolate Braddon's comparison of "the threat of native insurrection with that of feminist revolt[,] . . . displac[ing] the fiendish Indian sepoy with the seemingly innocent Englishwoman . . . and the martyred Englishwomen of Cawnpore [with Lady Audley's] victimized husband" (39). Nayder's fine argument points to important tensions in Braddon's fiction that suggest an often contradictory presentation of women's rights questions. I am interested in complicating Nayder's conclusions by asking, for example, how the gendered terms she employs here vex even her own claims. As Lady Audley is a sepoy is she not also the cruelly abused Englishwoman? Would not posi-

tioning George, Lady Audley's husband, as an Englishwoman suggest some defect in him as well? I would argue that Nayder's contention that the "mutiny" of British feminists, in the confines of the novel, "is successfully put down" (40) fails to consider not only the outcome of the mutiny, which was in many respects a movement toward an eventual termination of British rule (as early feminist efforts were steps toward enfranchisement and greater freedom for women), but also the significance of Lady Audley's fairly longstanding success in her rebellion. *Aurora Floyd* clearly represents the heroine's successes as more complete. In spite of her bigamy and her unladylike behavior, Aurora maintains her good name and bears the son who will inherit her husband's property, though, as Nayder notes, it would be difficult to identify Braddon as a feminist.

42. 3 Hansard 201 (24 May 1870), 1334.
43. Ibid., 1338.
44. See Foucault's *Discipline and Punish* on the creation of a criminal class. Although I agree with his basic tenet, I would argue that indeed physical torture was practiced on women who belonged to this demonized assembly.
45. 3 Hansard 201 (24 May 1870), 1314–15.
46. Ibid., 1315.
47. Poovey evaluates this move in terms of the introduction of chloroform into the medicalization of childbirth. The arguments of pro-chloroform physicians "fairly exult in the power with which chloroform could 'lay the most restless or ungovernable patient quiet on her pillow.' 'Screams . . . audible across the street' are silenced, and the unsuspecting patient is put under 'in spite of herself,' and even the most recalcitrant women express 'sincere gratitude' 'for saving them from their agonies'" (29). See chapter 2 of *Uneven Developments* for a complete discussion of these concepts.
48. 3 Hansard 201 (24 May 1870), 1265.
49. Ibid., 1320.
50. Ibid., 1313.
51. Ibid., 1335.
52. See Pamela K. Gilbert, *Desire, Disease, and the Body.*
53. 3 Hansard 203 (20 July 1870), 587–88.
54. Ibid., 1346.
55. Ibid., 601.
56. 3 Hansard 201 (24 May 1870), 1336.
57. 3 Hansard 203 (20 July 1870), 575.
58. See the discussion of Susan Gubar's "Blank Page" in chapter 2.

## IV. Sensational Violations

1. Vineta and Robert A. Colby (*The Equivocal Virtue*) note this honor bestowed by the Queen (xiii). Merryn Williams suggests in her biography of Oliphant that *Salem Chapel* was the writer's most popular and "most famous work" (76). This popularity is significant because it suggests that of Oliphant's mammoth oeuvre of ninety-two novels, this one, at some level, engaged the concerns of the period most powerfully. The same tensions the novel elucidated were also the subject of much legal and social debate at the time. Women's rights and identities as wives were of supreme concern during its publication: the Divorce Act was debated and researched throughout the

1850s and passed in 1857, and agitation for a Married Women's Property Bill began in the 1860s, leading to the passage of an act in 1870. See Mary Lyndon Shanley's *Marriage, Feminism, and the Law* for a full discussion of these legal debates.

2. This perception may be due in part to her widely quoted criticism of women's suffrage (a view she revised later in life) and what some saw as her puritanical critiques of sensational fiction and Thomas Hardy's novels. However, her nonfiction has certainly not been the only target. Some critics have maintained that even in Oliphant's fiction, we can look only for ideological orthodoxy. Joseph H. O'Mealy, although arguing for her place in the literary canon, suggests that feminist critics from Virginia Woolf to Sandra M. Gilbert and Susan Gubar have excluded Oliphant from consideration because "her novels do not question or challenge the prevailing patriarchy" (46). O'Mealy ultimately claims that "[i]n Oliphant's world everyone has to settle for the best she can get" (49).

3. In her 1862 essay "Sensation Novels" (which appeared in the same number of *Blackwoods Magazine* [xci] as the first volume of her own "sensation novel," *Salem Chapel*), Oliphant describes sensation as potentially "dangerous and foolish work, as well as false, both to Art and Nature" (567). Her essay also defines serial publication as a "violent stimulant . . . with [a] necessity for frequent and rapid recurrence of piquant situation and startling incident" (568).

4. I am interested in the theorization of mimesis and performance by critics such as Julia Kristeva and Jacques Derrida, who discuss the ways in which mimesis uncovers the artificial nature of these cultural delineations. Kristeva even suggests that the disturbance of these boundaries amounts to "social revolution" because it alters the very fabric of the symbolic ("Revolution in Poetic Language" 104–12). Judith Butler discusses a similar notion of the power of performance to alter gendered terms in *Gender Trouble*. She notes that "repetitive signifying [makes] a subversion of identity . . . possible" (145).

5. In *The Powers of Horror,* Julia Kristeva explains the dangers and benefits of this transgression of boundaries (see especially her chapters 1 and 7). These ruptures, such as menstrual bleeding, vomiting, and defecating, become culturally vile. Yet for Kristeva, they become symbolic of a form of creative power that may allow an author (certainly of action as well as of words) to invent. I would argue that this kind of invention may offer up possibilities that shift the cultural paradigm.

6. The presentation of familial horrors as melodramatic or sensational realities blurs the boundaries between sensation and the real. Perhaps fiction, and even more appropriately sensational fiction, is the site at which we should expect such an overflow of cultural institutions.

7. See Daniel Cottom's discussion of education and gentility in *Social Figures*.

8. I am indebted to Daniel Cottom for drawing my attention to the fact that both Kant and Freud theorized ways in which odors might dangerously betray boundaries that are aligned with civilization or morality, or as I discuss in this case, middle-class identity. Kant's *Critique of Judgment* "proscribed [odors] (in the form of perfumes) from the realm of art," and Freud argued in *Civilization and Its Discontents* that the upright stance of homo sapiens "placed their noses away from their own and others' genitals unlike other animals" for whom smell is much more significant in sexuality (Daniel Cottom, conversation with author, 5 December 1994).

9. See chapters 2 and 3 for further discussion of the cane/walking stick as an emblem of phallic power.

10. I do not intend to imply that there was more physical abuse in the working class than in the middle or upper classes. In fact, one of my goals is to demonstrate the ways in which such a belief served as a screen for middle- and upper-class domestic violence. Rather, this common stereotype about working-class families facilitated the production of vast quantities of literature concerning cruelty among laboring people.

11. Perhaps this complicates Foucault's notion of "bodies and pleasure" as a form of liberating rebellion (*History of Sexuality,* introduction) when examined on the axis of gender. In this context, male pleasure becomes a woman's terror.

12. See the discussion in chapter 2 of euphemistic and substitution phrases for physical violence in the Hansard Parliamentary Debates.

13. Gilbert and Gubar first elucidated the connections between madness, women's repressed speech, and political efficacy in *The Madwoman in the Attic.* Here, I point to the way in which the embodiment of this voice in the chief female character, a figure who moves across the boundaries of sanity and insanity, transports her threat into the safe domicile of the middle-class home, into the body of the middle-class maiden, and into realism, contaminating them and significantly remarking how these were understood.

14. See chapter 5 for a more thorough discussion of these specters.

15. Further, she is essentially disembodied by this gesture, made incapable of physical victimization and of assault. See the discussion in chapter 3 of Nancy Armstrong and the disembodiment domestic fiction can provide.

16. 3 Hansard 153 (5 April 1859]), 1380.

17. 3 Hansard 168 (24 July, 1862), 734. See also the introduction for a discussion of newspapers and the "real" stories they carried as a prelude to the sensation novel.

## V. Gwendolen's Madness

1. Ann Cvetkovich's *Mixed Feelings,* a discussion of sensation and feminism in Victorian Britain, also describes *Daniel Deronda* as a novel that demonstrates the impact of sensation on realism. Rather than focusing on the immateriality of affect as the province of sensation and the ways in which this depoliticized feminist issues, I am interested in the materiality of violence and the ways in which sensation offers potential for political change and generic transformation.

2. Although there has been increasing contemporary debate over the generic classification of Eliot's work, particularly in regard to the blurring of the distinction between realism and romance and the construction of the concept of realism, she was generally regarded in her day as a realist and has often been in ours as well. Critics such as Daniel Cottom (*Social Figures*), Karen Chase (*Eros and Psyche*), Richard Altick (*Presence of the Present*), and John McGowan (*Representation and Revelation*) have considered these issues at length.

3. In a 1994 discussion on the invaluable VICTORIA E-mail list regarding *Daniel Deronda,* the debate turned to the question of which plot line the subscribers liked better, Gwendolen/Grandcourt or Daniel Deronda/Mirah. Even among this distinguished body of Victorian scholars, many votes were tallied before a subscriber questioned the implications of segregating the two plot lines. Not only is there the obvious connection between Gwendolen and Daniel to take into account, but Daniel's relationship to Henleigh and Leonora's to Gwendolen, as well as the contrast between Gwendolen and Mirah. This "natural" rift—one that Eliot remarked

on with frustration in her nineteenth-century readers—is instructive. Certainly, this may be attributed to the trend that appeared in the Oliphant criticism, the relegation of one plot line to sensation and the other to realism. This distinction is fostered by the assumption that sensation and realism are such disparate modes of expression as to be utterly irreconcilable. (For the VICTORIA archives, see http://listserv.indiana.edu/archives/victoria.html.)

4. Gordon S. Haight, ed. *The George Eliot Letters*. 6 vols. New Haven: Yale University Press, 1955. 6:75. Cited in Putzell (37). I do not contend, as Putzell does, that Eliot transformed sensation fiction, but rather that realism was transformed by sensation and that Eliot employed the tools of sensation, calling into question the distinction between sensation and realism and achieving an end similar to those the sensation novels accomplished: speaking of issues that were otherwise difficult to approach, particularly domestic violence and women's response.

5. She insisted, in fact, on the connection between these plot lines, noting in an oft-quoted letter that she "meant everything in the book to be *related to everything else* there" (*George Eliot Letters* 6:290, cited in Putzell, 37).

6. Although Demaria argues that "Eliot insist[ed] on the personal and social destructiveness of the mercenary marriage" between Gwendolen and Henleigh (405), pointing to Gwendolen's desire for social power and her eleventh-hour recognition that she had "sold herself," this analysis neglects to take into account the complexity Eliot builds into Gwendolen's marriage. Significantly, Gwendolen believes that Henleigh is the first and only man she has encountered whom she might be able to love. He is the first suitor who does not bore or irritate her with worn petitions and gestures of affection. Further, despite the fact that his silence initially seems to imply a wider range of freedom for her, she admits that he has an authority over her, an ability to compel her, well before their marriage. Therefore, her relationship to Henleigh already implies that she will not be able to "operate powerfully" as Demaria suggests.

7. See chapter 2 for the discussion of the parliamentary construction of the "violent" man in debates over the Divorce Bill, passed into law in 1857.

8. See chapter 3 for a discussion of Aurora Floyd's whip and its significance.

9. The construct of the dangerous woman, something Gwendolen believes herself to be, arises out of an attempt to shift the responsibility for male sexual violence. See particularly the discussion of the Contagious Diseases Acts in chapter 3. Although sensation novels exploited this concept, the dangerous woman's power was a retributive act of violence that could go unpunished.

10. Note the similarities between the description of Henleigh's relationship to speech and that of *Aurora Floyd*'s Softy, a representative of violence within the domestic space.

11. In her study *Murder and Moral Decay*, Beth Kalikoff notes that popular middle-class journals, such as *Blackwoods Magazine*, *Household Words*, and *Cornhill Magazine*, tended to "guide the reader's response towards what the writer considered to be rational behavior" (75). This movement, which occurred at many levels in the culture, is what this novel attempts to interrogate.

12. Both Gwendolen's foresight and Henleigh's omniscience suggest Latimer's sight into the unspoken and horrifying reality that lies beneath the social in *The Lifted Veil*.

13. See especially chapter 3 on Aurora Floyd's and her dog Bow-wow's encounter with Softy.

14. See chapters 1 and 2 and the parliamentary debates concerning divorce laws.

15. The relationship between the tiny ornamental Maltese Fluff, which Henleigh holds in his lap, and the "beautiful" spaniel Fetch on the floor mirrors the relationship between Gwendolen, who is held merely for appearances, and Lydia, whose howling later leaves Henleigh unsettled. Ultimately, Henleigh rejects both, "depositing Fluff carelessly on the table" and ejecting Fetch.

16. Eve Lynch reads the specters in Braddon's fiction as a means of "carry[ing] the weight of her critical [social] examination." Lynch argues that Braddon was able to "indulge her desire for exploring the undercurrents of social problems within a genre ideally suited to adapting a double effect, the uncanny ghost story" (237). In this way, Braddon was able to garner an audience and still critique her culture.

17. Peter Brooks argues that the "processes that we can't readily explain through logic . . . must be given in narrative form, as a process" (251). My argument suggests that the narrative process that lends itself most readily to those "illogical" formations is (often layered) sensation. Ghosts sensationalize an already sensational narrative.

18. When Gwendolen considers leaving Henleigh, these are the avenues of criticism she anticipates: her rector uncle "would tell her to go back. Her mother would cry. Her aunt and [cousin] would look at her with wondering alarm. Her husband would [legally] have the power to compel her" (665).

19. Significantly, as Hermione is imprisoned by Leontes, Gwendolen becomes imprisoned by Henleigh, an event that will produce the same terror. However, unlike Susan (in *Salem Chapel*) and Hermione, Gwendolen does not play on the statuelike identity that Oliphant's novel seems to suggest is a form of reprieve from abuse.

20. Although critics often describe Mirah as the antithesis to Leonora (as well as to Gwendolen and Lydia) and her (their) performance, she escapes her abusive father by performing a submission to his will (which is that she marry/prostitute herself to a count, who, ironically, promises her she will never have to act again). Her fear that she will be put in a madhouse is thwarted by her decision to "*act* against" her father (260; emphasis added).

21. Winifred Hughes also notes Eliot's forays into sensationalism in her important study of sensation, *The Maniac in the Cellar.* Hughes does not see these gestures as integral, as I do, arguing that Eliot created one of her least effective plots in *Felix Holt* by employing sensation. I see the influence of sensation as more sweeping, and most critics read *Daniel Deronda* as a success, despite the sensation pervading it.

22. Elaine Showalter marks out the ways in which this association was detrimental to women throughout the century in *The Female Malady.*

23. This feat was often impossible, even to the woman who considered herself sane. Note the case of Georgiana Weldon, who was incarcerated by her husband (from whom she was separated) for her spiritualist beliefs and her interest in a small socialist orphanage and singing career. With the help of Louisa Lowe, Mrs. Weldon barely escaped entrapment. An overnight sensation, Mrs. Weldon was heralded by even the conservative *Times* and won case after case against the doctors who signed her lunacy order and against Forbes Winslow, whom she accused of libel for publicizing her supposed lunacy in the press. She successfully sought to have the proceeds of this case returned directly to her and succeeded in publicly chastising her money-seeking husband and the Lunacy Laws (Owen 160–66). See Alex Owen, *The Darkened Room,* and Daniel Cottom, *Abyss of Reason,* for excellent discussions of spiritualism, reason, and madness.

24. Showalter notes that sensation novels often used and critiqued the constructions of female madness (*Female Malady* 71, 48).

25. Contemporary psychology had noted the connection between madness in women and victimization through sexual violence and battery; this play on terms, then, might also have subversively transmitted the theme of abuse to the reader.

26. Showalter describes subscription to middle-class notions of feminine speech (and dress as well) as essential for a diagnosis of sanity (*Female Malady* 81, 84).

27. Athena Vrettos argues that "Gwendolen's hysteric visions reveal the tenuous boundaries between her private life and the world outside. The scene of Grandcourt's drowning punctuates this rift between public veneer and private violence" (573). Vrettos, however, represents the boundaries Gwendolen ruptures as those of mental health and argues that this violence is an aspect of Gwendolen's neurosis. I suggest that the tradition of reading the violence in this novel as solely Gwendolen's (mental health) problem, though it recognizes the cultural forces that come into play, does not examine the "lifted veil" of male violence as I do here, and derives from the same discourse in which the laws restricting dangerous women were written.

28. In *Bodies That Matter,* Butler describes citation "not as enslavement or simple reiteration of the original, but as an insubordination that appears to take place within the very terms of the original" (45). There is, she says, a "metonymic excess in every mime, indeed, in every metaphorical substitution, that is understood to disrupt the seamless repetition of the phallogocentric norm" (48). Lydia's citation of the failing boundary between reality and sensation distorts these phallogocentric norms in a way that makes her a threat to the structure from which Henleigh derives his power.

29. Vrettos agrees that in this scene, "Gwendolen's nervous sensibility temporarily displaces Grandcourt's mastery" (571). Although she says that this "reveals the division in Gwendolen's public and private narratives" (573), I would argue that it draws them together and displays the tensions between them.

30. Avengers of unpunished crimes, particularly the murder of the mother (Walker 327), the Furies are an apt threat to Henleigh, who has tortured Lydia and felt the sting of her revenge through Gwendolen.

31. Nina Auerbach compares Charcot's hypnotized women to performers, noting that "the versatility of these supposed mad women, their mesmerizing movement back and forth between demonism and saintliness [was] that of the Victorian actor. . . . Their hysteria [was] their aptitude at conversion" (*Private Theatricals* 82).

32. Certainly, people have participated in spectacular and sustained resistance to what had been considered real, valuing their reading of the social with such force in the space of cultural contradiction that the world was changed—as in the fights for suffrage and civil rights.

33. Robert McCarron suggests that this manifests in rape—what he describes as a "sadistic sexuality"—and beatings. He believes that these are metaphorically represented in the physical and verbal exchanges over the diamonds (80). Brooks concurs, calling Gwendolen's gems a "leitmotif of sociosexual display" and Grandcourt animalistic (250, 254). McCarron suggests, however, that Eliot chooses this method of presentation because she cannot represent physical abuse directly. Her novella "Janet's Repentance" defies that claim. What she does express in *Daniel Deronda,* however, is a much more subversive rhetoric of resistance rather than simply repentance on behalf of the abused woman.

34. In *Murder and Moral Decay,* Beth Kalikoff argues persuasively for a growing Victorian concern over moral decay. I read this concern as an anxiety about the shifting terms of morality that demonstrated its relativity, rather than universality and eternality. I identify this trend not as a concern about moral decay, but rather as a concern about the influence of the sensational on the real.

35. Several critics have commented on the threat to Daniel's male/masculine identity that lies in a name that seems to have no patriarchal precursor, his invisible father, and the shame he feels surrounding this disconnectedness.

36. The Victorian concept of play—as gambling, theatricality, and aesthetic theory—is developed in J. Jeffrey Franklin's *Serious Play.*

37. Jacques Lacan describes this phenomenon as the influence of the "Name of the Father." See "The Function and Field of Speech and Language" in *Ecrits* and "The Name of the Father" in *Four Fundamental Concepts.* Also see Mikkel Borch-Jacobsen's rendering of the function of the "Name of the Father" in the resolution of the Oedipal conflict (especially chapter 7, "Desire Caught by the Tail"), an issue that is clearly vexed for Daniel, whose "desire of the mother" is fiercely displaced by the "Name of the Father."

38. Mélusine, a fairy who occasionally became half-serpent/half-woman, unbeknownst to her human companions, not only grants this image the figure of plastic transformation, but also links Leonora to Gwendolen, whose serpentlike performance initially repels Daniel. Significantly, the Judeo-Christian tradition, with which Daniel will align himself exclusively, often identifies the serpent as an image of corruption. However, in many theological traditions (among them those of the Melanesians, the ancient Aegeans, Egyptians, and Hindus), the snake, whose shedding skin allowed for a new identity (like Leonora's performance), was a symbol of eternal life and also of conflict with the father. Echoes of this appear in the Judeo-Christian tradition in which the serpent in the Garden of Eden offers Eve that which God will not give her.

39. This passage calls to mind the suffrage movement. Though the suffragists were called mad, as are the characters here, they succeeded in countermanding "the will of generations." They had to encounter the violence of Black Friday, "cat and mouse" arrests, forced feedings, and threats on their lives in order to achieve such an end. This novel seems to suggest that violence is an inevitable response to threatened cultural shifts, but that the end result of the stresses that evoke a violent response may be a cultural change nonetheless. The mob of ghosts and shadows that threaten Gwendolen and Leonora into submission is resisted, perhaps, only through an equally communal response and resistance.

## Conclusion

1. Eliza Lynn Linton wrote social commentary and fiction and, though she lived an unconventional life herself, has often been noted for her resistance to women's rights legislation (see Nancy Fix Anderson's *Woman against Women*). Elizabeth Wolstenholme-Elmy, an ardent feminist political activist, founded the Ladies National Association with Josephine Butler to lobby for women's rights legislation. She agitated against the Contagious Diseases Acts and for women's suffrage, the Married Women's Property Act, and the Infant Custody Act.

2. *Time* artificially darkened O. J. Simpson's mug shot and used it as a cover shot the

week of his arrest. Claiming it had been an aesthetic decision, the editors attempted to avoid the question of how this case played into the racist fears that African-American men are still perceived as a threat to white women, particularly as sexual threats. The case spun out these fears, arguing sexual jealousy as part of the motive for the murder.

# Bibliography

Ackroyd, Peter. *Dickens*. New York: Harper Collins. 1990.

Althusser, Louis. "Ideological State Apparatuses." *Mapping Ideology*. Ed. Slavoj Žižek. New York: Verso, 1997. 100–140.

Altick, Richard D. *Deadly Encounters*. Philadelphia: University of Pennsylvania Press, 1986.

———. *The Presence of the Present*. Columbus: Ohio State University Press, 1991.

———. *Victorian Studies in Scarlet*. New York: W. W. Norton & Co., 1970.

Anderson, Nancy Fix. *Woman against Women in Victorian England: A Life of Eliza Lynn Linton*. Bloomington: Indiana University Press, 1987.

Anthon, Charles. *Classical Dictionary*. New York: Harper & Brothers Publishers, 1865.

Armstrong, Nancy. *Desire and Domestic Fiction*. Oxford: Oxford University Press, 1987.

———. "The Rise of the Domestic Woman." In *Feminisms*. Ed. Robyn R. Warhol and Diane Price Herndl. New Brunswick: Rutgers University Press, 1991. 894–925.

———, and Leonard Tennenhouse. *The Violence of Representation*. New York: Routledge, 1989. 1–26.

Auerbach, Nina. "Alluring Vacancies in Victorian Character." *Kenyon Review* 8, no. 3 (1986): 36–48.

———. *Private Theatricals*. Cambridge: Harvard University Press, 1990.

———. *Woman and the Demon*. Cambridge: Harvard University Press, 1982.

[B., E.] "The Sensation Novel." *Argosy* 18 (1874): 137–43.

Barrett-Durocq, Françoise. *Love in the Time of Victoria*. Trans. John Howe. New York: Penguin, 1991.

Barthes, Roland. *S/Z*. Trans. Richard Miller. New York: Hill and Wang, 1974.

Behagg, Clive. "Secrecy, Ritual and Folk Violence: The Opacity of the Workplace in the First Half of the Century." In *Popular Culture and Custom in Nineteenth Century England*. Ed. Robert D. Storch. Manuka, Australia: Croom Helm Ltd. 154–79.

Bhabha, Homi K. "Signs Taken for Wonders: Questions of Ambivalence and Authority under a Tree outside Delhi, May 1817." In *"Race," Writing, and Difference*. Ed. Henry Louis Gates Jr. Chicago: University of Chicago Press, 1986. 163–84.

Billington, Louis. "Revivalism and Popular Religion." In *In Search of Victorian Values*. Ed. Eric M. Sigsworth. New York: Manchester University Press, 1988. 147–61.

Bivona, Daniel. *Desire and Contradiction: Imperial Visions and Domestic Debates in Victorian Literature*. New York: Manchester University Press, 1990.

Booth, Alison. "Incomplete Stories: Womanhood and Artistic Ambition in *Daniel Deronda*." In *Writing the Woman Artist*. Ed. Suzanne W. Jones. Philadelphia: University of Pennsylvania Press, 1991. 113–30.

Borch-Jacobsen, Mikkel. *Lacan: The Absolute Master*. Trans. Douglas Brick. Stanford: Stanford University Press, 1991.

Boumelha, Penny. "George Eliot and the End of Realism." In *Women Reading Women's Writing*. Ed. Sue Roe. New York: St. Martin's Press, 1987. 13–36.

Bourdieu, Pierre. *Language and Symbolic Power*. Ed. John B. Thompson. Trans. Gino Raymond and Matthew Adamson. Cambridge: Harvard University Press, 1991.

Boyle, Thomas. *Black Swine in the Sewers of Hampstead*. New York: Viking, 1989.

Braddon, Mary Elizabeth. *Aurora Floyd*. New York: Garland Publishing, 1979.

———. *Lady Audley's Secret*. New York: Penguin Books, 1985.

Brantlinger, Patrick. *Fictions of State: Culture and Credit in Britain, 1694–1994*. Ithaca: Cornell University Press, 1996.

———. *Rule of Darkness: British Literature and Imperialism, 1830–1914*. Ithaca: Cornell University Press, 1988.

Britten, Emma Hardinge. *Nineteenth Century Miracles*. New York: Arno Press, 1976.

Brontë, Anne. *The Tenant of Wildfell Hall*. London: Penguin Classics, 1985.

Brontë, Charlotte. *Shirley*. New York: Penguin Classics, 1985.

Brooks, Peter. *Body Work: Objects of Desire in Modern Narrative*. Cambridge: Harvard University Press, 1993.

Butler, Judith. *Bodies That Matter*. New York: Routledge, 1993.

———. *Gender Trouble*. New York: Routledge, 1990.

Cameron, Deborah. "'That's Entertainment'?: Jack the Ripper and the Selling of Sexual Violence." In *Femicide: The Politics of Woman Killing*. Ed. Jill Radford and Diana E. H. Russell. New York: Twayne Publishers, 1992. 184–88.

Caputi, Jane. *The Age of the Sex Crime*. Bowling Green: Bowling Green State University Popular Press, 1989.

Caputo, John D. *Deconstruction in a Nutshell: A Conversation with Jacques Derrida*. New York: Fordham University Press, 1997.

Carpenter, Mary Wilson. "'A Bit of Her Flesh': Circumcisions and 'The Signification of the Phallus' in *Daniel Deronda*." *Genders* 1, no. 1 (1988): 1–23.

Chambers, Robert. *Chamber's Book of Days*. Vol. 2. London: W. & R. Chambers Ltd. 1914.

Chase, Karen. *Eros and Psyche*. New York: Methuen, 1984.

Chittick, Kathryn. *Dickens and the 1830s*. New York: Cambridge University Press, 1990.

Clark, Anna. *Women's Silence, Men's Violence*. New York: Pandora Press, 1987.

Cobbe, Frances Power. "Wife Torture in England." *Contemporary Review* 32 (1878): 55–87.

Cohen, William A. *Sex Scandal: The Private Parts of Victorian Fiction*. Durham: Duke University Press, 1996.

Colby, Vineta, and Robert A. Colby. *The Equivocal Virtue: Mrs. Oliphant and the Victorian Literary Market Place*. Hamden, Conn.: Archon Books, 1966.

Collins, Philip. *Dickens and Crime*. 3d ed. New York: St. Martin's Press, 1994.

Collins, Wilkie. *Man and Wife*. London: Chatto and Windus, 1907.

———. *The Woman in White*. New York: Penguin, 1985.

*The Complete Newgate Calendar*. London: Privately printed for the Navarre Society, 1926.

Connor, Steven. "'They're All in One Story.' Public and Private Narratives in *Oliver Twist*." *The Dickensian* 85 (1989): 3–16.

Cottom, Daniel. *Abyss of Reason: Cultural Movements, Revelations and Betrayals*. New York: Oxford University Press, 1991.

———. *Social Figures: George Eliot, Social History, and Literary Representation*. Minneapolis: University of Minnesota Press, 1987.

Curtis, Jeni. "The 'Espaliered' Girl: Pruning the Docile Body: M. E. Braddon's *Aurora Floyd*." In *Beyond Sensation: Mary Elizabeth Braddon in Context*. Ed. Marlene Tromp, Pamela Gilbert, and Aeron Haynie. New York: State University of New York Press, 2000. 77–92.

Cvetkovich, Ann. "Ghostlier Determinations: The Economy of Sensation and *The Woman in White*." *Novel* 23 (Fall 1989): 24–43.

———. *Mixed Feelings: Feminism, Mass Culture, and Victorian Sensationalism*. New Brunswick: Rutgers University Press, 1992.

David, Deirdre. *Rule Britannia: Women, Empire, and Victorian Writing*. Ithaca: Cornell University Press, 1995.

Davidoff, Lenore, and Catherine Hall. *Family Fortunes: Men and Women of the English Middle Class, 1780–1850*. Chicago: University of Chicago Press, 1987.

de Lauretis, Teresa. "The Violence of Rhetoric: Considerations on Representation and Gender." In *The Violence of Representation*. Ed. Nancy Armstrong and Leonard Tennenhouse. New York: Routledge, 1989. 239–58.

Deleuze, Gilles. *Masochism*. New York: Zone Books, 1991.

Demaria, Joanne Long. "The Wondrous Marriages of Daniel Deronda: Gender, Work, and Love." *Studies in the Novel* 22, no. 4 (1990): 403–17.

Derrida, Jacques. *Acts of Literature*. Ed. Derek Attridge. New York: Routledge, 1992.

Dickens, Charles. *Oliver Twist*. New York: Oxford University Press, 1966.

Doggett, Maeve E. *Marriage, Wife-Beating and the Law in Victorian England*. Columbia: University of South Carolina Press, 1993.

During, Simon. "The Strange Case of Monomania: Patriarchy in Literature, Murder in *Middlemarch*, Drowning in *Daniel Deronda*." *Representations* 23 (1988): 86–104.

Eliot, George. *Daniel Deronda*. Ed. Barbara Hardy. London: Penguin Classics, 1986.

———. "Janet's Repentance." In *Scenes of Clerical Life*. New York: Penguin Classics, 1985.

———. *The Lifted Veil*. New York: Virago Modern Classics, 1985.

Ellis, Kate F. *The Contested Castle*. Chicago: University of Illinois, 1989.

Ellis, Sarah Stickney. *Wives of England*. London: Fisher, 1843.

Faludi, Susan. *Backlash: The Undeclared War against American Women*. New York: Crown, 1991.

Fisher, Judith L. "The 'Sensation Scene' in Charles Dickens and Dion Boucicault." In *Dramatic Dickens*. Ed. Carol Hanbery MacKay. New York: St. Martin's Press, 1989. 152–67.

Foucault, Michel. *Discipline and Punish*. Trans. Alan Sheridan. New York: Vintage Books, 1975.

———. *The History of Sexuality*. Vol. 1, *An Introduction*. Trans. Robert Hurley. New York: Pantheon Books, 1978.

———. *Power/Knowledge: Selected Interviews and Other Writings, 1972–1977*. Ed. and trans. Colin Gordon. New York: Pantheon Books, 1978.

Franklin, J. Jeffrey. *Serious Play: The Cultural Form of the Nineteenth-Century Realist Novel*. Philadelphia: University of Pennsylvania Press, 1999.

Frederick, Kenneth. "The Cold, Cold Hearth: Domestic Strife in *Oliver Twist*." *College English* 27 (1966): 465–70.

Gallagher, Catherine. "George Eliot and Daniel Deronda: The Prostitute and the Jewish Question." In *Sex, Politics, and Science in the Nineteenth-Century Novel*. Ed. Ruth Bernard Yeazell. Baltimore: Johns Hopkins University Press, 1986. 39–62.

———. *The Industrial Reformation of English Fiction*. Chicago: University of Chicago Press, 1980.

Gibson, Ian. *The English Vice: Beating, Sex and Shame in Victorian England and After*. London: Duckworth, 1979.

Gilbert, Pamela K. *Desire, Disease, and the Body in Victorian Women's Popular Novels*. New York: Cambridge, 1997.

Gilbert, Sandra M., and Susan Gubar. *The Madwoman in the Attic: The Woman Writer and the Nineteenth-Century Literary Imagination*. New Haven: Yale University Press, 984.

Ginsburg, Michael Peled. "Truth and Persuasion: The Language of Realism and of Ideology in *Oliver Twist*." *Novel* 20 (1987): 220–36.

Gray, Beryl. "Afterword." In *The Lifted Veil*. George Eliot. New York: Penguin, 1985.

Greenfield, Meg. "In Defense of Sensationalism: The Media and the O. J. Simpson Case." *Newsweek* 124, no. 13 (1994): 72.

Grugel, Lee E. *Society and Religion during the Age of Industrialization: Christianity in Victorian England*. Washington, D.C.: University Press of America, 1979.

Gubar, Susan. "'The Blank Page' and Issues of Female Creativity." In *Writing and Sexual Difference*. Ed. Elizabeth Abel. Chicago: University of Chicago Press, 1982. 73–94.

Hadley, Elaine. *Melodramatic Tactics: Theatricalized Dissent in the English Marketplace, 1800–1885*. Stanford: Stanford University Press, 1995.

Haining, Peter, ed. *A Circle of Witches: An Anthology of Victorian Witchcraft Stories*. New York: Taplinger Publishing Co., 1971.

Hammerton, A. James. *Cruelty and Companionship*. New York: Routledge, 1995.

Hansard Parliamentary Debates, 3d series. Great Britain.

Hartman, Mary S. *Victorian Murderesses*. New York: Schocken Books, 1977.

Hazlitt, W. Carew. *Dictionary of Faiths and Folklore*. Vol. 2. London: Reeves & Turner, 1905.

Helmstadter, Richard J., and Bernard Lightman, eds. *Victorian Faith in Crisis*. Stanford: Stanford University Press, 1990.

Helsinger, Elizabeth K., Robin Lauterbach Sheets, and William Veeder, eds. *The Woman Question: Society and Literature in Britain and America 1837–1883*. New York: Garland, 1983.

Hollingsworth, Keith. *The Newgate Novel 1830–1847: Bulwer, Ainsworth, Dickens, and Thackeray*. Detroit: Wayne State University Press, 1963.

Houston, Gail Turley. "Broadsides at the Board: Collations of *Pickwick Papers* and *Oliver Twist*." *Studies in English Literature* 31 (1991): 735–55.

———. "Mary Braddon's Commentaries on the Trials and Legal Secrets of Audley Court." In *Beyond Sensation: Mary Elizabeth Braddon in Context*. Ed. Marlene Tromp, Pamela Gilbert, and Aeron Haynie. New York: State University of New York Press, 2000. 17–30.

Hughes, Winifred. *The Maniac in the Cellar: Sensation Novels of the 1860s*. Princeton: Princeton University Press, 1980.

[James, Henry.] Review of Wilkie Collins's *The Woman in White*. *Nation* 1 (9 November 1865): 593–95.

Jasper, David, and T. R. Wright, eds. *The Critical Spirit and the Will to Believe*. New York: St. Martin's Press, 1989.

Jay, Elisabeth. *Faith and Doubt in Victorian Britain*. London: Macmillan Education Ltd., 1986.

Jeffords, Susan. "Performative Masculinities: Or, 'After a Few Times You Won't Be Afraid of Rape at All.'" *Discourse* 13, no. 2 (1991): 102–18.

Kahane, Claire. "Hysteria, Feminism, and the Case of *The Bostonians*." In *Feminism and Psychoanalysis*. Ed. Richard Feldstein and Judith Roof. Ithaca: Cornell University Press, 1989. 280–97.

Kalikoff, Beth. *Murder and Moral Decay in Victorian Popular Literature*. Michigan: UMI Research Press, 1986.

Kaplan, Fred. *Sacred Tears: Sentimentality in Victorian Literature*. Princeton: Princeton University Press, 1987.

Kent, John. "Religion and Science." In *Nineteenth Century Religious Thought in the West*. Ed. Ninia Smart, John Clayton, Steven Katz, and Patrick Sherry. Cambridge: Cambridge University Press, 1985. 1–36.

Kincaid, James R. "Performance, Roles, and the Nature of the Self in Dickens." In *Dramatic Dickens*. Ed. Carol Hanbery MacKay. New York: St. Martin's Press, 1989. 11–26.

King, Alice. "A Few Words about Novel Writing by a Novelist." *Argosy* 13 (1872): 48–53.

Kristeva, Julia. *Powers of Horror: An Essay on Abjection*. New York: Columbia University Press, 1982.

———. "Revolution in Poetic Language." In *The Kristeva Reader*. Ed. Toril Moi. New York: Columbia University Press, 1986. 89–136.

Krueger, Christine L. *The Reader's Repentance*. Chicago: University of Chicago Press, 1992.

Kucich, John. *Repression in Victorian Fiction*. Berkeley: University of California Press, 1987.

Lacan, Jacques. *Ecrits*. Trans. Alan Sheridan. New York: Norton, 1977.

———. *The Four Fundamental Concepts of Psycho-Analysis*. Ed. Jacques-Alain Miller. Trans. Alan Sheridan. New York: W. W. Norton & Co., 1978.

Lambertz, Jan. "Feminists and the Politics of Wife-Beating." In *British Feminism in the Twentieth and the Nineteenth Century*. Ed. Harold L. Smith. Hants, England: Edward Alger Publishing, 1990. 25–43.

Langbauer, Laurie. "Women in White, Men in Feminism." *Yale Journal of Criticism* 2, no. 2 (1989): 219–43.

Langland, Elizabeth. "Enclosure Acts: Framing Women's Bodies in Braddon's *Lady Audley's Secret*." In *Beyond Sensation: Mary Elizabeth Braddon in Context*. Ed. Marlene Tromp, Pamela Gilbert, and Aeron Haynie. New York: State University of New York Press, 2000. 3–16.

———. *Nobody's Angels: Middle-Class Women and Domestic Ideology in Victorian Culture*. Ithaca: Cornell University Press, 1995.

Leach, Robert. *The Punch and Judy Show: History, Tradition and Meaning*. Athens: University of Georgia Press, 1985.

Lees, Sue. "Naggers, Whores and Libbers: Provoking Men to Kill." In *Femicide: The Politics of Woman Killing*. Ed. Jill Radford and Diana E. H. Russell. New York: Twayne Publishers, 1992. 267–88.

Levine, George. *The Realist Imagination*. Chicago: University of Chicago Press, 1981.

Loesberg, Jonathan. "The Ideology of Narrative Form in Sensation Fiction." *Representations* 13 (1986): 115–38.

Lukacs, Georg. *The Theory of the Novel*. Trans. Anna Bostock. London: Merlin Press, 1971.

Lynch, Eve. "Spectral Politics: M. E. Braddon and the Spirits of Social Reform." In *Be-*

*yond Sensation: Mary Elizabeth Braddon in Context*. Ed. Marlene Tromp, Pamela Gilbert, and Aeron Haynie. Albany: State University of New York Press, 2000. 235–54.

Mansel, Henry Longeville. "Sensation Novels." *London Quarterly Review* 113 (1863): 251–68.

Maynard, Jessica. "Telling the Whole Truth: Wilkie Collins and the Lady Detective." In *Victorian Identities*. Ed. Ruth Robbins and Julian Wolfreys. New York: St. Martin's Press, 1996.

McCarron, Robert. "Evil and Eliot's Religion of Humanity: Grandcourt in *Daniel Deronda*." *Ariel* 11, no. 1 (1980): 71–88.

McGowan, John P. *Representation and Revelation: Victorian Realism from Carlyle to Yeats*. Columbia: University of Missouri Press, 1986.

McGowan, Randall. "Punishing Violence, Sentencing Crime." In *The Violence of Representation*. New York: Routledge, 1989. 140–56.

McNay, Lois. *Foucault and Feminism: Power, Gender, and the Self*. Boston: Northeastern University Press, 1993.

Meckier, Jerome. *Hidden Rivalries in Victorian Fiction*. Lexington: University of Kentucky Press, 1987.

———. "Wilkie Collins' *The Woman in White*: Providence against the Evils of Propriety." *Journal of British Studies* 22, no. 1 (1982): 104–26.

Meyer, Susan. *Imperialism at Home*. Ithaca: Cornell University Press, 1996.

Michie, Helena. *The Flesh Made Word*. New York: Oxford University Press, 1987.

Miller, D. A. *The Novel and the Police*. Berkeley: University of California Press, 1988.

"Miss Braddon." *The Nation* 1 (1865): 593–94.

"Miss Braddon's Novels." *Dublin University Magazine* 75 (1870): 513–20.

Mitchell, Sally. *The Fallen Angel: Chastity, Class, and Women's Reading, 1835–1880*. Bowling Green: Bowling Green State University Popular Press, 1981.

Moi, Toril, ed. *The Kristeva Reader*. New York: Columbia University Press, 1986.

Montweiler, Katherine. "Marketing Sensation: *Lady Audley's Secret* and Consumer Culture. In *Beyond Sensation: Mary Elizabeth Braddon in Context*. Ed. Marlene Tromp, Pamela Gilbert, and Aeron Haynie. New York: State University of New York Press, 2000. 43–62.

Morgan, Thaïs E., ed. *Victorian Sages and Cultural Discourse: Renegotiating Gender and Power*. New Brunswick: Rutgers University Press, 1990.

Morrell, Caroline. *"Black Friday" and Violence against Women in the Suffragette Movement*. London: Women's Research and Resources Centre Publications, 1980.

Morris, Virginia B. *Double Jeopardy: Women Who Kill in Victorian Fiction*. Lexington: University of Kentucky Press, 1990.

Nayder, Lillian. "Rebellious Sepoys and Bigamous Wives: The Indian Mutiny and Marriage Law Reform in *Lady Audley's Secret*." In *Beyond Sensation: Mary Elizabeth Braddon in Context*. Ed. Marlene Tromp, Pamela Gilbert, and Aeron Haynie. New York: State University of New York Press, 2000. 31–42.

———. *Wilkie Collins*. New York: Twayne Publishers/Prentice Hall, 1997.

Nenadic, Stana. "Illegitimacy, Insanity, and Insolvency: Wilkie Collins and the Victorian Nightmares." In *The Arts, Literature, and Society*. London: Routledge, 1990. 133–62.

"Novels in Relation to Female Education." *Dublin University Magazine* 85 (1875): 513–20.

Oliphant, Margaret. *Salem Chapel*. New York: Garland Publishing, 1976.

[———.] "Sensation Novels." *Blackwoods Magazine* xci (May 1862): 565–74.

O'Mealy, Joseph H. "Mrs. Oliphant, *Miss Marjoribanks,* and the Victorian Canon." In *The New Nineteenth Century: Feminist Readings of Underread Victorian Fiction.* Ed. Barbara Leah Harman and Susan Meyer. New York: Garland Publishing, 1996. 63–76.

O'Neill, Philip. *Wilkie Collins: Women, Property, and Propriety.* Totowa, N.J.: Barnes and Noble, 1988.

Oplinger, Jon. *The Politics of Demonology: The European Witchcraze and the Mass Production of Deviance.* London: Associated University Press, 1990.

Oppenheim, Janet. *The Other World: Spiritualism and Psychical Research in England 1850– 1914.* Cambridge: Cambridge University Press, 1985.

"Our Female Sensation Novelists." *Living Age* 78 (1863): 352–69.

"Our Novels." *Temple Bar* 29 (1870): 488–503.

Owen, Alex. *The Darkened Room: Women, Power and Spiritualism in Late Victorian England.* Philadelphia: University of Pennsylvania Press, 1990.

Page, Norman, ed. *Wilkie Collins: The Critical Heritage.* Boston: Routledge & Kegan Paul, 1974.

Paroisien, David. "*Oliver Twist* and the Contours of Early Victorian England." *The Victorian Newsletter* 83 (1993): 14–17.

Patmore, Coventry. *The Angel in the House.* Boston: Ticknor and Fields, 1856.

Pearsall, Ronald. *The Worm in the Bud.* Toronto: Macmillan, 1969.

Perkins, Pamela, and Mary Donaghy. "A Man's Resolution: Narrative Strategies in Wilkie Collins' *The Woman in White.*" *Studies in the Novel* 38 (1990): 392–402.

Pleck, Elizabeth. "Feminist Responses to 'Crimes Against Women,' 1868–1896." *Signs* 8 (1983): 451–71.

Poovey, Mary. *Uneven Developments.* Chicago: University of Chicago Press, 1988.

Putzell, Sara M. "The Importance of Being Gwendolen: Contexts for George Eliot's *Daniel Deronda.*" *Studies in the Novel* 19, no. 1 (1987): 31–45.

Pykett, Lyn. *The "Improper" Feminine: The Women's Sensation Novel and the New Woman Writing.* New York: Routledge, 1992.

———. *The Sensation Novel: From* The Woman in White *to* The Moonstone. Plymouth, England: Northcote House, 1994.

Rae, W. Fraser. "Sensation Novelists: Miss Braddon." *North British Review* 43 (1865): 92– 105.

Raina, Badri. "*Daniel Deronda:* A View of Grandcourt." *Studies in the Novel* 17, no. 4 (1985): 371–81.

"Recent Novels: Their Moral and Religious Teaching." *London Quarterly Review* 27 (1866): 100–124.

Restuccia, Frances L. "Literary Representations of Battered Women: Spectacular Domestic Punishment." In *Bodies of Writing, Bodies in Performance.* Ed. Thomas Foster, Carol Siegel, and Ellen E. Berry. New York: New York University Press, 1996. 42–71.

Rooney, Ellen. "Criticism and the Subject of Sexual Violence." *Modern Language Notes* 98 (1983): 1269–78.

Rose, Jacqueline. "Where Does the Misery Come From? Psychoanalysis, Feminism and the Event." In *Feminism and Psychoanalysis.* Ed. Richard Feldstein and Judith Roof. Ithaca: Cornell University Press, 1989. 25–39.

Rosenberg, Brian. "The Language of Doubt in *Oliver Twist.*" *Dickens Quarterly* 4 (1987): 91–98.

Rosenman, Ellen B. "Women's Speech and the Roles of the Sexes in *Daniel Deronda*. *Texas Studies in Literature and Language* 31, no. 2 (1989): 237–56.

Rowe, Margaret Moan. "Melting Outlines in *Daniel Deronda*." *Studies in the Novel* 22, no. 1 (1990): 10–18.

Rowlinson, Matthew. "Reading Capital with Little Nell." *Yale Journal of Criticism* 9 (1996): 347–80.

Rush, Florence. "A Victorian Childhood." In *The Best-Kept Secret: Sexual Abuse of Children*. Blue Ridge Summit, Pa.: TAB Books, 1980. 56–73.

Said, Edward W. *Culture and Imperialism*. New York: Knopf, 1993.

Saunders, Mary. "Lady Dedlock Prostrate: Drama, Melodrama, and Expression in Dickens's Floor Scenes." In *Dramatic Dickens*. Ed. Carol Hanbery MacKay. New York: St. Martin's Press, 1989. 68–80.

Scarry, Elaine. *The Body in Pain*. New York: Oxford University Press, 1985.

———, ed. *Introduction to Literature and the Body*. Baltimore: Johns Hopkins University Press, 1986.

Scobie, Stephen. *Signature Event Context*. Edmonton: NeWest Press, 1989.

Sedgwick, Eve Kosofsky. "Nationalisms and Sexualities in the Age of Wilde." In *Nationalisms and Sexualities*. Ed. Andrew Paker, Mary Russo, Doris Sommer, and Patricia Yaeger. New York: Routledge, 1992. 235–45.

Shakespeare, William. *The Winter's Tale*. In *The Complete Works of Shakespeare*. Ed. David Bevington. Glenview, Ill.: Scott, Foresman, and Co., 1980. 1459–96.

Shanley, Mary Lyndon. *Feminism, Marriage and the Law in Victorian England*. Princeton: Princeton University Press, 1989.

Showalter, Elaine. "Desperate Remedies." *Victorian Newsletter* 49 (1976): 1–5.

———. *The Female Malady*. New York: Pantheon Books, 1985.

Silverman, Kaja. *The Acoustic Mirror*. Bloomington: Indiana University Press, 1988.

Sims, George. *How the Poor Live*. London, 1883.

Smith, Grahame. *Charles Dickens: A Literary Life*. New York: St. Martins Press, 1996.

Spivak, Gayatri Chakravorty. "Three Women's Texts and a Critique of Imperialism." In *Feminisms*. Ed. Robyn R. Warhol and Diane Price Herndl. New Brunswick: Rutgers University Press, 1991. 798–814.

Sroka, Kenneth M. "Dickens' Metafiction: Readers and Writers in *Oliver Twist, David Copperfield,* and *Our Mutual Friend*." *Dickens Studies Annual* 22 (1993): 35–66.

Stanley, Liz. *The Diaries of Hannah Cullwick, Victorian Maidservant*. New Brunswick: Rutgers University Press, 1984.

Stewart, Garrett. "'Beckoning Death': *Daniel Deronda* and the Plotting of a Reading." In *Sex and Death in Victorian Literature*. Ed. Regina Barreca. London: Macmillan Press Ltd., 1990. 69–106.

———. *Dear Reader: The Conscripted Audience in Nineteenth-Century British Fiction*. Baltimore: Johns Hopkins University Press, 1996.

Stokes, John. "Rachel's 'Terrible Beauty': An Actress among the Novelists." *English Literary History* 51, no. 4 (1984): 771–93.

Strange, G. Robert, ed. *The Poetical Works of Tennyson*. Boston: Houghton Mifflin Co., 1974.

Strawbridge, Sheelagh. "Darwin and Victorian Values." In *In Search of Victorian Values*. Ed. Eric M. Sigsworth. New York: Manchester University Press, 1988. 102–15.

Taussig, Michael. *Shamanism, Colonialism and the Wildman*. Chicago: University of Chicago Press, 1986.

Taylor, Jenny Bourne. *In the Secret Theatre of the Home*. New York: Routledge, 1988.

————. "Psychology and Sensation: The Narrative of Moral Management in *The Woman in White*." *Critical Survey* 2, no. 1 (1990): 49–56.

Tomes, Nancy. "A 'Torrent of Abuse': Crimes of Violence between Working-Class Men and Women in London, 1840–1875." *Journal of Social History* 11 (1978): 328–45.

Trodd, Anthea. *Domestic Crime in the Victorian Novel*. New York: St. Martin's Press, 1989.

Trollope, Anthony. *An Autobiography*. New York: Oxford University Press, 1950.

Vrettos, Athena. "From Neurosis to Narrative: The Private Life of the Nerves in *Villette* and *Daniel Deronda*." *Victorian Studies* 33, no. 4 (1990): 551–79.

————. *Somatic Fictions: Imagining Illness in Victorian Culture*. Stanford: Stanford University Press, 1995.

Walker, Barbara G. *The Women's Encyclopedia of Myths and Secrets*. San Francisco: Harper & Row, 1983.

Walkowitz, Judith. *City of Dreadful Delight: Narratives of Sexual Danger in Late-Victorian London*. Chicago: University of Chicago Press, 1992.

————. *Prostitution and Victorian Society*. Cambridge: Cambridge University Press, 1980.

Wallace, Alfred Russel. *Miracles and Modern Spiritualism*. New York: Arno Press, 1975.

Walsh, Susan. "Bodies of Capital: *Great Expectations* and the Climacteric Economy." *Victorian Studies* 37, no. 1 (1993): 73–98.

Walvin, James. *Victorian Values*. Athens: University of Georgia Press, 1987.

Webb, Peter. "Victorian Erotica." In *The Sexual Dimension of Literature*. London: Vision & Barnes and Noble, 1982. 90–121.

Weeks, Jeffrey. *Sex, Politics and Society: The Regulation of Sexuality since 1800*. 2d ed. Essex, England: Longman Group, 1989.

Williams, Merryn. *Margaret Oliphant: A Critical Biography*. New York: St. Martin's Press, 1986.

Wolff, Robert Lee. *Sensational Victorian: The Life and Fiction of Mary Elizabeth Braddon*. New York: Garland Publishing, 1979.

*The Woman in White*. Unsigned review. *Critic* xxi (25 August 1860): 233–34.

————. Unsigned review. *Sixpenny Magazine* i (September 1861): 366–67.

————. Unsigned review. *Spectator* xxiv (28 December 1861): 1428.

Worth, George J. *Dickensian Melodrama: A Reading of the Novels*. Lawrence: University of Kansas Press, 1978.

Wright, T. R. "*Middlemarch* as a Religious Novel, or Life without God." In *Images of Belief in Literature*. Ed. David Jasper. New York: St. Martin's Press. 138–52.

Yaeger, Patricia. "Violence in the Sitting Room: *Wuthering Heights* and the Woman's Novel." *Genre* 21 (1988): 203–29.

Young-Bruehl, Elisabeth. *Freud on Women*. New York: W. W. Norton & Co., 1990.

Zainaldin, Jamil S. "The Emergence of a Modern American Family Law: Child Custody, Adoption, and the Courts, 1796–1851." *Northwestern University Law Review* 73 (1979): 1038–89.

Žižek, Slavoj. "The Spectre of Ideology." In *Mapping Ideology*. Ed. Slavoj Žižek. New York: Verso, 1997. 1–33.

# Index

# Victorian Literature and Culture Series

S
N
L